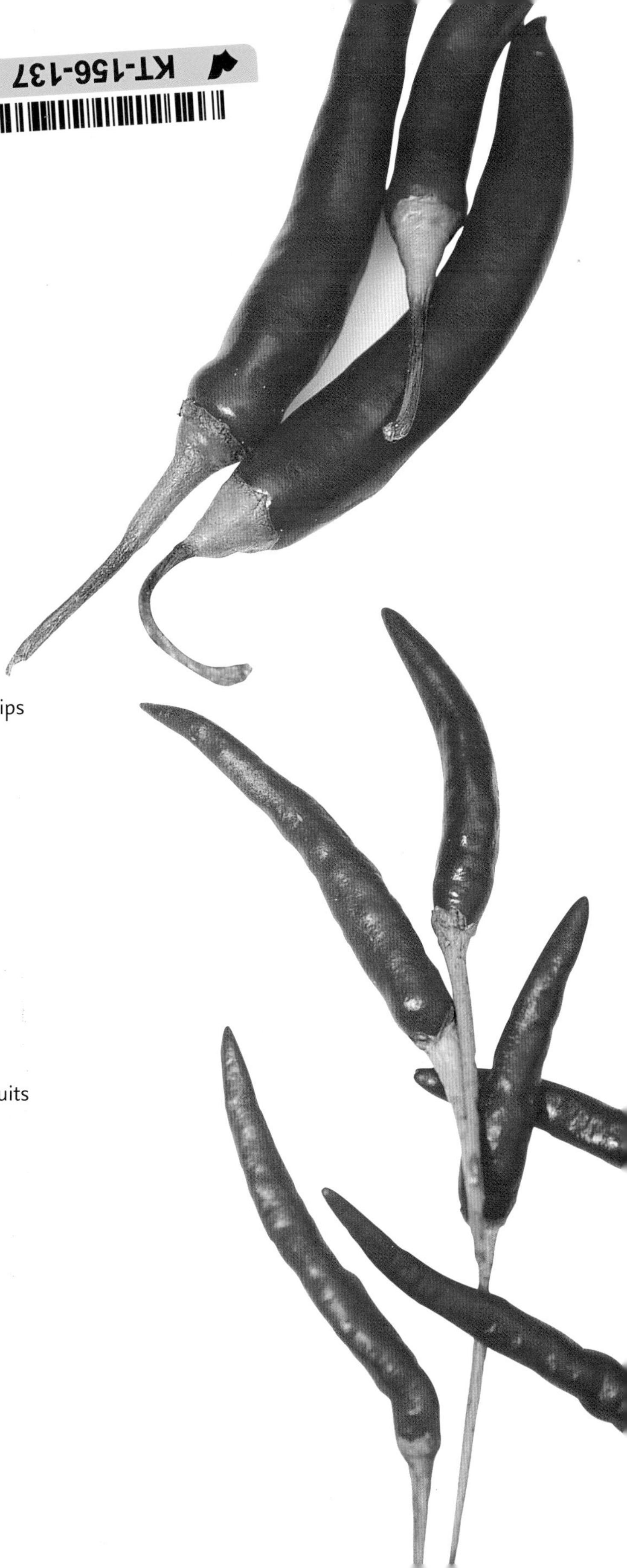

Contents

4   Why Cook?

5   Techniques and General Tips

12   Soups, Starters and Eggs

62   Pasta, Pizza and Rice

92   Meat and Poultry

134   Stir-frying

144   Fish

168   Vegetables and Salads

198   Puddings, Cakes and Biscuits

237   Index

Why Cook?

Good question. Why should you learn to cook at all? You'll get by just fine on take-aways, ready-meals, sandwiches, crisps and chocolate. Nobody needs to cook at all these days, as long as they own a microwave, a kettle and a toaster.

This is potentially a good thing, and certainly hugely liberating. Before you throw the book down in disgust, let me explain. Cooking should be and can be a thoroughly enjoyable life-enhancing task. There is such pleasure to be had from working with beautiful, fresh, natural produce, from combining ingredients to expose their finest, most enticing flavours, a kind of magic that is there to be discovered by every person who walks into a kitchen with appetite and hunger. All this before you even get to the climax of the whole endeavour – the eating itself.

How miserable then, when cooking becomes a tyranny, which it can when there is a day-in-day-out obligation to put a proper cooked meal on the table. So to me, the ideal is a balanced compromise between real cooking as often as possible, and convenience food as back-up for those days when work or play has sapped your energy. There's nothing wrong with beans on toast every now and then.

There are considerable health benefits to be had from cooking your own food, too. This is not a book about nutrition, but the fundamental principles of healthy eating are straightforward: variety, moderation, loads of veg and fruit. With you as head honcho in the kitchen, you can make yours a healthy, delicious way of eating that allows for occasional indulgences without guilt.

To do that though, you will have to know how to cook. It's really not at all difficult. It just takes a bit of practice and it will stand you in good stead for the rest of your life. Encapsulated in the recipes in this book are most of the basic techniques you will need to cook a myriad of dishes. It is not a 'complete' or 'comprehensive' course - that would be quite impossible. I've skipped over certain skills you can manage without for the time-being (e.g. making pastry). I have included a wide range of recipes covering both familiar foods and some that may be new to you, to get your culinary imagination in full working order.

And finally, a kitchen motto that has worked well for me, ever since the day when I moved into my first bedsit, and began the task of learning to cook for real: **don't panic**. If the worst does come to the worst (we all have off days) and you bodge it up completely, bin it, and send out for a pizza!

Techniques and General Tips

How to Read a Recipe

Skip this if you want to; I know it sounds superfluous. Any fool can read a recipe, but do they know how to interpret what they read? Mostly it is common sense, just a list of instructions that you should follow in the right order to end up with something enjoyable to eat. It is, however, worth noting that these instructions are nothing more than guidelines, not hard and fast rules inscribed in granite.

For instance, I cannot tell you exactly how long to cook a sauce or a gratin; your pans and dishes are unlikely to be exactly the same size or style as mine; your stove will not be the same as mine; and your idea of a medium heat will not be identical to mine. But, assuming that you and I concur roughly on these three parameters, my suggested cooking times will be roughly right. So, treat them as estimates. Use your own senses to judge when dishes are perfectly cooked – check the look, the smell (a waft of burning cheese is a dead giveaway that you've massacred your cheese on toast), the taste, the feel (with cakes this is essential), and even the sound – sizzling is the best indicator of the heat of fat, for instance. The more you cook, the easier this all becomes.

When you decide to cook a particular recipe, read it through carefully before you even write your shopping list. Do you have all the right equipment (no good tackling a gratin if you don't have a suitable shallow ovenproof dish)? If not, it may be worth adding what you lack to your list.

Do you understand the various cooking terms? If not, look them up in this book, or another reference book, or phone somebody who might be able to explain them to you. Don't give up instantly if you are not quite clear – often something makes much more sense as you are preparing or cooking real ingredients, and it's only by practising that you will become proficient. How long does it take to cook? Can you prepare some of it in advance?

It is worth noting that in a well-written recipe, the ingredients are usually listed in the order they are used. This can be useful when you are cooking. As a novice cook, it makes sense to measure and prepare all ingredients as described in the ingredients list before you actually start on the cooking proper. The exception to this is when one part of the recipe needs to be made in advance (you might need to marinate something for several hours before cooking and making the sauce), but if you've read your recipe carefully you'll already be aware of this. As you gain experience and confidence you will know what has to be chopped or sliced initially, and what else can be done while the first batch of ingredients is sizzling away in the pan.

Weights and Measures

Recipes, as I've already said, are merely a set of guidelines and recommendations. This is as true of the ingredients list as of the method. As a beginner it is advisable to stick to the given quantities and suggested ingredients – as you become more familiar with a particular recipe, you can start to play around to a certain extent. In some instances it is fine to deviate slightly from given amounts where common sense dictates. Suppose, for instance, that a potato salad calls for 450g (1 lb) potatoes – there is no need to cut off a third of one new potato to get exactly the right amount; a tiny bit more or less will make little difference.

The standard advice is to stick with either metric or imperial measurements and not to mix the two. This is probably what you will do anyway, but in truth it won't make much difference in most recipes if you do mix them up. And always taste as you cook; adjust seasonings and balance of flavours to suit your taste and your ingredients. The one area demanding strict accuracy is baking.

Surprisingly small differences in the ratios of flour, fat, sugar, eggs and so on affect the way the cake turns out. So, no guess work, or slapdash weighing out here.

Spoon measurements Spoon measurements in this book are all rounded, unless otherwise indicated. I use a 5ml teaspoon, a 10ml dessertspoon and a 15ml tablespoon.

A sprig, a stem, a bunch or a handful? At first these terms will seem infuriatingly vague, but try to view them as opportunities to exploit your own personal tastes. If you really love the aroma of a certain herb, then make your sprig or handful big and generous. If it is new to you, you may prefer to err on the side of caution at first – reduce that sprig to a couple of inches, grab a petite handful. Soon the deliberate vagueness will become endearingly familiar.

Preparing Common Vegetables and Other Ingredients

Chopping Onions

The most important advice here is to make sure you have a sharp knife before you begin (see knives and knife sharpeners below). Chopping an onion is easy when the blade glides smoothly through the layers, a right pain when you have to push hard and saw your way through. As so many savoury recipes begin with chopping an onion, it will improve your kitchen life considerably if this basic operation is painless and swift.

1 First cut the onion in half, slicing from stalk to root (photo 1). Place one half flat on the chopping board and cut off the upper stalk end (photo 2). Now pick up the onion and peel the brown skins

back towards the root, without ripping them right off – it isn't disastrous if they do come right away, but left attached to the onion root, they act as a handle to grip hold of when chopping. So bend the skins back, away from the onion (photo 3).
2 Place your left hand (or right if you are left-handed) flat on top of the onion to hold it still,

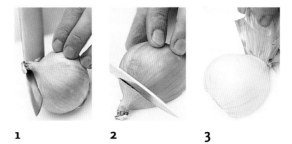

1   **2**   **3**

then slice it horizontally, stem end towards the root, but stopping just short of the root, so that the pieces stay together (photo 4).

3 Now, keeping the onion flat on the work surface, grasp the skin handle holding the onion steady, and make parallel vertical cuts, from root end towards the stalk end (photo 5).

4 Finally, make parallel cuts at right angles to the previous set of cuts, working your way from stem end back to the root.

And there you have it: a mound of perfectly chopped onion (photo 6).

Slice off the base and the tip of the clove (photo 2). If you are going to chop or crush the garlic, the easiest way to get the skin off is to place the clove flat on the chopping board, then press the bowl of a wooden spoon down on it firmly, crushing it gently (photo 3). Now the skin will almost fall off.

If, on the other hand, you intend to slice the clove, or keep it whole, pull the skin away bit by bit with your fingers. Any skin that sticks can be loosened by running the blade of the knife, held at an angle to the clove, firmly down the skin.

4　　　　**5**　　　　**6**

1　　　　**2**　　　　**3**

Slicing Onions

Easy. Peel the onion completely, and trim ends. For rings, turn the onion on its side and slice downwards, thinly or thickly as you wish. Leave whole or separate into rings. For half-moons, halve the peeled onion through its equator. Set cut-side down, and slice.

Peeling Garlic

Remove outer layers of papery skin from the head of garlic, then ease out as many cloves as you need for your recipe (photo 1). Store the rest of the head in a cool, dry place, but not in the fridge, where it may taint milk and eggs and other foods.

Chopping Garlic

Garlic is chopped in much the same way as onion, but scaled down appropriately. If you've crushed it virtually flat when removing the skin, then you obviously won't be able to slice it horizontally.

Crushing Garlic

A garlic crusher is quick but wasteful. A lot of good garlic gets left behind or stuck in the holes. A knife does the job more efficiently, though it takes a little practice.

Peel the garlic and chop it very roughly into three or four pieces. Sprinkle with a good pinch of salt (this diminishes slippage). Press the flat of the blade of the knife down on the pieces, crushing them, then drag the sharp end of the blade, at an angle to the board, over the smashed pieces. Push them all back together, and repeat the dragging and crushing until you have a smooth paste. The dismaying thing is how little you end up with, but don't fear – the impact of the smoothly crushed garlic will be epic.

Chopping Herbs

Pile the leaves up together on the chopping board. Grab the biggest knife you own (but not a serrated knife). Hold the handle with your right hand, and the tip with your left (reverse this if you are left-handed). Hold the knife over the herbs, the tip in contact with the board close to one side of the heap. Now hold the tip steady on the board, and bring the knife firmly and quickly down on the herbs, again and again, swinging it backwards and forwards. Push the herbs back together in a pile, and repeat the whole operation. Keep doing this until the herbs are chopped as you want them. With practice this becomes an easy, quick and rhythmic operation.

This is also the method to use for fine chopping garlic or onion, once they have been roughly chopped in the usual way.

Skinning Tomatoes

Cut a small cross in each tomato, opposite the stalk end (photo 1). Place in a bowl and cover with boiling water (photo 2). Leave for a minute, then pick the tomatoes out of the water. The skin will now pull away from the tomato with ease (photo 3). If it doesn't, repeat the process – the tomatoes must have been under-ripe.

1   2   3

Deseeding Tomatoes

Method 1 For tomatoes that are to be cooked in a sauce or stew or soup. Halve the tomatoes through the equator, i.e. cutting halfway between stalk end and base (photo 1). Squeeze each half over a bowl or bin, just as if you were squeezing out lemon juice (photo 2). The seeds will ooze out.

Method 2 For when you want perfect looking pieces of tomato. Halve the tomatoes as for method 1, then scoop out the seeds with a teaspoon (photo 3).

1   2   3

Deseeding Peppers

Begin by slicing off the stem end as if it were a lid. Turn the pepper upside down and tap the base firmly several times to loosen the seeds. Shake them out, and scrape out any malingerers with a knife. When you want to keep the pepper whole, perhaps for stuffing, or cut it into rings, you should also scrape out the white ribs (not 100% necessary, but it does improve the flavour a mite). For quartered peppers or long strips, cut the cup into four from one corner to the other, to give flattish pieces. This makes them easier to cut into strips, or grill. Remove the odd seed and cut away the white ribs if you haven't already. Now cut into strips if required.

Handling Chillies

It is the capsaicin in chillies that makes them hot. When you handle chillies, capsaicin transfers itself to your fingers, so you need to be extremely careful that you don't rub your eyes, or worse still, especially for men, go to the loo, before cleaning your hands thoroughly. The results can be painful. Capsaicin is not water-soluble, so you need to use a good deal of soap, or some alcohol-based cleanser to get rid of it all. Either that or wear rubber gloves when working with chillies, not a bad idea if you

have sensitive skin. The plus side of this is that you absolutely need to drink some kind of alcohol with a hot curry, if you want to soothe your mouth and throat. Water just won't do.

Deseeding Chillies

Halve the chillies lengthways and scrape out the seeds and cores with a knife. These are the hottest parts, although the flesh too is hot (as described above).

Chillies vary in heat, and there seems to be a correlation between size and heat – often the smallest chillies are the hottest!

Topping and Tailing Beans

Most fresh green beans need to be topped and tailed. This means cutting off the tips on both ends. I like to do them individually, as long as there is something interesting to listen to on the radio. When I have a huge pile to work through, I'm inclined to become more

wasteful – taking a bunch of beans at a time, lining up the ends and then just slicing them all off in one fell swoop.

Grating Lemons

The zest of all citrus fruit contains aromatic oil, and this adds wonderful flavour to many dishes, along with the juice. Rub the surface of the (washed) fruit to and fro on the fine grid of a flat grater several times to remove the zest without any of the bitter white pith. Move around the fruit, covering different areas, until it is denuded. Only then squeeze the juice!

Recommended Kitchen Utensils

It is impossible to make one definitive list of the essential cooking implements and utensils you will need. Absolute basics are fairly obvious – with nothing but one sharp knife and a frying pan or saucepan, you could turn out a fair number of severely streamlined meals. After that, the list is dictated as much by what you like to cook as anything else.

View your 'batterie de cuisine' (cooking equipment) as a long-term collection that you will build up over the years. Sadly, the general rule is that the more you spend, the better the quality, and better quality often makes for easier, more enjoyable cooking. So, no long list but instead a few notes and recommendations on useful kitchen kit, and recommended buys.

Casserole Every home should have one (unless, of course, you loathe stews of any sort). Best bet is a flame- and heatproof casserole that can go both on the hob and in the oven. It should also look good enough to go straight from the oven to the table. It is better to buy a larger casserole dish than a smaller one, allowing plenty of room. After all, most stews improve in flavour if kept for a day or two in the fridge, or can be frozen if necessary, so making a big potful is a pretty sensible thing to do, even if you are just cooking for one or two.

Chopping Boards Hard to do without, so again, buy the best and biggest you can afford. It is far more useful to have one really big wooden chopping board, than several small book-sized ones. Chopping boards should be made of wood (which scientists now consider perfectly hygienic as long as you wash them after use) or plastic.

Food Processor You can manage very well without one, but your kitchen life will become a good deal easier with. Here, as so often, you should probably head for the best you can afford. Choose one with a relatively large capacity, and several different speed settings. Several models have small inner bowls that can be fitted to process small amounts – very useful for making curry pastes and spice rubs, amongst other things.

Frying Pan, Non-stick Another investment item. A really tip-top heavy-based non-stick frying pan does not come cheap, but is worth every penny. Choose one that is fairly large with high sides so that as well as frying, you can also cook a chicken stew and the like in it. Incidentally, modern non-stick surfaces are very tough, so it is usually all right to use metal implements in them.

Graters Don't get too fancy. An old-fashioned box grater does the job very nicely. I like the modern Microplane graters, too, especially for orange and lemon zest, or Parmesan, or nutmeg.

Kitchen Tongs These do make turning practically anything in a frying pan or under the grill ten times easier and quicker.

Knives Buy the best you can afford (or ask some nice relative with more money than you to make a gift of them). A good knife will last you a lifetime. They're not cheap, but since you will be using them constantly, knives should be seen as a major investment. You will need, at the very least, one fairly big chef's knife (around 17.5–20cm /7–8in), one smaller 15cm (6in) knife and a bread knife. A smaller serrated knife (around 10cm/4in) is great for cutting tomatoes.

Knife Sharpener As essential as the knives. A small hand-held knife sharpener is easier.

Liquidiser   If I had to choose, I'd say that a liquidiser is more essential than a processor and a darn sight cheaper, too. Liquidisers are important for making soup and smoothies amongst other things. For more on liquidisers, turn to page 17.

Pestle and Mortar   Two most important characteristics: firstly, that the mortar needs to be heavy, so that it doesn't slip and slide around on the table. Secondly, the interior must feel rough. If it is smooth it will make grinding and pounding hard work. Best pestles are rough at the wider end, rather than smooth.

Saucepans   You'll need one small one, one medium-sized one and one large. And no doubt you will add more over the years. When choosing your saucepans, look for solid, heavy bases that will conduct heat evenly.

Sieve   I prefer metal, but modern nylon sieves are fine. More important than the material is the mesh size. This should be fairly large. If the mesh is too fine, then it can makes things like sieving a soup a complete nightmare. Never buy a sieve which doesn't have one or two hooks on the rim opposite the handle, so that you can sit the sieve securely over a bowl or saucepan.

Weighing Scales   Digital scales are far more accurate than most dial scales. Buy scales with a flat top, so that you can use any bowl or pan on them, resetting the display to zero before weighing out ingredients.

Cooking Terms

Baking and Roasting both refer to cooking in the oven, and the differences between them are not always clear. Generally, however, roasting is done at a high temperature without covering the food, so that it browns, while baking is undertaken at a slightly lower temperature and the food may sometimes be covered or not.

Frying means to cook something in hot fat, either in a shallow frying pan (sometimes also called pan-frying), or in a deep pan, half filled with oil, which is known as deep-frying.

Grilling means to cook food under a hot grill.

Sautéing is a form of frying. Unlike ordinary frying, which is verging on sedate, sautéing is an energetic business. The word 'sauter' is literally the French for 'to jump' and that describes the method well. When sautéing the idea is to keep all the pieces of food moving more or less constantly, so that they brown and cook evenly on all sides, and never have a chance to stick on the base of the pan.

Searing and Griddling   Searing means cooking food with the minimal amount of fat, on a searingly hot flat surface - probably a heavy-based frying pan. Griddling is similar, but a ridged, heavy griddle pan is used instead.

Simmering means cooking something in simmering water, in other words water that is so hot that a few small bubbles are lazily making their way up to the surface, but not much more than that. The surface of the water will move and tremble gently. In most instances water is first brought up to the boil (i.e. when crowds of bubbles rise ebulliently to the surface), the item that is to be cooked is tipped in, which reduces the temperature of the water below simmering point, and then the whole lot is warmed up again until the water is simmering.

Sweating means cooking over a low heat, with a small amount of fat, the lid clamped on tightly.

chapter one

Soups, Starters and Eggs

Soups

I'm a great believer in soup. Here is a dish that fulfils a multitude of functions, the prime amongst them being that it satisfies the soul. Oh – and the stomach. A big steaming bowlful of soup can really hit the spot. It makes a good first course and it makes the heart of a handsome lunch or supper, eked out with loads of soft-centred, crisp-crusted bread, a big hunk of cheese, and healthy fruit or something more indulgent to follow. Make one big batch and it will feed a crowd, or just feed you on your own quickly and easily over several days.

Types of Soup

Soups divide, fundamentally, into three categories. The first is the puréed soup, with vegetables aplenty boiled up together, then liquidised to silky smoothness (or if you prefer, rustic chunkiness). The second is the bits and bobs, meal-in-a-bowl soup, where a pleasing medley of this and that is simmered in broth, which may or may not be thickened. The third is the incredibly elegant upmarket consommé – a beautiful limpid concoction, intensely flavoured, served in suitably small quantity with maybe a single oyster or whatever floating in its centre. This is restaurant soup, not impossible to make at home by any means, but a good deal of work. If you want a recipe for this type of soup, look elsewhere.

Tips and Techniques

Making soup is all about extracting the maximum flavour from a set of ingredients. Certain techniques, like sweating vegetables and thickening or thinning the soup, are essential to a good result, while others, like stock-making, can be circumnavigated but are worth learning because they have the potential to turn a pedestrian but acceptable soup into a first-rate one. If you want to get the best soup on to your table, read these tips and techniques before you get out the saucepan.

First, a word about the basic structure of a soup. Most soups start off with a group of base ingredients (e.g. onion, garlic, butter or olive oil) that give the soup a background flavour. The main ingredients are what give the soup its predominant flavour – carrots, perhaps, or parsnips, or a medley of vegetables and beans.

Aromatics are the complementary ingredients that scent or spice the soup – usually herbs and spices. The commonest of these is a 'bouquet garni' which is a bundle of different herbs, tied together with string so that it can be easily removed before liquidising or serving the soup (see page 20).

All soups need some sort of liquid otherwise they wouldn't be soups at all! And then last, but not at all least, they need to be seasoned with salt and pepper, or maybe cayenne pepper for a dash of colour and heat combined.

Sweating without Perspiration

Most puréed soups and many meal-in-a-bowl soups start off with a spot of sweating. Not the sort that requires a cold shower, but sweating of the culinary sort. Foodie sweating means cooking vegetables and often herbs with a little fat, over a very low heat, with the lid clamped firmly on the saucepan. Once they are on the stove-top, you barely need to bother with them for a good 10–15 minutes, apart from giving them a quick stir once or twice, but no more. This process develops the full depth of flavour of the vegetables so don't try to rush it. As long as the heat is low, they'll produce enough liquid to prevent them sticking or burning.

Thick, Thicker, Thickest

Somewhere among the ingredients will usually be one that serves primarily as a thickener, to give body to the soup. Potatoes are the commonest, but rice, beans or lentils play a similar role. A few more starchy vegetables, e.g. parsnips, need no thickener, as they are quite capable of doing the job themselves.

Liquid Essentials

Obviously soups need some type of liquid to dilute the main ingredients. In certain cases, where there is already a considerable depth of flavour present, water may be quite adequate. Milk can sometimes be used too. The rest of the time you really need a decent stock. This is the backbone of the soup. You can't taste it specifically, but it is what all the other ingredients rely on for support. An insipid or tasteless stock will produce an indifferent soup. An absolutely tip-top home-made stock will transform the soup into something outstanding.

Stock-cubes and powdered 'bouillon' are tolerable stand-bys though not half as good as the real McCoy. Make them up slightly weaker than suggested on the packet so that the factory-brewed overtones are not so evident. You can buy real liquid stocks in supermarkets (sold in small tubs, often stacked alongside the chilled meat) and they come in second best.

By far and away the best option, however, is to make stock yourself. Whenever you have had a roast chicken, say, or find a selection of odds and ends of vegetables hanging around in your veg drawer, knock some stock up, and then freeze it for another day.

Microwave Chicken Stock

This is the ideal list of ingredients, but as long as you have the chicken carcass (most butchers will sell off raw ones cheap, and they do the best job), the onion, the carrot and one or two of the herbs, you can turn out a fine stock. Remember not to add salt to a stock. Why? Just in case you want to boil it down to concentrate the flavour, or add it to other ingredients that are already salty.

1 chicken carcass, raw or cooked
1 onion, peeled and quartered
1 carrot, peeled and quartered
1 leek, quartered
1 celery stalk, quartered
1 bay leaf
2 parsley stalks
1 thyme sprig
8 black peppercorns

1 Break the chicken carcass up roughly. Put all the ingredients into the largest microwaveable bowl you own. Pour over enough boiling water to cover everything.
2 Cover with a tight layer of clingfilm, and then microwave on full power for 25 minutes. Let the whole lot stand for a further 25 minutes, then strain.

Classic Chicken Stock

1 Use the same ingredients on page 15.

2 Pile them into a roomy saucepan, and add enough water to cover generously. Bring up to the boil, then turn the heat down low and simmer very gently – the water should just tremble – for 3 hours, adding more hot water every now and then as the liquid level falls.

3 Once cooked, strain.

Vegetable Stock

The greater the variety of vegetables you add, the better balanced the taste. Avoid potatoes (which make the stock cloudy) and globe artichokes (which make the stock bitter). The sulphurous scent of over-cooked brassicas, such as cabbage, broccoli or Brussels sprouts, is not too pleasant either, so leave them out. This is a good way of using up fresh vegetable trimmings and parings, as long as the vegetables were washed.

1 onion, peeled and roughly chopped
1 carrot, peeled and roughly chopped
1 leek, roughly chopped
2 celery stalks, sliced
2 bay leaves
1 large thyme sprig
3 parsley sprigs
8 black peppercorns
whatever other vegetables you have to hand
  (e.g. green beans, runner beans,
  courgettes)

1 Put all the ingredients into a saucepan and cover with water. Bring up to the boil, and simmer very gently for 30 minutes.

2 Strain and chill or freeze.

need to know

STORING STOCK Stock will keep for two days in the fridge. If you want to keep it for longer than that, pour it into a wide, deep frying pan and boil down until reduced in volume by about two-thirds. Cool, and then pour carefully into ice-cube trays. Freeze, and then store your own home-made frozen stock cubes in an airtight container in the freezer. When you come to use them, melt and dilute with water to taste, to restore your stock to its original state.

Machinery If you like smooth soups, then you will need to invest in some type of liquidiser. Jug liquidisers are surprisingly cheap and make a far smoother soup than a processor, which is far more expensive anyway. Hand-held wand liquidisers are also a bargain. Although it takes longer to liquidise a saucepanful of soup, you have a greater degree of control, so that if you wish you can vary the texture from rough and chunky to silky smooth.

Before liquidising, let the soup cool a little, so that odd splashes won't burn you. With a jug liquidiser, always make sure that the lid is firmly clamped on. Don't over-fill – it is better to liquidise the soup in three or four batches, than to risk it squirting out all over the kitchen.

Liquidising with a hand-held wand.

Even the toughest liquidiser can't reduce absolutely everything to a smooth cream, so every now and then you will come across a soup that also needs sieving (such as the roast tomato and onion soup on page 24). The trick here is to make sure that you have a sieve with a comparatively loose mesh, i.e. with big enough holes to make sieving bearable. A sieve with a very tight mesh is fine for, say, sifting flour, but a nightmare when it comes to soups and sauces, as you have to work really, really hard for relatively small returns. So, go check your sieves and if necessary invest in a new, wide-meshed one as soon as possible. With that in hand, sieving a soup should be an easy enough matter. Use the largest wooden spoon you own to push the solids through the mesh of the sieve, scraping the puréed matter that clings to the underside off into the rest of the soup fairly frequently.

Alternatively, you could buy a mouli-légumes, or a food mill, which will do a similar job with efficiency.

Thinning Down   Once your soup is liquidised, you can assess the consistency properly. You may like it just as it is, but if you want to thin it down to a lighter consistency, stir in a little water if it needs only minor adjustment, or more stock, or perhaps some milk, if appropriate. Add a little at a time, stir in and then taste. Be careful not to overdo the extra liquid, or you will end up with a soup that tastes of precious little at all.

Dressing Up   An unadorned naked bowl of soup is a fine thing in itself, but there are times when all of us, soup included, benefit from a spot of dressing up. Some garnishes go particularly well with specific soups, whilst others are universally a good thing. Here is a list of some of the best, to be used on their own or in tandem with others

Fresh herbs   Shredded basil leaves on any tomato-based soup; coriander leaves on soups with a hint of spice; chopped parsley or chives will give a lift to most soups; tarragon leaves bring a hint of aniseed – use your imagination.

Cream   A drizzle or swirl of cream looks classy and enriches soup. It doesn't matter a great deal whether it is single, whipping or double cream. Lightly whipped cream, seasoned with lime juice or herbs, floats on top of the soup, melting gently in the heat. Soured cream, crème fraîche and yoghurt (especially Greek-style yoghurt) need to be dolloped on gently. Yoghurt has a tendency to sink.

Croûtons   The traditional croûton is a small, crisp golden cube of fried bread which adds a welcome contrast in texture to most soups. I find it easier to bake croûtons in the oven: toss cubed bread (crusts removed) with a little oil, turning well, then spread out on a baking sheet and bake at 190°C/375°F/Gas Mark 5, turning occasionally until golden brown, about 5–10 minutes. Although any decent loaf of bread will do, you can make extra-fancy croûtons with, say, olive bread or sun-dried tomato bread.

Croûtes   Croûtes are larger versions of croûtons. Small slices of bread (either quarter large pieces, or use slices of a baguette) can either be toasted, or brushed with olive oil and baked in the oven until crisp (the best method, I think, see the croûtons section above). You could top each one with a smear of pesto (bought or home-made, see page 71), or tapenade (an olive and caper purée that can be bought in small jars from the deli). Or try a small swirl of crème fraîche, or you could pile some grated Gruyère cheese on top. Whatever you do, the idea is then to float it in the soup as it is served.

Fresh herbs: from top left, coriander, chives, flat-leaf parsley and tarragon.

Croûtes, one with a swirl of crème fraîche.

Croûtons.

Cheese Grated or very finely diced cheese is a good garnish for chunky soups, such as the Italian vegetable and bean soup on page 26. Parmesan is wonderfully piquant, but grated mature Cheddar brings oodles of flavour, too. The sweetish, nutty taste of Gruyère is another winner.

Olive oil A drizzle of a really fruity extra virgin olive oil works well in many more Mediterranean soups, bringing a fresh, light richness that invigorates all the other flavours in the soup. For a powerful injection of energy, fry 1 or 2 chopped garlic cloves and a deseeded chopped red chilli in olive oil until the garlic is golden, then spoon over the surface of the soup, still hot and sizzling, just before serving.

Bacon Choose good-quality dry-cured streaky bacon (it crisps up better than back bacon), and cook in rashers until brown and crisp (see page 21).

Diced tomato, cucumber or pepper These add an appealing freshness to a soup, as well as a splash of colour. Deseed tomatoes and peppers, but don't skin them, before dicing small. I really can't see the point in deseeding cucumbers, but if you really want to, that's fine. Diced celery can also work well, but a fair number of people aren't so keen on it.

Good Vegetable Soup

This is a basic primer recipe for puréed vegetable soup. It's ideal for using up the odds and ends of vegetables that gather in the bottom of the fridge or in the vegetable rack (as long as they are not too old and mouldering), but you can also use it to make a purer mono-veg soup, such as the curried parsnip soup below.

Serves 4–6

BASE INGREDIENTS

2 tablespoons olive or sunflower oil, or 30g (1oz) butter
1 onion, peeled and chopped
1 garlic clove, peeled and chopped

AROMATICS

1 bouquet garni (the classic one below)
and/or   1–2 fresh red chillies, deseeded and chopped
or   1 teaspoon or more curry paste or curry powder or spices, e.g. cumin, fennel seeds, cinnamon, etc.

MAIN INGREDIENTS

1 potato, or other thickener if needed, peeled and cut into chunks
500g (18oz) vegetables, prepared as appropriate (see page 27) and roughly chopped

LIQUID

1–1.5 litres (1¾– 2¾ pints) Vegetable or Chicken Stock (see pages 15–17), or vegetable cooking water, or a mixture of water
and milk

SEASONINGS

salt and pepper

1 Heat the oil or butter gently in a large saucepan, then add the base ingredients, the aromatics and the main ingredients. Stir around to coat everything in the fat, then sweat very gently for 10–15 minutes.

2 Add the smaller amount of stock or other liquid, saving the rest for thinning down (if necessary), and season with salt and pepper. Bring up to the boil, then simmer gently for about 20 minutes until all the vegetables are tender.

3 Liquidise in several batches, and return to the pan. Thin down with the reserved stock, water or milk as required, and check the seasoning.

4 Reheat when needed, and eat.

need to know

BOUQUET GARNI This is a bundle of herbs, that gives flavour to stocks, soups and stews. Classically it is a bay leaf, a sprig of parsley and a sprig of thyme tied together with string. Other flavours can be added – leek leaves, alternative herbs or lemon zest.

Potato, Parsley and Garlic Soup

This yummy, comforting soup can be served as a first course, or in larger quantities whenever you are need of a bit of inner warmth. I love it with a touch of cheese and some crisp, salty bacon bits stirred in, but neither is utterly essential. You might just want to scatter over a few chopped chives instead, or spoon on some nuggets of golden-fried chopped garlic and chilli with a drizzle of olive oil.

Serves 4–6

BASE INGREDIENTS
1 onion, peeled and chopped
30g (1oz) butter

AROMATICS
1 bouquet garni (2 strips lemon zest,
    1 bay leaf, 1 sprig thyme)

MAIN INGREDIENTS
leaves of 1 bunch parsley, roughly
    chopped
1kg (2¼lb) potatoes, peeled and
    thickly sliced
1 whole garlic bulb, separated into cloves,
    peeled

LIQUID
1.2 litres (2 pints) Vegetable or Chicken
    Stock (see pages 15–17)
300ml (10fl oz) milk

SEASONINGS
salt and pepper
freshly grated nutmeg
½ lemon

DRESSING UP (OPTIONAL)
a handful of grated Gruyère cheese
4–6 rashers streaky bacon, cooked until
    crisp (see right), and crumbled

1 Follow the basic method opposite, adding the stock only, plus salt, pepper and nutmeg at stage 2. When liquidised, stir in the milk, and add a squeeze or two of lemon juice (this highlights flavours, but shouldn't be so much that the soup tastes lemony).

2 Reheat, and serve with the cheese and bacon if you wish.

need to know

CRISPY BACON To get bacon appetisingly crisp you will need to start off with a pack of streaky bacon. The higher fat content is what makes it go so irresistibly crunchy and golden. A dry-cure bacon is a better option than cheaper bacon which will probably have been pumped up with water and other additives. The best cooking method, I find, is to lay the bacon on a rack over a roasting tin and cook it in a hot oven, around 200°C/400°F/Gas Mark 6, for about 20 minutes until it is golden brown. Grilling is the second best option and not so dissimilar – keep the bacon about 10cm (4in) away from the grill and move it around the grill rack every few minutes so that it grills evenly. Either way, let it cool a little before attempting to crumble it.

need to know

HOW BIG IS A BUNCH? 'A bunch of parsley' is, I admit, infuriatingly vague. Actually, it's deliberately vague, and I hope you will consider it empowering in a very small, kitcheny sort of a way. It's a permission-giver of a term. So, if you quite fancy the idea of loads of parsley giving the soup a definite green tint, then you use a big bunch. For an altogether tamer affair, take it down to posy-ish size. The point, really, is that the exact size is not critical to the success of the soup; it just changes the taste a little... or a lot. Hey – you're the cook here. It's up to you how the food turns out. Embrace the responsibility!

Curried Parsnip Soup

When my Mum, the food writer Jane Grigson, came up with this wonderful soup way back in the 1970s, it seemed quite radical. Now, almost everyone has caught up with it, and variations on the theme abound. The original combination of humble parsnips and curry remains one of the best.

Follow the **Good Vegetable Soup** recipe on page 20, using a ½ tablespoon curry paste (or a little more if you like things extra spicy) as the aromatic element, and replacing potato and vegetables with 500g (18oz) parsnips, which are starchy enough to thicken the soup without aid. Smaller parsnips should be peeled, then sliced, discarding the top. After peeling, larger parsnips will need to be cut into chunks, then quartered lengthways to reveal the tougher inner core. Cut this bit out and chuck it in the bin. Use what is left for the soup.

This is a soup that takes particularly well to being finished with a little cream swirled into each bowl and a scattering of croûtons.

Carrot and Coriander Soup

This is another modern classic, but one that is often misinterpreted. It is coriander seed that works so magically with carrots, rather than coriander leaf (although this is welcome as a finishing touch).

Follow the recipe for **Good Vegetable Soup** on page 20, using a tablespoon of whole coriander seeds as the aromatic element, replacing the potato with 1 tablespoon of rice (any white rice: long-grain, pudding or risotto), and using carrots alone, with no other vegetables. Serve the soup with a scattering of fresh coriander leaves on top.

Curried parsnip soup with croûtons and a swirl of cream.

Roast Tomato and Onion Soup

Roasting the vegetables for a soup gives a great depth of flavour, and a hint of something darker and treaclier distilled from the heat-charred edges. It also happens to be a particularly simple way of setting about soup-making. Everything bar the stock is piled into a roasting tin and slid into the oven. You go away for 45 minutes or so, and then all you need do is liquidise the whole lot. And sieve it. Finito.

Serves 4–6

BASE AND MAIN INGREDIENTS

1.5kg (3lb 5oz) reddest tomatoes you can find, cut in half
1kg (2¼ lb) onions, peeled and cut into eighths
6 garlic cloves, unpeeled
3 big thyme sprigs
4 tablespoons olive oil

SEASONINGS

2 teaspoons caster sugar
salt and pepper

LIQUID

900ml (1½ pints) Vegetable or Chicken Stock (see pages 15–17)

DRESSING UP (optional, but really good)

50ml (2fl oz) whipping cream
a small handful of basil leaves, chopped

1 Preheat the oven to 220°C/425°F/Gas Mark 7.

2 Put all the base and main ingredients and the seasonings into a large roasting tin. Use your hands to turn the vegetables so that they all get coated in oil and evenly seasoned. Roast uncovered for 45 minutes, stirring once, until patched with brown and phenomenally soft and tender. If the onions still appear a little firm, give the whole lot another stir and return to the oven for a further 15 minutes. Remove the thyme stalks.

3 Liquidise in batches with big slurps of stock to keep the whole lot moving (in a processor, or with a hand-held wand liquidiser). Sieve the resulting soup back into the pan, with any remaining stock. Stir well, then taste and adjust seasoning.

4 Reheat when needed, or serve chilled on a hot day.

Coat the vegetables with oil and roast uncovered.

Roast tomato and onion soup.

5 The dressing-up basil cream is easy. Put the cream and most of the basil, together with a couple of pinches of salt, in a bowl and whisk together until the cream just holds its shape. Don't over-do it or you will end up with butter. Not at all the idea. Drop a spoonful of the basil cream into the centre of each bowl of soup and top with a little of the remaining basil before passing around.

Liquidise and sieve the soup, and whisk up the basil cream.

Italian Bean and Vegetable Soup

This is a brilliant, filling chunky soup just like the ones mama makes all over Italy.

Serves 6–8

BASE INGREDIENTS
4 tablespoons olive oil
1 onion, peeled and chopped
3 garlic cloves, peeled and chopped
2 carrots, peeled and diced

AROMATICS
2 sprigs each of thyme and rosemary
4 tablespoons chopped parsley

MAIN INGREDIENTS
200g (7oz) dried cannellini beans, soaked
   overnight, or 1 x 400g can cooked
   cannellini beans
450g (1lb) potatoes, peeled and cut into 2 cm
   (¾ in) cubes
about 300g (10oz) prepared weight of at least
   2 of the following: courgettes, winter
   squash such as butternut, turnips, fennel,
   celery, leeks (see opposite)
1 x 400g can chopped tomatoes
110g (4oz) peas, fresh or frozen and thawed

LIQUIDS
1.2 litres (2 pints) water

SEASONINGS
salt and pepper

DRESSING UP
freshly grated Parmesan cheese (or Cheddar
   or Gruyère)
the very best extra virgin olive oil

1 If cooking the beans yourself, drain after soaking. Cover with 1.8 litres (3 pints) fresh water, add half the aromatics, and bring to the boil. Boil hard for 5 minutes, and then simmer until the beans are just cooked and tender, around 40 minutes.

2 Drain the cooked or canned beans. If you have cooked them yourself, save the cooking water.

3 Sauté the base ingredients in a good large, heavy-based pan until soft and lightly browned. Don't rush this. Allow a good 10–15 minutes and keep on stirring, so that the full sweet, caramelised flavour has time to develop.

4 Add the remaining aromatics and all the remaining main ingredients except for the beans, peas, courgettes or leeks (or whichever vegetables you are using). Pour in the liquid (use the bean cooking water if you have it). Season with salt and pepper and bring up to the boil.

5 Simmer gently until the potatoes are almost cooked (around 15 minutes), then stir in the peas and courgettes and leeks if using, along with the beans. Simmer for a further 4–5 minutes. Taste and adjust the seasoning.

6 Serve in big bowls, passing the cheese and olive oil around the table so that everyone can add just the amount they like to their soup.

Italian Vegetable Soup with Pasta

Follow the recipe for **Italian Bean and Vegetable Soup** opposite, replacing some, all or none of the beans (depending on how much carbohydrate you crave), with a handful or two of small macaroni, or other small pasta shapes. Throw the pasta into the soup when it has been boiling for about 10 minutes, and check that it is cooked al dente (see page 65) before taking the pan off the heat. You may need to add a little extra water (say around 100–150ml/4–5fl oz) to the pan, as the pasta will absorb some of the liquid.

need to know

PREPARING VEGETABLES

COURGETTES: slice thickly and quarter each slice.

WINTER SQUASH (any from pumpkin to butternut squash, to onion squash and so on): cut away the hard rind and scrape out the seeds. Cut the flesh into 2cm (¾in) cubes.

TURNIPS: if they are young and small there is no need to peel. Older chunkier turnips have older thicker skin, so it's best to remove it. Cut what remains into 2cm (¾in) cubes.

FENNEL: trim off the stumps of the stalks, which tend to be stringy. Cut a thin slice from the base, and if the outer layer is damaged and browned, discard that too. Quarter from base to stalk end, then slice each quarter.

CELERY: wash and slice, removing as many strings as possible.

LEEKS: slice off the tougher dark green leaves, and trim off the roots. Make a cut through the centre of the leek, from the leaf end, down its length for around 7.5cm (3in), and then make a second cut, the same length, at right angles to it. Fan this end of the leek out under running water to clean out any trapped particles of earth. Shake off excess water. Now slice the leek into rings about 5mm (¼in) thick.

Smoked Haddock and Shrimp Chowder

Chowders are big, hearty soups, quick to make and a delight to eat. Essential items are potatoes, carrots, celery, bacon and milk, and from then on you can extemporise. Fish of some sort is usual in a chowder – it was, after all, originally a fisherman's on-board meal – but not absolutely critical (see below). Smoked haddock gives a particularly fine flavour (buy the undyed, pale honey-tan fish, not the garish yellow), while a handful of shrimps or prawns lifts it above the ordinary.

Serves 4 as a main course, 6 as a starter

BASE INGREDIENTS
1 onion, chopped
30g (1oz) butter
4 rashers back bacon, cut into small strips

AROMATICS
1 bay leaf
2 tablespoons chopped parsley

MAIN INGREDIENTS
2 large carrots, peeled and thickly sliced
2 celery stalks, thickly sliced
1 green pepper, deseeded and cut into postage-stamp squares
2 medium-sized potatoes, peeled and cut into 1cm (½in) cubes
30g (1oz) plain flour
250g (9oz) skinned smoked haddock fillet
110g (4oz) peeled, cooked shrimps or prawns

LIQUIDS
600ml (1 pint) milk
150ml (5fl oz) water

SEASONINGS
salt and pepper

DRESSING UP
a handful of freshly grated Cheddar cheese

1 Fry the onion and bacon gently in the butter in a large saucepan until the onion is translucent and soft.

2 Now add the aromatics, using only half the parsley, and all the vegetable main ingredients. Stir around, then sprinkle over the flour, a little salt (not too much as both the bacon and the haddock may be salty) and plenty of pepper. Stir again for some 30 seconds or so to make sure the flour is more or less evenly distributed.

3 Now add a third of the milk and stir well, before adding the remaining milk, the water, and some more salt and pepper if needed.

4 Bring up to the boil, stirring frequently to prevent catching (i.e. burning) on the base. Turn the heat down low and simmer very gently for around 15–20 minutes until the vegetables are all tender. Stir frequently to prevent catching. If the mixture seems too thick, add a little more milk or water.

5 While the soup simmers, cut the smoked haddock fillet into chunks about 2.5cm (1in) square, discarding any bones you may come across. Stir the haddock and the shrimps or prawns into the chowder and simmer for a further 3–4 minutes until the haddock is just cooked through.

6 Sprinkle with the remaining parsley and plenty of cheese. Make a meal of this one, serving it in deep generous bowlfuls with warm bread.

Starters

This time, you've decided, you're going for the full works. Entertaining proper, with starter, main course and pudding. Any time-challenged cook (and that's most of us these days) needs a bevy of almost effortless starters up their sleeves for occasions like these. Starters that will look good, taste fabulous, and take the edge off hunger during the wait for the main course. This is where the deli counter, be it at the supermarket or a proper delicatessen shop, comes into its own, able to provide the makings of a superb first course that demands little more effort on your part than a spot of arranging on pretty plates.

It's worth pointing out, too, that any of these ideas below would also make a nifty light lunch. All you need do to flesh them out is add a couple of salads: maybe a green salad or a tomato salad, and a potato salad (see pages 188–89 and 191).

The one important thing to remember with these simple starters is that they all need to be served at room temperature (except for the grilled goat's cheese, which obviously needs to be served hot), not straight from the fridge, as cold kills the taste of so many foods. So, lay them out at least half an hour before eating and cover with clingfilm until your guests congregate near the table.

Four Mediterranean Medleys

All around the Mediterranean, people love to start a meal with a selection of little dishes to get the gastric juices flowing. One up from a picnic, this mini-feast can consist of no more than two or three items, or stretch to a sea of bits and bobs to nibble on. The point is that they should all have lively, vivid flavours, so a selection will usually include cured meat or fish, cheese, and pickles of one sort or another. Now that our supermarkets stock so many Mediterranean ingredients, it is incredibly easy to put together the same sort of starter here, and the brilliant thing is that it requires next-to-no effort on the part of the provider.

How Much? It's almost impossible to be precise about quantities here, as so much depends on the rest of the meal, the appetites of your guests, and how many different bits and bobs you put on the table. As a rough guide, make sure that there is enough of each item for everyone to get a decent taste. The more different items you have, the less you need of each one. Provide plenty of bread as well, and don't worry.

Presentation   You have two options here. **Option A** is to make up individual platefuls of hams and cheeses and whatever for each of your guests. That way no-one is going to squabble over the last slice of Parma ham. And if you are worried that quantities may be a little skimpy, you can pad each plateful out with a small handful of rocket or watercress or other salad leaf, or even just an artful sprig or two of fresh parsley, basil or other herb if you happen to have some to hand.

Option B, which happens to be the one that I prefer, is to lay your collection of delicacies out on serving plates or platters and arrange them in the centre of the table so that everyone can help themselves. This way everyone can take what they like and ignore what they don't without feeling embarrassed. And it's wonderful how a bit of passing this or that around can get the conversation flowing, and invoke a cheery atmosphere.

Provençal Hors d'Oeuvre

In the south of France, they do the pick'n'mix starter with much grace. A classic hors d'oeuvre selection may include pâtés and cured hams, or delicious pungent dips and spreads.

Tapenade   Buy a jar of this blend of olives, capers and anchovies. Pile it into a pretty little bowl, and finish with a sprig of parsley.

Fromage frais aux fines herbes   As a complete contrast, make up your own bowl of creamy pale cheese flecked with green herbs. Buy a pot or two of creamy young goat's cheese (chèvre frais) and beat in either a little crushed garlic or finely chopped shallot, lots of chopped fresh herbs (parsley, mint, tarragon, chives or whatever you have to hand) and a few spoonfuls of cream or milk if the mixture is still too thick to work as a dip. Then scrape into a bowl and place on the table.

Crudités   Serve these with the two dips – in other words, carrot sticks, strips of pepper, celery sticks, pink and white radishes and so on.

French bread   The ready-to-bake half baguettes are usually better than the ubiquitous French stick.

French olives   These are easy to find. Amongst the best are small, dark, wrinkled Niçoise olives and green picholine olives.

Silvery marinated anchovies   Although these may actually have come from Italy or elsewhere, they fit nicely into this southern French ensemble.

Two full plates of Mediterranean medleys: Spanish chaciñas (top, with Manchego cheese and bread), and Italian antipasti (right, with bocconcini and baby artichokes).

Italian Antipasti

For a really special occasion, track down your nearest Italian deli for a classy selection of imports, but the rest of the time, scour the shelves of your local supermarket for some of the following:

Parma ham or **San Daniele ham** The most famous of Italy's many cured raw hams (prosciutto crudo), sliced paper thin.

Bresaola Cured beef, thinly sliced and dressed with a squeeze of lemon juice and a drizzle of extra virgin olive oil.

Italian salami.

Pecorino A sheep's milk cheese, which may be either hard or soft.

Provolone A softer cow's milk cheese which may be young and mild (dolce) or more mature and punchy (piccante).

Buffalo mozzarella Mozzarella di bufala is the real thing, softer and milkier than cow's milk mozzarella. It comes in packets in its own brine. Serve it drained, torn into pieces and dressed with lemon or balsamic vinegar, extra virgin olive oil, salt and pepper and a little chopped parsley, mint, or even fresh tarragon. You could also add some sliced halved cherry tomatoes for contrast, or 'bocconcini di mozzarella', walnut-sized mini-mozzarellas, served whole and dressed as above.

Olives Choose whichever type you like best as long as they are not those ghastly stoned black olives that taste of soap.

Sun-dried tomatoes in olive oil.

Canned marinated grilled peppers.

Marinated baby artichokes These come in glass jars. Serve them sliced in halves or quarters.

Ciabatta bread Many supermarkets now sell 'ready-to-bake ciabatta' which comes out of the oven crisp and golden outside, soft and slightly chewy inside, with the most tantalising smell. Warm ciabatta always seems to disappear with remarkable speed, so buy a loaf or two more than you think you will need.

Spanish Chaciñas Plate

Over recent years we have been introduced to more and more of the excellent cured pork products and cheeses of Spain, via a handful of delicatessens and now the supermarkets. These are usually referred to as 'chaciñas', which translates more or less as 'cold cuts', but taste a good deal more exciting than that sounds. To make up a Spanish chaciñas plate, take your pick from:

Jamón serrano The Spanish equivalent to Parma ham, cured high in the hills.

Chorizo A spicy salami, with a reddish hue from generous seasoning of paprika. It can either be 'dulce' or mild, or 'piccante' or chilli-hot.

Manchego cheese Spain's most renowned cheese with a gorgeous flavour, which can either be mild or mature and is often served with 'marmelada' or quince paste.

Caper berries The fruit of the caper plant that grows wild around the rocky shores of the Mediterranean. Capers are the buds, but the berries or seed-pods are like tiny maracas that have been pickled in vinegar – delicious.

Olives Spain specialises in huge 'gordo' green olives which are sometimes sold here, but any juicy, plump-looking olive, black or green, will look good on the plate.

Canned 'pequillo' peppers Something of a speciality in Spain, you can sometimes find them on supermarket shelves here. Look out too for the small green padron peppers which are just beginning to hit the shops in this country.

Bread Spanish bread hasn't made much of a mark here, so choose any handsome-looking loaf of bread to accompany your chaciñas. A sourdough pain de campagne or sturdy rye bread, warmed through in the oven, would be a good choice.

Greek/Middle Eastern Mezze

From Greece and the Middle East come some of the best ready-made starters and snacks – from hummus and taramasalata to pitta bread and now the floppier, larger Arab bread. Put them all together and you can create a magnificent 'mezze', a pick'n'mix of a first course.

Hummus This is the obvious starting place for any Greek-inspired 'mezze' and a pot of two of bought hummus can easily be dolled up to look glamorous. First of all, add a little crushed garlic if you wish to liven up the flavour, then scrape it into a small bowl, and dust the top lightly with paprika or cayenne pepper, and a drizzle of extra virgin olive oil. A small sprig of parsley in the centre adds a final splash of colour. If you have the time, you could also sprinkle over or stir into the hummus a handful of pine nuts, that have been dry-fried until golden brown for a sophisticated finish.

Taramasalata This has to be next on the list, but try to find some that has not been dyed a virulent bright pink. Natural taramasalata is a softer, honeyed colour. Again, scrape into a bowl and sprinkle over a little cayenne pepper and some chopped parsley.

Crudités Provide a selection of raw vegetables to dip into the hummus and taramasalata – carrot sticks, strips of pepper, celery sticks and so on, as well as plenty of warm pitta bread.

Gigantes beans in tomato sauce If you haven't tasted these before, this is the moment to try them out. Usually sold in glass jars, they are similar to butter beans, bathed in a well-flavoured tomato, dill and olive oil sauce.

Canned dolmades Little parcels of flavoured rice wrapped in vine leaves, these are surprisingly good and just need to be transferred to a plate.

Purple black Kalamata olives are fat and juicy with taut skins and tip-tilted pointy ends.

Pickled green chillies These are a hot favourite in Greece, in both senses of the word – find them in jars, somewhere near the olives.

Some Classic Quick Starters

Here is a handful of quick and easy starters that never fail to please. Original? Well, maybe not, but the reason they've been enjoyed for so many decades is that they work so well, and cause so little angst to the cook!

Tuna and Bean Salad

This is a great (mainly) storecupboard stand-by that I often serve as a first course, or as part of a salad-based meal. It takes 10 minutes max to put together, and needs no more than some great, chunky bread as an accompaniment.

For four people you will need 1 x 400g can of cannellini beans, drained and rinsed, and a 198g can of tuna (the stuff in oil tastes nicer, but is higher in calories), drained and flaked. Mix them together with 1 small garlic clove, crushed, 1 shallot that has been finely chopped (or you could use ½ small red onion), and about ½ tablespoon chopped fresh marjoram or 1 level teaspoon dried oregano. Whisk together 1½ tablespoons lemon juice, 3–4 tablespoons extra virgin olive oil, salt and pepper, and stir into the tuna mixture. Make a bed of rocket on a serving plate, and pile the tuna and bean salad on to it. Serve at room temperature.

Bruschetta

At its most elemental, bruschetta (pronounced 'broos-ket-ah') is no more than a slice of griddled or char-grilled bread, rubbed with garlic and drizzled with olive oil. This most straightforward form of bruschetta is an ideal accompaniment to antipasti (see above). For a stand-alone bruschetta that is interesting enough to make a first course in its own right, the basic bruschetta is surmounted with any one of hundreds of toppings. A serving of three pieces of bruschetta, each with its own individual character, makes a substantial starter, although you should remember when planning the meal that the bruschette (that's the proper Italian plural) will need to be made no earlier than half an hour before guests arrive. Even better, they should be griddled and made up at the very last minute so that the bread is still warm, but that may prove just too tricky in terms of timing.

Two bruschette: one with tomatoes and ham (left), the other with pesto, mozzarella, sun-dried tomatoes and basil (right).

The key to success with bruschette is to source good-quality sturdy bread; if in doubt buy a loaf of pain de campagne or a sourdough loaf. Slice thickly and cut huge slices in half, or even into thirds. Then toast under the grill, or better still griddle to achieve the all-important slightly smoky flavour with a hint of charring (but no more than a hint, please!). It could also be done on the barbecue, but it seems a little excessive to get it going just for a few slices of bread! The toaster is completely out of bounds.

To griddle the bread, you will need to have a ridged griddle pan. Place over a high heat and leave to get really, really hot – allow some 5 minutes for this. Cram as many slices of bread on to it as possible, and turn once the underneath is striped with dark brown. Griddle the other side in the same way.

After rubbing the grilled bread with garlic, drizzle it with some olive oil.

While the bread is toasting cut a couple of cloves of garlic in half. Rub the garlic lightly over one side of each piece of grilled bread, then drizzle a scant ½ teaspoon of extra virgin olive oil over each piece.

With the toppings, you can really let your imagination go, but to kick-start you, here are three straightforward ideas.

1 Halve several well-flavoured tomatoes (you can use cherry tomatoes if necessary), and rub them over the bread, pressing down firmly so that the juices and some of the flesh are smeared over the surface. Top with slices of jamón serrano, or Parma or San Daniele ham.

2 Instead of drizzling with olive oil, spread each slice with pesto, then top with sliced buffalo mozzarella, a piece of sun-dried tomato and a sprig of basil.

3 Top with rocket, drizzle with a little balsamic vinegar, and finish with shavings of Parmesan. To shave Parmesan, take a vegetable peeler and pull it across the surface of the block of Parmesan to create thin shavings of cheese (see left).

Melon or Figs with Parma Ham

This is one of summer and autumn's most perfect combinations. The key is learning to choose ripe fragrant fruit. In midsummer it is the melon you should go for, whilst in the autumn the fig reigns supreme. Although you may occasionally find a magnificent melon in midwinter, it is rare, so ignore temptation in the colder months.

For this you are looking for an orange-fleshed melon, in other words a cantaloupe or charentais melon. The paler, white/green-fleshed varieties have a duller taste – not to be sneezed at, but less of a success with salty Parma ham. Use your nose. A ripe melon will smell fragrant and sweet. Press the stalk end gently: if it gives slightly then you are probably on to a winner, but double-check that there are no soft squidgy patches indicating over-ripeness or a mouldy taint. One large melon will be enough for four people.

Ripe figs are tender and fairly soft. Pick them out carefully, avoiding any that are showing patches of brown. Handle them reverently, and place them side by side in a paper bag, settling the bag on top of the rest of your purchases as ripe figs are easily squashed. One or two figs per person is fine.

To serve the melon, cut into eight wedges. Scrape out the seeds and discard. Arrange the slices on individual plates and drape two or three thin slices of Parma ham (or jamón serrano) over each serving.

With the figs, nip the hard stalk tip off each one, then quarter, cutting down towards the base, but stopping just short of it, so that the quarters stay together. Splay them out slightly like the petals of a flower. Place on individual plates, and arrange two or three thin slices of Parma ham (or jamón serrano) alongside them on each plate.

Melon (here cantaloupe and piel de sapo), with Parma ham.

Grilled Goat's Cheese Salad

Now something of a bistro classic, this is still a great way to start a meal, but does require a brief spell of last-minute work in the kitchen. Keep this to a minimum by preparing everything in advance, so that it's all ready to go. Choose small drum-shaped goat's cheeses for this – the sort with a soft, white rind.

For each person you will need a handful of mixed salad leaves (I favour a mix of rocket and spinach, but the choice is entirely yours), about ½ tablespoon of a good vinaigrette (see page 189), a ½ goat's cheese, a small sprig of rosemary or parsley, a trace of oil (olive or sunflower) and some good (walnut) bread.

Preheat the grill thoroughly and line the grill rack with foil. Arrange the ½ cheese cut-side up on the foil. Brush the cut side with a little oil, then slide under the grill until browned. Meanwhile, toss the salad with the vinaigrette and divide between plates. Top each salad with a sizzling, browned ½ goat's cheese and finish with a sprig of herb. Serve immediately with toast.

Guacamole

Quick and easy to prepare, guacamole makes a brilliant starter served with warmed pitta bread or tortilla crisps. Alternatively, use it as a sort of relish to serve with grilled fish or meat, or roll up with chicken and peppers in a 'fajita' (see page 108).

If you use the smaller Hass avocados you will need three, but with larger avocados two will suffice. The avocados must be ripe and buttery for guacamole.

Serves 4 as a starter

2 tomatoes
1–2 fresh red chillies
a handful of coriander leaves
2–3 ripe avocados
½ red onion, peeled and finely diced
juice of 1 lime
salt and pepper

1 Deseed and finely dice the tomatoes. Deseed (depending on strength) and finely chop the chillies. Chop the coriander. Skin the avocados, and remove the stones.

2 Working quickly, roughly mash the avocado flesh with a fork in a bowl, then mix in all the remaining ingredients. Taste and adjust flavouring, adding more lime if needed. Cover the surface with clingfilm to exclude as much air as possible, thus diminishing the inevitable browning of the avocado. Chill.

3 Bring back to room temperature before serving, then stir and scoop into a clean serving bowl.

Grilled goat's cheese salad.

Eggs

A decent meal is never far away if you have a stash of eggs in your kitchen. And if you think egg dishes are boring, you'd better revise your thinking right now. An omelette, for example, is an extraordinary vehicle for any number of other ingredients from the minimalism of a grating of Cheddar to the Mediterranean delights of a frittata. The humble fried egg is given a new lease of life with a spot of chilli and garlic, while scrambled eggs take to the fresh zing of citrus juice with consummate ease. One of the best of all egg and cheese combinations, needing just a little butter and flour for substance, is the wicked French gougère, a gorgeously indulgent, gooey cheese pastry that I often knock up for supper or a light lunch. The great thing about all of these simple dishes is that you can tailor them to your own requirements – once you get the basic principles sorted, the imagination can take over (even if it is only to the extent of using up the odds and ends left in the back of the fridge).

Buying Eggs

Eggs are no longer just mere eggs. Oh no. Nowadays there is a bewildering series of choices to be made when buying eggs: four-grain, barn-fresh, perchery, free-range, organic, Colombian this, and something else that. In fact, buying eggs is not half as confusing as it may first seem when you are facing the high-stacked egg shelves. Ultimately there are really only three critical choices to make: size, the well-being of the laying birds, and freshness.

Size Eggs are sorted into size bands according to weight: extra large (more than 73g), large (63–73g), medium (53–63g) and small (less than 53g). All the eggs used in testing recipes for this book were large, so if you want to be sure of getting a good result with my recipes, these are the ones to go for. When you are using other cookbooks, particularly if you are baking cakes, it is worth checking the beginning of the book, where there should be a short section telling you what size eggs are to be used, as well as other useful basic cook's information.

Happy Chooks By the year 2012, the very worst space-depriving cages for egg-laying chickens will have been banned in the EU. About time too, for they are grim and deeply objectionable. Hard to believe that a nation of so-called 'animal-lovers' could have let them exist for so long. Meanwhile, unless you really don't care one iota about animal welfare, pay the few extra pence to buy free-range eggs. The law guarantees that the chickens that lay these eggs at least have continuous daytime access to outdoor runs. In other words, they can peck around and stretch their wings, even if they don't live in quite the idyllic circumstances one might imagine. Organic eggs are by definition free-range.

Freshness Crack open a perfectly fresh egg on to a saucer and the yolk stands proud above the white, which clings thickly around it. In an older egg the yolk is flatter and flabbier, while the white is more liquid and spreads in a dilute fashion around the saucer. Luckily you don't have to crack open each egg to ascertain its age. Look on the box instead, where you will find a 'best before date'. The eggs were laid 21 days, in other words three weeks, before this date.

For some cooking methods (poaching in particular) ultra-freshness is critical, whilst for others (e.g. boiling) a small scrap of maturity is a positive boon.

Salmonella The doom-laden spirit of salmonella contamination still lingers on in many people's minds. The truth is that these days the chances of developing salmonella poisoning from semi-cooked or raw eggs is verging on negligible. That time-honoured hazard of falling under a bus is far, far more likely to happen to you than a spot of salmonella sickness.

All eggs that are stamped with the 'lion' symbol (which represents the Lion Quality Mark) come from flocks of chickens that have been vaccinated against salmonella, and are regularly checked to make doubly sure they are clean. If you are buying wonderful extra-free-range eggs from a local farmer, then the likelihood is that his or her flock has also been vaccinated, but if in any doubt, just ask.

Salmonella bacteria are killed by high temperatures, so eggs that are hard-boiled or cooked thoroughly in, say, a cake batter cannot possibly cause any harm. Many of the most delicious ways of cooking eggs, however, demand that they are semi-cooked, with the yolk still runny and this is where, in the very, very unlikely event that they are infected, the problem lies. For most healthy people, the worst that could happen is a nasty bout of stomach upset and diarrhoea, but it is not worth risking even this extraordinarily unlikely event with anyone susceptible to illness. In other words, the elderly, invalids, pregnant women and very young children should all steer clear of semi-cooked or raw eggs. End of scare stories.

None. The colour of the eggshell is totally irrelevant and tells you nothing about the inside or the way it was produced. Even more surprisingly, the colour of the yolk isn't much to go on, either. A deep, rich, almost orange hue might suggest a grain-rich diet for its mother hen, but it may just as well indicate the inclusion of dyestuffs in the feed. Appearances can be deceptive.

Storage

In an ideal world, you would keep your eggs in a cool larder, temperature around 15°C or less. Oh? You don't have a cool larder where you live? How very awkward of you! You'll just have to keep your eggs where most people store them: in the fridge. It's the second best option and it's done me fine for the past twenty something years, so I don't think there's any need for concern. Try to remember to get them out of the cold and into the warmth of the kitchen 15 minutes or so before cooking, particularly if you are boiling or poaching them – again, counsel of perfection, but easier to achieve than the cool larder.

Separating Eggs

Separating the yolk and white of an egg is essentially an easy process, but it may nonetheless take two or three attempts to get it right. So make sure that you have a couple of eggs in reserve, just in case. Fresher eggs (up to a week old) are easier to separate than older ones.

Before you start, gather together a large bowl to hold the whites (assuming you intend to whisk them after separating), and two smaller bowls. The first of the smaller bowls is for the yolks. The second is for the white of the egg that you are in the midst of separating, before you tip it into the larger bowl. Why do you need this extra bowl? Insurance. Just one small drop of fat in amongst the whites will be enough to prevent them whisking up properly. Yolks are very fatty. There is nothing more dismaying than successfully separating four eggs, and then breaking the yolk of the fifth so that it contaminates the whole lot. An infuriating waste of eggs and time. For the same reason, you should always make sure that both of the bowls for the whites are scrupulously clean before you begin, with no trace of grease.

1 Hold the egg comfortably in your hand, pointed end towards your thumb, rounded end towards your little finger (or vice versa), fingers wrapped around.
2 Tap the exposed side firmly against the edge of a bowl, cracking the shell. The skill here is to use enough force to crack the shell without actually smashing the whole egg. A bowl with a narrow edge is better than one with a thick rim.

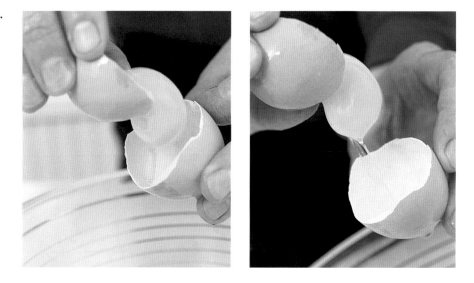

3 Turn the egg cracked side upwards and ease the tips of both thumbs into the crack, pulling the two halves of the shell apart, over the bowl, so that the yolk settles neatly into one side, while some of the white falls out of the other into the bowl.
4 Gently tip the yolk from one half of the shell into the other, allowing the white to dribble out into the bowl. Two or three goes at this should be quite enough. Slide the yolk into a small bowl.

Whisking Egg Whites

Whisked egg whites are used to lighten cakes, mousses, soufflé omelettes and other dishes. The whisking process traps small bubbles of air within the egg whites to make a foam. The more you whisk, the thicker and firmer the foam. For cooking you need to whisk egg whites either to soft peak or firm peak stage (see overleaf). But it is possible to go too far. Over-whisked eggs turn lumpy and it is impossible to incorporate them evenly into a batter. Nor will they give nearly so much lift.

When properly whisked whites are cooked, the air bubbles expand in the heat, lifting the mixture, at the same time as the egg white sets to hold the bubbles in place. Uncooked whisked egg whites are distinctly unstable, so must be used as soon as they have been whisked. If left standing around, they will collapse and liquefy and cannot be re-whisked successfully.

It is possible to whisk egg whites with a fork if all else fails, but it is extremely hard work. A balloon whisk is more efficient, but still tiring on the arms. An electric hand-held whisk is a brilliant luxury that makes quick work of whisking egg whites to the lightest foam.

Make absolutely sure that both bowls and whisk (or fork!) are completely grease-free before you separate eggs and start whisking the whites. It takes no more than a smear of grease to prevent egg whites whisking successfully.

How to whisk egg whites with a balloon whisk or a fork

1 Hold the bowl containing the egg whites firmly with one hand, tilting it slightly towards the other hand.

2 Move the whisk in a continuous circular movement, using your wrist rather than the whole arm, taking the whisk down through the whites then up and around and back down into them again.

3 Keep going and have faith. Eventually (assuming they haven't been contaminated with fatty yolk or grease), the whites will bulk up in volume, transformed into a fluffy cloud of whiteness.

4 For the vast majority of recipes, you will need to whisk the whites either to 'soft peak' or 'firm peak' stage. To test, pull the whisk slowly out of the whites. If the whites just slump back down into the bowl, you've not reached either stage yet. If they form a peak, the tip of which flops over as the whisk is withdrawn, then they have reached soft peak stage. If the tip of the peak remains pointing straight up at the ceiling, they have reached 'firm peak'. Whisk no more!

Whisking egg whites.

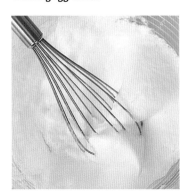  

Folding in When it comes to blending whisked egg whites (or whipped cream) into another mixture, you must do your very best to keep as much air as possible trapped in the whites, whilst at the same time mixing evenly. You wouldn't want to waste all that effort, now would you? This demands a special technique, called folding in.

First of all, search out a large metal spoon. Wooden spoons have thick edges, which break lots of bubbles releasing more air, whereas the thin edge of a metal spoon keeps damage to a minimum. Take a spoonful of the whites and just stir them straight into the other mixture (which should, incidentally, be no more than lukewarm). This loosens it up a little, making it easier to fold in the remaining whites. Now tip the rest of the whites on top. Slide the spoon, edge first, down into the whites and underlying mixture, right to the bottom, then curl it back up in one continuous movement, scooping up some of the contents of the bowl. As the spoon emerges tip what it brings up with it back over into the bowl. Keep going, turning the bowl every now and then, until the whites are evenly mixed in, with no lingering traces of white. Work swiftly and with confidence.

Primary Cooking Methods

Boiling First of all, get your eggs out of the fridge at least 15 minutes before cooking if at all possible. This reduces the likelihood of shell-cracking in the heat of the sauccpan. Pour enough water to submerge the eggs, into a pan that is just large enough to hold the eggs in a single layer (an over-large pan encourages the eggs to ricochet off the sides and each other, which is another reason they may crack). Bring the water up to the boil, then lower the eggs on a spoon into the water, one by one. Reduce the heat so that the water is simmering rather than bubbling violently. Set your timer to 5 minutes for soft-boiled eggs with a runny yolk and just set white, or 8 minutes for just hard-boiled eggs (firm white, creamy set yolk), 10 minutes for fully hard-boiled eggs.

Presumably you will be eating your soft-boiled egg while still hot from the water, so dish up immediately. If a hard-boiled egg is for a salad, or other cold dish, plunge it straight into cold water as soon as it is cooked, to prevent the formation of a discoloured green-black ring around the yolk. Not an attractive sight.

To shell a hard-boiled egg, tap the egg against the work surface, turning to break the shell all over. Pull off the shell, along with the thin membrane that lies underneath (easier to do with fresher eggs).

Frying There are many ways to fry an egg, but I shall attempt to keep things simple by offering just two of them: firstly the more traditional method, using butter; secondly a more vigorous method, using oil. If you have an excellent non-stick frying pan, you can also cook your eggs with virtually no fat at all (use the first method without the butter), though whether this technically counts as frying is debatable. Fresh eggs (up to a week) produce neater fried eggs than older ones.
Smooth and buttery method   Melt a good knob of butter in your frying pan over a moderate heat. When it is foaming, swiftly break your egg(s) into the pan – the

older they are the more room you will have to allow for spreading whites. Spoon some of the hot butter over the whites of the egg. Turn the heat down a little and then cover the pan with a lid or a large plate. Cook for about 2 minutes. Lift the lid and inspect the whites of the eggs. If they are still translucent and runny around the yolk, spoon over more hot butter, then replace the lid and leave for another 1–2 minutes by which time they should be done. Once the white has set to a glassy white opacity right up to the edge of the yolk, they are ready. Lift out of the pan with a fish slice and eat right away.

Crisp and bubbly method   I love fried eggs with a crisp browned edge to contrast with the smoothness of the rest of the whites, and the richness of a runny yolk, and to achieve this you need heat. Butter burns too quickly, so oil is the preferred frying medium. Spoon 1–2 tablespoons of extra virgin olive oil, or sunflower or vegetable oil into your frying pan, and heat over a fairly high heat. Break the egg(s) carefully into the oil, which should be hot enough to sizzle and spit a little. Spoon the oil over the whites to help them set. Once the eggs have browned a little at the edges, reduce the heat to moderate and continue cooking until the whites are cooked through to the yolk, occasionally spooning the fat over the whites. Lift out of the pan with a fish slice and tuck in.

Scrambling   The very best, creamiest scrambled eggs are those cooked slowly and lovingly in a bowl set over a pan of simmering hot water – try it one day when you have plenty of time (it can take 20 minutes or more of fairly constant attention). Meanwhile, stick with this quicker, not-quite-so-ideal method, which is better suited to the normal pace of life. Remember that scrambled eggs should never, ever be cooked in advance and kept warm. That way you end up with ghastly over-cooked, rubbery, institutionalised scrambled eggs instead of the luxuriously creamy, tender confection that properly scrambled eggs should be.

Break two eggs per person (or three if ravenous) into a bowl and whisk together. Season well with salt and pepper but do not add milk or water. Place a small saucepan or frying pan over a low heat and add a good knob of butter. Let it melt, then pour in the egg. Stir constantly with a wooden spoon or spatula, scraping the base and sides of the pan as the egg sets on them. Keep going until the saucepan contains a creamy, thick primrose-yellow scramble of eggs. Whip off the heat swiftly, scrape the scrambled egg straight on to plates or toast and dish up.

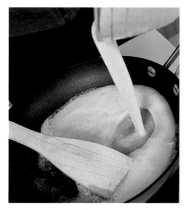

Scrambling eggs.

Smart scrambled eggs   Sunday brunch or breakfast with someone special is the time to dress up your scrambled eggs in full finery. Something as simple as stirring chopped fresh herbs into them as soon as they are cooked brings a touch of glamour – try chopped chives, tarragon or coriander. More fancy is the addition of strips of smoked salmon and some chopped chives, or sautéed sliced mushrooms, cooked alongside in a frying pan. I also love diced deseeded tomato or sun-blush tomato and roughly torn-up basil, again stirred in just as the scrambled egg reaches the perfect creamy consistency.

Poaching   Beautifully poached eggs are things of great purity. Some people love them on toast for breakfast, though I happen to prefer them at lunch or supper perched on top of a nice piece of grilled smoked haddock with a mound of spinach, or on pasta tossed with (ready-made) red pesto and rocket leaves, or on a warm spinach and bacon salad. There is something so very inviting about their wibbly-wobbly exterior, just begging to be breached, allowing the yolk to flow out in a flood of molten gold.

As I have discovered the hard way, over a number of years, it is only worth trying to poach eggs that are extremely fresh – up to four days, or at a pinch a week. In this state the thick white clings closely to the yolk, swaddling it in a protective layer. This is exactly what you want when poaching an egg. After a week or so, the white thins and no longer holds fast to the yolk. Result – when slid into hot water, the white floats off in disintegrating ribbons and your poached egg is a barely salvageable disaster. Don't say I didn't warn you.

How to poach an egg

1 Take a non-stick, high-sided frying pan, or a wide shallow saucepan. Fill it to a depth of at least 2.5cm (1in) with cold water and season with salt. Bring up to a boil, then reduce the heat so that the surface of the water trembles provocatively, with only the occasional burp of a bubble.

2 Break the first egg gently into a teacup or small ramekin or glass. Swirl a small whisk round and round in the trembling hot water to form a vortex. Remove the spoon and swiftly tip the egg into the centre of the vortex. As the water settles back down, use the bowl of a spoon to nudge any straying white back on to the yolk. Cook for approximately 3 minutes.

3 Cook no more than two or three eggs in the pan at any one time. Once the white has set, lift the poached egg out carefully, with a draining spoon if you have one (allowing water to drain back into the pan). Set it down on a plate lined with a double layer of kitchen towel to mop up dampness, then serve.

Fried Eggs with Coriander, Cumin and Balsamic Vinegar

These are fried eggs with attitude – jumping and sizzling with flavour. The recipe is based on the brilliant breakfast I tasted down at the wholesale vegetable market in Bogota in Colombia, many years ago. There's something about chilli and garlic and runny egg yolk first thing in the morning that is decadent and exotic and kicking. A great way to start the day.

Per person

olive oil
2 eggs
¼ red chilli, deseeded and finely sliced
¼ teaspoon cumin seeds
½ garlic clove, peeled and chopped
1–2 slices toasted bread to serve
½ teaspoon balsamic vinegar, or lime juice
coarse salt
a handful of chopped coriander

1 Pour enough oil into a heavy frying pan to cover the base. Heat over a fairly generous heat and then carefully break the eggs into it. Fry as usual (see page 48), spooning hot oil over the eggs to help them set.

2 When they are about half cooked, add the chilli, cumin and garlic to the pan and continue cooking until the white is set.

3 Lift the eggs out on to the bread, together with the bits of chilli and garlic, then spoon over a little of the oil. Drizzle over the balsamic vinegar, season with salt and scatter over lots of chopped coriander. Eat immediately.

Lemon scrambled egg
on toasted bagel, with
some smoked salmon
– good for a first
course.

Lemon Scrambled Eggs on Toasted Bagels

Quite the classiest scrambled eggs, these, ideal for a special breakfast or brunch. The lemon takes the edge off the richness and gives them a big boost. If you are feeling in a particularly indulgent mood, you might embellish them even further with a slice of smoked salmon apiece. I also serve these lemon scrambled eggs cold with smoked fish as a first course. Sounds a bit weird, but they actually taste great. As soon as they are cooked, scrape into a cool bowl to stop them thickening any further. Cool, then arrange a slice of smoked salmon, or cold-smoked trout, or smoked eel on each plate, with a mound of the lemon scrambled eggs beside it.

Serves 2

6 eggs
2 tablespoons double cream
finely grated zest of ½ lemon
juice of 1 lemon
salt and pepper
15g (½ oz) butter
2 plain or onion bagels, split open
1 teaspoon chopped parsley or chives
   (optional)

1 Whisk the eggs with the cream, lemon zest, half the juice, and some salt and pepper.

2 Melt the butter in a small saucepan over a low heat and add the beaten egg. Cook as for ordinary scrambled eggs (see page 49), until creamy. Taste and add more lemon juice, and salt and pepper if needed.

3 Toast the bagel halves lightly, and arrange on plates. Spoon the scrambled eggs over and scatter with parsley or chives if using.

Omelettes

A good omelette is a beautiful object, with the gold-yellow of the eggs burnished with softly glistening, honeyed brown, plump and curvaceous in shape, with a definite come-hither look to it. Quick and easy too. What a seductive little beast.

Cooking   There is no great mystery to making a good omelette, as long as you bear the following in mind:

- **The eggs have got to be good quality** – there's not much else to mask imperfections. So, opt for free-range eggs, and make sure that they are at most two weeks old.
- Though quick, **omelettes need constant attention** while they cook. Therefore it is not a good idea to attempt feeding the whole gang on omelettes. This is a treat for one or two people only.
- **Butter is the cooking medium for a French omelette** – the magic combination of fresh eggs and butter is the whole point.
- **Do not attempt to 'stretch' the eggs** by adding water or milk to them. The liquid evaporates anyway, and makes the omelette a little tougher in the process.
- **You do not need a special omelette pan**. A good non-stick frying pan is ideal. If you use a non-non-stick frying pan, then it should have a thick base, and you must make sure that you get temperatures just right, otherwise the omelette will stick.
- **Pan size is critical**. For a three-egg omelette you should use a 17–20cm (7–8in) frying pan, but for a six-egg omelette (to be shared) the frying pan must be around 25cm (10in) in diameter. A frying pan that is too large will produce a thin, tough omelette, and in a pan that is too small, the egg is likely to burn before it sets adequately.
- **Don't over-cook** your omelette. It is done when the top is 'baveuse', a French term which means still moist and a little teensy bit runny. Remember that the omelette will continue cooking in its own heat for several minutes, so to take it any further in the pan would result in an over-cooked rubbery omelette.
- **Omelettes should never, ever be kept waiting**. Cook them only when you are ready to eat, and make sure that all fillings and accompaniments are ready to serve.

Fried onion and pancetta omelette.

Classic French Omelette aux Fines Herbes

There is no end to the ways you can liven up a plain omelette, either by mixing flavourings into the beaten eggs themselves (as in the omelette here) or by wrapping the omelette around them. Some of the best omelettes I've ever made have been one-offs, created from odds and ends and leftovers nestling in the fridge. Then again, some of the old standards are hard to beat. Following this basic recipe are a few ideas to launch your career as an omelette-creationist-extraordinaire.

Serves 1

3 eggs
1 tablespoon chopped chives
1 teaspoon chopped parsley
½ teaspoon chopped tarragon
salt and pepper
a knob of butter (about 15g/½oz)

1 Whisk together the eggs, herbs, salt and pepper.

2 Melt the butter over a frisky heat in a 17–20cm (7–8in) frying pan. As soon as it starts to foam, pour in the egg mixture. Reduce the heat a little and let the omelette begin to set around the sides, turning the pan if necessary so that it cooks evenly.

3 As the edges begin to set, use a fork or a spatula to lift up the sides here and there around the perimeter of the omelette, nudging them towards the centre and allowing

Use a fork or spatula to lift up the sides of the omelette, nudging them towards the centre (here, the classic French omelette aux fines herbes).

Flip one side of the omelette over on to the centre, then tilt the pan towards the waiting plate.

After flipping the omelette on to the plate, it will be folded neatly in three (here a fried onion and pancetta omelette).

runny egg to slide down into the gap. Continue cooking in this way until the omelette is almost set, but still moist on top. Remind yourself that it will carry on cooking in its own heat after it leaves the pan, so don't cook it to desiccated death.

4 Flip one side over on to the centre of the omelette, then tilt the pan towards the awaiting plate, and flip the omelette gently out on to it, so that it folds neatly in three. Eat straightaway.

Double Cheese Omelette

Stir a handful of grated mature Cheddar or a couple of tablespoons of freshly grated Parmesan into the eggs. Mix a couple of tablespoonfuls of cream cheese (or young goat's cheese) with lots of chopped chives, salt, pepper and a grating of fresh nutmeg. Cook the omelette as opposite. As soon as it is 'baveuse' (see page 52), turn off the heat, spoon the cream cheese mixture down the centre, then fold and slide out on to a plate.

Mushroom Omelette

Sauté about 110g (4oz) sliced button mushrooms in butter, adding a chopped garlic clove when almost done, and a scattering of chopped parsley. Season and keep warm. Make a plain omelette – as opposite, but without the herbs – and as soon as it is 'baveuse' (see page 52), spoon the mushrooms down the centre, fold and slide on to a plate.

For an even more luxurious version, sauté the mushrooms in butter, then add the parsley and a small slug of dry sherry or white wine. Let it bubble up, stirring the mushrooms around at the same time, then mix in 2 tablespoons of double cream or crème fraîche, salt and pepper. Let it bubble until the sauce is thickened. Keep warm and use to fill the omelette.

Tomato and Basil Omelette

Deseed and dice a medium tomato and chop a small garlic clove. When the omelette is almost done (see page 54), melt a knob of butter in a small frying pan, add the garlic and fry for a few seconds, then add the tomato, with a little salt and pepper. Toss in the hot butter for about 30 seconds to 1 minute to heat through, then take off the heat and mix in around 6 basil leaves, roughly torn up. As soon as the omelette is 'baveuse' (see page 52), spoon the tomato mixture down the centre, fold and slide out on to a plate.

Fried Onion and Bacon or Pancetta Omelette

Halve and slice a medium onion. Fry in a mixture of butter and oil until patched with brown and very tender. Season with salt and pepper. Cut a rasher (or even two) of streaky bacon or pancetta into short strips. Heat a small splash of sunflower or vegetable oil in your omelette pan and fry the bacon strips briskly until they start to brown. Now tip in the beaten eggs, and cook your omelette as on page 54. When it is done, spoon plenty of the fried onions down the centre, fold and flip out on to a plate.

Sauteéd Courgette, Prawn and Chorizo Omelette

Cut about 60g (2oz) chorizo (Spanish spicy salami, available from delis and good supermarkets) into cubes. Dice a medium courgette. Heat a trickle of olive oil in a frying pan and sauté the chorizo in it until sizzling. Add a chopped garlic clove and the courgette and sauté until the courgette is tender and patched with brown. Now add a diced, deseeded tomato, and fry for another minute or so, then finally add a small handful of peeled prawns. Fry just long enough to heat through, and season with salt and pepper. Use this mixture to fill your omelette as above.

Frittate

The frittata is the Italian omelette, hovering somewhere between the purity of a classic French omelette, and the bold chunkiness of a Spanish omelette or tortilla. The 'filling' is right there in the very body of the omelette, mixed amongst the eggs as they cook. Those eggs are usually well flavoured, probably with plenty of Parmesan, and with herbs such as parsley or basil or marjoram, or the warm fragrance of newly grated nutmeg. The other defining characteristic is that it is cooked top and bottom, then served in wedges, like a cake.

You can pad a frittata with all kinds of items, from the simplicity of just Parmesan and lots of parsley, to something more substantial, such as chunks of sausage and red pepper, or even sautéed potatoes or leftover pasta. Imagination is the key, though restraint is no bad thing, either. A frittata should never be a dustbin dish, but it is an ideal way to use up small quantities of this and that.

Cooking Although frittate (that's the proper Italian plural) are often cooked in butter in Italy, I love the taste of olive oil with the eggs and cheese, and besides, it is less likely to burn. Either way, make sure that the fat is pretty hot when you pour in the eggs, then immediately reduce the heat so that they cook through slowly. I find that the easiest way to set the upper side of the omelette is to slide the whole pan under a well preheated grill, fairly close to the heat. As soon as the top has set, with just a hint of brown here or there, pull it out again, so that the frittata remains moist and juicy inside.

Serving One of the great joys of a frittata is that it is excellent hot, warm or at room temperature. So very well behaved. When still hot from the grill, team it up with buttered lightly cooked cabbage, or green beans, and with new potatoes or sauté potatoes. Warm frittata is lovely with a tomato and olive or basil salad unless there is tomato in the frittata itself, in which case a green salad or bean salad would be more appealing. Alternatively, eat it warm or at room temperature as the Italians often do, in a sandwich. A crusty roll is the very best casing for it, but whatever bread you have to hand will do fine.

Tomato and Spring Onion Frittata

The taste of the tomato, cooked so lightly that it doesn't have time to collapse, and the sprightly spring onion, make this a light and fresh-tasting frittata.

Serves 2–3

4 large eggs
4 tablespoons freshly grated Parmesan
   cheese
salt and pepper
freshly grated nutmeg
1 tablespoon olive oil
1 large garlic clove, or 2 small, peeled and
   chopped
4 spring onions, trimmed and sliced
2 medium tomatoes, deseeded (see page 8)
   and roughly chopped

1 Preheat the grill.

2 Beat the eggs with the Parmesan, salt, pepper and plenty of nutmeg.

3 Heat a 25cm (10in) frying pan, preferably non-stick, over a medium heat. Add the oil, and after about 30 seconds, the garlic. Fry, stirring, until beginning to take on a little colour. Quickly add the spring onions and tomatoes and stir around. This lowers the heat in the pan swiftly, which will prevent the garlic burning. Cook for a further minute or so, to let the tomato heat through and the spring onion to begin to soften. Don't over-do this stage, or else the tomatoes will collapse to start forming a sauce.

4 Give the eggs one more quick whisk, and pour in. Tilt and swirl the pan a little so that the eggs settle evenly and nudge the pieces of tomato around so that they are more or less evenly distributed. Without disturbing the eggs, let the frittata cook gently for another 5 minutes, give or take. The top should still be runny.

5 Slide the frying pan under the grill, fairly close to the heat, and grill until the top is set and golden brown, but no more! This will take a matter of minutes, so hang around. Slide the frittata on to a plate, and either eat immediately or leave to cool, and eat at room temperature.

Add the tomatoes and spring onions to the oil and soften slightly.

Pour in the eggs.

Nudge the bits of tomato to distribute them evenly.

Grill until the top of the frittata is golden brown.

Serve hot or at room temperature.

Tomato and spring onion frittata.

Mushroom and Pancetta (or Bacon) Frittata

Replace the tomato and spring onion with 225g (8oz) button mushrooms, washed and sliced and 3 slices of pancetta or rashers of streaky bacon, snipped into small strips. Heat 2 tablespoons of olive oil in the frying pan over a medium heat and add the bacon. Fry for about 1 minute, then raise the heat high and toss in the mushrooms. Fry briskly until tender and patched with brown, then add the garlic and fry for a further minute or so until beginning to colour.

Pour in the eggs, already beaten with the Parmesan, salt, pepper and nutmeg, plus 2 tablespoons chopped parsley, then immediately reduce the heat. Finish cooking as for the **Tomato and Spring Onion Frittata** on page 58.

Red Pepper and Basil Frittata

Instead of using tomato and spring onion, this frittata is filled out with sweet red pepper and fragrant basil. Here's how. Quarter and deseed one red pepper, then cut into thin strips. Fry these in 1 tablespoon olive oil until tender, and then add the garlic. Sauté for a further minute or so until the garlic begins to colour.

While the pepper cooks, beat the egg with the Parmesan, salt and pepper, but no nutmeg. Instead, add a handful of basil leaves, roughly torn up. Pour the mixture into the frying pan with the peppers. Reduce the heat and continue as on page 58.

Pasta Frittata

So, you have some leftover pasta from last night's supper? With a bit of sauce still clinging on hopefully? Good, because that's what you need for this frittata. Anything from penne to spaghetti will do fine, with practically any sauce, though a tomato-based one is particularly good.

Leave out the tomato, spring onion and garlic in the original frittata (see page 58). Instead, whisk the eggs with the Parmesan, salt, pepper and 2 tablespoons finely chopped parsley instead of the nutmeg. Stir a cereal bowlful of the leftover pasta into the eggs, breaking up any clumps.

Heat 1 tablespoon olive oil in the frying pan over a high heat. Pour in the eggs and pasta, smooth down, reduce the heat and continue cooking as above.

chapter two

Pasta, Pizza and Rice

Pasta

How did we ever manage without pasta? When I was a child (oh God, here she goes…) it was something of a novelty, the kind of thing that you ate once in a blue moon, verging on risky or risqué, depending on your viewpoint. Now, of course, that's hard to imagine. Pasta is just the best-ever storecupboard treasure, always there ready and waiting, cheap, easy and quick to cook, satisfying and reassuring, pleasing to both vegetarians and omnivores and open to endless variation. No wonder the Italians eat it every day.

Which Type?
With increasing popularity comes increasing variation. If you have ever stood, confused and bemused, in front of the wide stretch of shelves that houses the dozens of different sorts of pasta now available, this brief guide may be of use.

Dried Pasta   There is no shame in choosing dried pasta over fresh. Your average Italian household appreciates the value of dried pasta for most everyday cooking, so don't ever look down on it. I would even go so far as to say that dried pasta often has a better texture and flavour than mass-produced fresh. It has a magnificently long shelf life (check the use-by date on the packet) and costs less than fresh. An unopened packet of dried pasta can be stored anywhere that is convenient – even in your sock drawer if you're really pushed for space. Once opened, either cover the opening completely with clingfilm, or transfer to a resealable plastic bag.

Fresh Pasta   Fresh pasta is extremely handy for those occasions when time is severely limited, as it takes only a few minutes to cook. The texture is usually softer than that of dried pasta, with less bounce. It really comes into its own with the multitude of stuffed pastas (you can get dried stuffed pasta, but it is generally pretty dire). Stuffed pasta, such as ravioli (plump square cushions), tortellini (small navel-shaped filled pasta) or tortelloni (larger navel-shaped filled pasta), is more expensive than standard pasta, but can be delicious. It needs only the simplest of sauces, such as melted butter, infused with sage leaves (melt butter in a small saucepan, then add a small handful of fresh sage leaves, turn the heat down to its lowest setting, cover and leave for 5–10 minutes), or a simple tomato sauce (see page 67) and freshly grated Parmesan. Most fresh pasta is made on a commercial scale, but if you are lucky enough to have a deli near you that makes its own, splash out occasionally to see how good fresh pasta can be when hand-made.

Fresh pasta should be kept in the fridge. If it comes in a sealed airtight packet, be guided by the use-by date. Once opened, use it up within two to three days. When buying tip-top hand-made fresh pasta, you really should use it within one or two days at most to appreciate it at its best. Although the fridge is the best place for it, don't be tempted to wrap it tightly in clingfilm, as it may well become soggy and sticky. Keep it in its box or paper bag.

Egg or No Egg? The cheapest pasta is made with no more than flour (hopefully, good durum wheat semolina flour) and water and perhaps a touch of salt. More luxurious is egg pasta, where copious quantities of beaten egg replace the water. This has a silkier texture and is considered superior. Storage is not affected.

What Shape?

The official line is that long-stranded pasta (spaghetti, tagliatelle, pappardelle, etc.) is best for the smoother, clingier sauces that will cling to each strand, coating it nicely, whilst smaller shapes (penne, farfalli, conchiglie, etc.) are more suited to 'bitty' sauces, because they catch the bits and pieces in their folds and hollows. When buying pasta for a specific dish, it's worth bearing this in mind.

You can also buy very small pasta shapes, which are meant for soups.

How Much?

As a rough guide you need about 100g (3½oz) dried or fresh pasta per person. So a 500g pack of dried pasta will feed four to five people.

Cooking

1 Take the largest pan you have, fill it two-thirds full with water, and place on a high heat. Add some salt – throw in a small handful, not just a pinch. Adequate seasoning with salt makes an amazing difference to the taste of the pasta, especially important when serving it with some of the simplest, olive-oil-based sauces. There is no need to add any oil to the water, as long as there is plenty of it.

2 Cover the pan (it will heat up more speedily) and bring up to a rolling boil. Now remove the lid, tip in the pasta and bring back to the boil. Start timing from this point. Stir the pasta once or twice as it cooks, to prevent sticking.

3 Perfectly cooked pasta is 'al dente', in other words offers a slight resistance as you sink your teeth into it. If it is soft and pappy then it has been over-done. The best way to test is just to take a piece or strand out of the pan, and bite into it. As soon as it is ready, whip the pan off the heat, set a colander in the sink, and tip the pasta and its cooking water into it. Drain well.

4 Pasta doesn't like to be kept waiting. It really, really should be introduced to its sauce and eaten straightaway. If the worst comes to the worst and you have to keep it hanging around for a while, toss it with a spoonful of olive oil or a knob of butter, so that each piece or strand is coated, preventing it sticking.

5 When cooking pasta for a cold pasta salad, drain as soon as it is 'al dente', then immediately rinse under the cold tap to halt the cooking process. Drain thoroughly, then toss with a little olive oil before it has a chance to become sticky. Better still, toss it with the vinaigrette for the salad, which will then soak right into the pasta.

Getting Spaghetti into the Pan

To the uninitiated this is one of the great kitchen conundrums: just how do you get those long, long strands of brittle dried spaghetti into a pan of boiling water without breaking them (or using an impossibly deep pan)? If this still puzzles you, here is the answer. Grab the spaghetti firmly in one hand and plunge the lower part down into the boiling water. Let go, and now use the palm of your hand to slowly nudge down the upper ends as the lower ends soften in the heat of the water. When you get them down as far as the rim of the pan, replace the palm of your hand with the bowl of a large wooden spoon and continue pushing the pasta down, letting it curl round the pan as it softens. Let it boil for a minute or so, and stir to separate the strands. Then just cook as normal.

Which Cheese and Why?

King of the cheeses for grating over pasta is Parmesan, or 'Parmegiano Reggiano' to give it its proper name. No doubt about it. Because all Parmesan has been matured for a minimum of one year, and often longer. As a result, it is totally packed with flavour, and what a flavour – intense and powerful, but never overwhelming. A little goes an awfully long way, which means that a) it works out less expensive than it appears at first, and b) that it introduces less greasiness to the pasta dish. It also seems to match almost everything that you are likely to put on to pasta. In Italy, they never put any cheese at all with seafood pasta, but I've broken this rule on occasion, and have enjoyed the combination. Grana padano cheese is almost identical to Parmesan, but made just outside the Parmesan area, and subject to less rigorous manufacturing controls.

There is one other Italian cheese with similar qualities to Parmesan, though a subtly different taste, and that is pecorino, a sheep's milk cheese. You will need the hard, matured variety of pecorino that can be grated. This is the proper cheese to use for a home-made pesto, but is harder to find outside Italy than Parmesan.

Whichever one of these you use, the key is to grate it to order. The ready-grated Parmesan that you buy in small tubs can be perfectly vile, enough to put anyone off the cheese for the rest of their lives. So, buy a whole chunk of Parmesan or grana padano or pecorino, store it in the fridge, wrapped in clingfilm or silver foil, and grate as much as you need while the pasta is cooking.

Three Extremely Quick Ways with Pasta

1 When you are ravenous, there is little that is more restorative than freshly cooked pasta, tossed with plenty of butter (or a little extra virgin olive oil), freshly grated Parmesan and freshly ground black pepper. If you can be bothered to chop a little fresh parsley, that's even nicer, but not critical.

2 For something a touch perkier, heat up some olive oil in a small frying pan, while the pasta is boiling. Add a chopped garlic clove and a chopped, deseeded fresh chilli, if you have one, and fry until the garlic is beginning to colour. Draw off the heat. If you don't have fresh chilli, then you can substitute either dried chilli flakes, or oodles of freshly ground or roughly crushed black pepper, but add them only a few seconds before the garlic is done, so that they don't burn. Pour the oil, garlic and chilli over the drained pasta, toss and serve with Parmesan.

3 While the pasta is boiling, halve and slice an onion thinly, and chop a garlic clove. Heat a good layer of olive oil in a frying pan, fry the onion, stirring frequently, until beginning to brown, then add the garlic and continue cooking for another minute or so. Toss into the hot, drained pasta, together with torn-up basil or chopped parsley, or the freshly grated zest of a lemon, and freshly grated Parmesan.

Tomato and Other Sauces for Pasta

When tomatoes are at their ripest and cheapest, in late July and August, tomato sauces are hard to beat. The first takes about half an hour, while the Salsa Cruda needs no cooking at all. Once you've mastered the art of making a standard tomato sauce, you open the door to a hundred and one different variations on the theme. Made from either fresh or canned tomatoes (in winter the latter usually have a better flavour than fresh ones, and are certainly better value), onion and garlic, the sauce can be lifted with herbs, other vegetables, bacon, chilli, beans, tinned tuna, shellfish, fresh fish and many, many other ingredients.

Sugo al Pomodoro (Tomato Sauce for Pasta)

Serves 4

4 tablespoons extra virgin olive oil
1 onion, peeled and chopped
3 garlic cloves, peeled and chopped
2 x 400g cans chopped tomatoes in their
    juice, or 1 kg (2¼lb) fresh tomatoes,
    skinned, deseeded and roughly chopped
1 tablespoon tomato purée
1 bay leaf
1 sprig thyme
1 teaspoon caster sugar
salt and pepper

1 Heat the oil in a wide frying pan over a gentle heat. Add the onion and fry, stirring frequently, until translucent. This stage should take around 10 minutes. Now add the garlic and cook for a further 2 minutes to soften.

2 Tip in the tomatoes, the tomato purée, the bay leaf and thyme, the sugar, and some salt and pepper. Bring up to the boil, then reduce the heat and simmer very gently for 20–30 minutes, stirring frequently, until the tomatoes have reduced down to a thick sauce. You may need to add a little water.

3 Taste and adjust the seasoning. Discard the herbs. Reheat when needed, and toss with hot pasta.

Sugo al Pomodoro e Basilico

Just before tossing the **Tomato Sauce for Pasta** above with the pasta, stir in a really generous handful of fresh basil leaves, roughly torn up. The heat of the sauce will release their full flavour, but too much heat destroys it, so don't put them in until the very last minute. I sometimes also stir mozzarella, cut into small cubes, into the sauce along with the basil. One regular ball of Italian mozzarella, preferably buffalo mozzarella, of around 150g (5 oz) will be plenty.

A bowl of spaghetti with tomato sauce, fresh basil and shavings of Parmesan.

Sugo all 'Arrabiata

In other words, 'angry sauce' because it is aflame with the heat of chilli. Make a standard **Tomato Sauce for Pasta** as on page 67, using a whopping 5 garlic cloves, chopped, and adding ½ teaspoon crushed chilli flakes.

Sugo all 'Amatriciana

A sauce from the Apennines, where it is made with pork jowl. Pancetta is an easier option here. Cut 8 rashers of pancetta into short thin strips. Fry with the onion in the **Tomato Sauce for Pasta** on page 67, then add the garlic and a couple of pinches of crushed chilli flakes. Cook for a further minute, then pour in 110ml (4fl oz) dry white wine. Turn the heat right up and let the wine bubble until it has virtually all evaporated. Next tip in the tomatoes and purée, season and continue cooking as above. This is traditionally served with grated pecorino, though Parmesan is good with it too.

Salsa Cruda

Or in other words, raw sauce…. Made with ripe tomatoes, this becomes one of summer's highlights. Chop and mix the sauce together an hour or two in advance, then toss the cool sauce into piping hot spaghetti, which releases the full flavour.

Serves 4

1kg (2¼lb) fabulous tomatoes, deseeded (see page 8) and finely diced
1 small red or white onion, or 3 small shallots, peeled and very finely chopped
6 tablespoons extra virgin olive oil
2 tablespoons lemon juice or balsamic vinegar or sherry vinegar
2 garlic cloves, peeled and very finely chopped
a good handful of basil leaves, torn up
salt and pepper
caster sugar (optional)

1 Mix all the ingredients together, seasoning to taste, and adding a pinch or two of sugar if you think the tomatoes need pepping up. Cover and chill for about an hour (this lets the juices run out from the tomatoes and take on the scent of basil and garlic).
2 Taste and adjust seasonings, which should be fairly vigorous, before tossing into hot pasta.

Penne with Gorgonzola, Spinach and Hazelnuts

Gorgonzola is a creamy yet pungent Italian blue cheese that melts easily into this rich sauce. It clings seductively to the tubes of penne, lightened by the presence of barely cooked spinach leaves, and toasted hazelnuts. A fabulous combination.

Serves 4

400–450g (14–16oz) dried penne
salt
300g (10oz) fresh small spinach leaves
45g (1½oz) shelled hazelnuts, toasted,
   skinned and chopped
freshly grated Parmesan

GORGONZOLA SAUCE
110g (4oz) mild Gorgonzola cheese
   (Gorgonzola dolce)
100ml (3½fl oz) milk
100 ml (3½fl oz) double cream

1 Put a large pan of water on to boil for the penne, adding plenty of salt. When it has reached a rolling boil, tip in the penne. Bring back to the boil and then cook the penne until al dente – around 10 minutes, but check the packet for more precise timing.

2 Meanwhile, put the Gorgonzola, milk and some salt and pepper into a heavy-based saucepan. Stir over a low heat until the Gorgonzola has melted into the milk to form a thick sauce.

3 Now stir in the cream and raise the heat to medium. Cook for a further 4–5 minutes until it has thickened to a good coating consistency (see page 220). If the pasta is not yet ready, turn the heat right down low and keep the sauce warm.

4 As soon as the pasta is al dente, throw the spinach into the saucepan, give it one quick stir, and drain immediately. Tip back into the saucepan, add the hazelnuts and 4 tablespoons Parmesan, and then pour over the Gorgonzola sauce. Toss to mix thoroughly, and serve straightaway, with more freshly grated Parmesan in a bowl for those who want it.

need to know

TO ROAST HAZELNUTS Preheat the oven to 190°C/375°F/Gas Mark 5. Spread the hazelnuts out on a baking tray and slide into the oven. Roast for about 4–8 minutes, checking frequently, until they have begun to brown, and the skin is flaking off. Don't forget about them, as they hurtle from perfectly browned to burnt in a remarkably short space of time. Roll the nuts around in a tea-towel so that all the flaky skin separates from the nuts. Pick out the denuded nuts and discard the skins.

Roasting hazelnuts browns them and helps remove the flaky skin.

Penne with Gorgonzola, spinach and hazelnuts.

Home-made Pesto

The difference between home-made pesto and bought pesto in a jar is phenomenal. It's like two completely different sauces. Real pesto is a stunning bright green, and has an extraordinary pungent fragrance that is utterly irresistible.

If you have a processor, then real pesto can be made in minutes. Even if you have to chop the ingredients by hand, it is still very quick to put together, with a pleasingly knobbly texture that is extremely fashionable, as well as an inestimable pleasure to eat.

Fresh pesto will keep in the fridge, in a covered bowl, for two to three days, and can be frozen very successfully. Handy if you come across a source of cheap basil, which does occasionally happen.

Serves 4 on pasta

85g (3oz) basil leaves
60g (2oz) Parmesan and/or mature pecorino, broken up into small chunks
60g (2oz) pine nuts
2 garlic cloves, peeled and roughly chopped
100ml (3½fl oz) extra virgin olive oil

1 To make knobbly pesto (i.e. without a processor), pile the basil in the centre of a large chopping board, and top with the cheese, pine nuts and garlic. Now wield the largest, sharpest knife you own. Chop all the ingredients together, over and over again, until they are all very finely chopped. Mix with the olive oil, and there it is – knobbly pesto, ready to toss into hot pasta.

2 For creamy pesto, put the basil leaves into the bowl of the processor with the cheese, pine nuts and garlic. Pulse-process until very finely chopped. Scrape down the sides, then set the blades whirring again. Gradually trickle in the olive oil to give a creamy sauce.

Knobbly pesto – ingredients finely chopped and mixed with olive oil.

Spaghetti with Meatballs

This is one of my all-time favourite pasta dishes, based on a tomato sauce again, but this time with meatballs cooked in with it. Although purists will insist on serving it with freshly grated Parmesan, I like it best with grated mature Cheddar. Incidentally, this is a sauce that can be made a few hours in advance and reheated when needed, as long as you are careful not to break up the meatballs.

Serves 4

400g (14oz) dried spaghetti
1 tablespoon extra virgin olive oil
freshly grated Parmesan or mature Cheddar,
   to serve

MEATBALLS AND SAUCE

1 thick slice white bread, crusts removed
4 tablespoons milk
350g (12oz) lean minced beef or pork
3 tablespoons finely chopped parsley
3 garlic cloves, peeled and crushed
salt and pepper
1 egg, beaten
2 tablespoons extra virgin olive oil
2 x 400g cans chopped tomatoes
2 tablespoons tomato purée
1 teaspoon caster sugar
2 teaspoons dried oregano

1 For the meatballs, tear the bread into small pieces, put in a large bowl with the milk and leave to soften for 5 minutes. Add the minced meat, half the parsley, half the garlic, and some salt and pepper. Mix thoroughly, kneading the mixture with your hands, so that the bread dissolves and disappears into the mixture. Add just enough egg to bind the mixture without making it sloppy. Now roll into walnut-sized balls.

2 Put a large pan of salted water on to boil for the spaghetti.

3 Take the widest frying pan you have and place over a medium heat. Add the oil. When it is hot, add the meatballs in a single layer. They should sizzle as they meet the hot fat. If they don't then it is not hot enough, so raise the heat a little. Once you have placed them all in the pan, resist the temptation to start moving them around. Leave them alone for 2–3 minutes until they have begun to brown underneath, then turn and continue until they browned all over.

4 Lift the pan off the heat, and tilt it carefully to allow excess fat to drain off into a heatproof bowl. Return to the heat.

5 Now add all the remaining sauce ingredients, including the remaining parsley and garlic, and carefully stir the sauce and meatballs around to mix everything up. Simmer very gently, covered, for around 25–30 minutes, stirring occasionally. Taste and adjust the seasoning.

6 About 10 minutes (check the packet for cooking times) before the sauce is done, add the spaghetti to the pan of now boiling water. Boil until al dente, then drain and return to the pan. Tip over the meatball sauce, toss to mix, and serve.

Tagliatelle Bolognaise

It is really worth learning how to make a good 'ragù bolognese' or bolognaise sauce. It is wonderful with pasta but has other uses too (see overleaf). In Bologna, ragù bolognese is often served with tagliatelle, and almost never with spaghetti! Choose whichever you like best.

The longer the sauce is cooked the better – the best Italian cooks let it simmer gently for 3 hours or so, constantly adding more liquid. You can get away with a mere 1 hour, however, which is just long enough to develop the flavours and soften the meat.

Serves 4

400g (14oz) dried tagliatelle
freshly grated Parmesan, to serve

RAGÙ
1 tablespoon sunflower oil or vegetable oil
30g (1oz) butter
1 onion, peeled and chopped
2 garlic cloves, peeled and chopped
2 carrots, finely diced
2 celery stalks, finely diced
450g (1lb) minced beef
salt and pepper
freshly grated nutmeg
1 x 400g can chopped tomatoes
300ml (10fl oz) milk

1 For the ragù, heat the oil and butter in a wide, heavy frying pan over a medium heat. Add the onion, garlic, carrot and celery and stir, then reduce the heat and leave to fry very gently, stirring every now and then, until the vegetables are tender and patched with brown here and there (but not burnt). Do not rush this – it should take at least 15 minutes!
2 Add the minced beef, breaking it up into smaller pieces that can be mixed with the vegetables and spread out to cover the base of the pan completely. Leave for about 5 minutes, letting all the juice boil off. By now the underneath should have browned, but if not, give it another few minutes. If you turn it too early, then your bolognaise sauce turns out unappealingly pale. Once the underneath has

From red at first, the beef for tagliatelle bolognaise turns an appetising brown.

browned, turn and break up the meat again, mixing in the browned bits. Flatten out once more, and fry for another 3–4 minutes until the underneath is good and brown.

3 Stir the meat, and add salt, pepper and a good grating of nutmeg. Add the tomatoes and half the milk. Leave to simmer very gently, until the liquid has almost all evaporated. Stir in the remaining milk.

4 Now just leave the sauce simmering very quietly for another 40 minutes or even longer, occasionally adding a little water if it threatens to boil dry and burn. Don't rush it.

5 Taste and adjust the seasoning. Either use immediately, or reheat thoroughly when needed.

6 Put a large pan of salted water on to boil. Once it has reached a rolling boil, add the tagliatelle and cook according to packet instructions, usually around 10 minutes. Once the pasta is al dente, drain and return to the pan. Add the sauce, toss to mix and serve immediately with lots of freshly grated Parmesan.

need to know

OTHER USES FOR RAGÙ It's really not worth cooking less than this amount of ragù, even if you are only feeding one or two. Instead of serving it with pasta for several nights in a row, try spooning it over baked potatoes and topping with a spoonful of soured cream, or rustle up a Mexican (ish) fiesta, by wrapping the sauce in warm tortillas, together with slices of avocado, pickled jalapeño peppers, soured cream and grated Cheddar. For a more anglophile approach, use the ragù as a basis for a cottage pie. Tip into a pie dish and top with mashed potato beaten with an egg. Make wavy lines on top with the tines of a fork, dot with butter and bake at 200°C/400°F/Gas Mark 6 for about 20–30 minutes until lightly browned and very hot.

Tagliatelle bolognaise.

Pizza

I just love making pizza. I may not turn out something quite as perfect as a master pizzaiolo (pizza-maker) in the back-streets of Naples, but what emerges from the oven is all my own creation and tastes all the better for it. That's the joy of DIY pizza – you can go for classics like pizza margherita, or let your imagination rip.

Here then, to set you going, is a bunch of starter pizzas. Whatever pizza you decide to try, remember that the key to a classy pizza is classy ingredients. Tomatoes should be ripe and sweet, the mozzarella must be bona fide Italian mozzarella, the basil must be fresh and peppery, and the olive oil is, of course, extra virgin.

Pizza Know-how

Timing
You can't make a pizza in half an hour. The actual cooking itself is a matter of a few minutes, but you must allow plenty of time for the dough for the base to rise. Let us assume that your kitchen is comfortably warm. In this case, you must start on the dough 1½–2 hours before you intend to sit down and eat the finished pizza. Once you've kneaded the dough to a perfect smoothness, it will need roughly 1 hour to rise, which leaves you just enough time to flatten it out, smear on the tomato sauce and other toppings, bake it and get it on to a plate. If your kitchen is chilly, then either transfer the dough to a warm airing cupboard to rise, or allow more time.

Should it be more convenient to make the dough in the morning, for supper later on, that's no problem. Just store it, in its bowl covered with clingfilm, in the fridge, where it will rise extremely slowly. Remember to bring it back to room temperature before using, i.e. out of the fridge at least half an hour in advance.

What Flour?
A pizza is really no more than a flattened piece of bread surmounted with a host of delicious bits and pieces. Therefore it needs to be made with proper bread flour, which is also sold as 'strong flour'. Plain flour will not work, as it doesn't contain enough gluten. Strong flour is rich in gluten, which gives bread its bouncy texture.

Yeast
Yeast is what makes the pizza dough rise and comes in one of three forms – fast-working dried 'easy-blend' or 'easy-rise' yeast, ordinary dried yeast and fresh yeast.
Fast-working yeast The dried micro-granules of fast-working yeast are the most convenient. They keep for months in the cupboard, and can be mixed straight into the flour. This is what I have used in the dough recipe overleaf.

Fresh yeast   Doughs made with fresh yeast usually rise more speedily than those made with dried (of either sort) and the flavour of the cooked pizza base is a little better. Fresh yeast can be bought from many bakers and some delicatessens. It keeps for a week or so in the fridge and can even be frozen for up to a month. You need twice as much fresh yeast as dried yeast. To use fresh yeast, crumble it into some of the liquid used in the dough, warmed to blood temperature. As a rough and ready guide, stick your finger into the water and count slowly to ten. If you can just about keep your finger in the hot water until you reach ten, but no longer, then the temperature is about right. You can also add a teaspoon of sugar or honey at this point, though it is not strictly necessary. Stir the mixture to soften and dissolve the yeast, then leave in a warm place (e.g. on a radiator or in the airing cupboard) for about 10 minutes, by which time the mixture will be very frothy, indicating that it is ready to use. Supposing, by some sad mishap, there is barely any evidence of activity and no froth to mention, you will just have to throw the mixture out – the yeast is dead. Either the water you used was too hot, or the yeast was too old.
Ordinary dried yeast   Start off as for fresh, but you don't have to crumble it.

How Much Water?   It is quite impossible to tell you exactly how much water will be needed to produce a pizza dough of the correct consistency. One batch of flour will absorb more than another, and on a humid day you may need less water. Instead, consider the dough itself. When it is first mixed the dough should be quite soft and slightly (but only slightly) sticky. A dough that is too dry will be hard to knead and shape, but is easily corrected by sprinkling with more water and kneading until absorbed. A dough that is too wet to knead easily is no problem either – just dust it with flour (several times if need be), and carry on kneading until smooth and elastic.

Kneading by Hand   Bread doughs are usually kneaded twice before baking. The first bout of kneading is the process that develops the gluten in the flour, to give an elastic dough as smooth as a baby's bottom. As you knead the dough you will also trap tiny bubbles of air in the mixture – essential if your yeast is to work properly. When you come to bake the pizza the thousands of air bubbles expand in the heat of the oven to give the base its characteristic light bready texture. The second bout of kneading is much briefer, to even out the distribution of air bubbles in the dough.

Kneading requires some determination but is the ideal way to work off latent aggression. Sprinkle the work surface lightly with flour and rub a little on to the palms of your hands. Place the dough in front of you and push the heel of your right hand (or left, if you are left-handed) into the dough and then away from you, anchoring it steady with your other hand. The idea is to stretch the dough out. This becomes progressively easier as the gluten develops. Fold the stretched bit back over on to the rest of the dough, then turn the dough and repeat. Once you get the knack of it, you will develop a comfortable rhythm, punctuated only by the occasional break to rest your arm. Keep going for at least 5 minutes and probably longer, until the dough is as smooth as satin, and extremely stretchy and elastic.

Machine Kneading Most food processors come armed with a dough hook which can be used for kneading small quantities of dough. Follow the manufacturer's instructions but be aware that it is possible to ruin the motor if a) the dough is too stiff, or b) you send the hook round too fast, or c) you knead the dough for too long. Food mixers are stronger, but again take it gently and follow the manufacturer's instructions.

Rolling out the Dough Divide the dough into two pieces and roll each one into a ball. Dust two baking sheets with flour (or brush with oil). Dust the work surface with flour. Dust the rolling pin with flour and roll the dough out to form as large a circle as you can. This is a frustrating business as the beautifully elastic dough shrinks back to a smaller circle each time you roll it out.

To get it even thinner and larger, try to imitate professional pizza-makers, by picking the dough up and stretching it with your hands working your way around the circle, but trying not to tear holes in it. You could even have a go at whirling it around in a circle. Fun, but not always successful. Once you have stretched it as far as it will go (aim for about 25cm/10in in diameter), lay the dough circles on the baking sheets. Let them rest for 5–10 minutes before adding the toppings.

Cooking Pizza You can bake pizzas on a baking sheet, but if you want to ensure an extra crisp base, buy either a special pizza tin (a perforated circle of metal with a rim around the edge), or splash out on a pizza stone which does an even better job.

In all cases the critical thing is to get the oven thoroughly hot, preheated to 230°C/450°F/Gas Mark 8. To get the maximum heat bake the pizzas at the top of the oven. With two pizzas on different shelves, swap them over halfway through the cooking time, so that they both have a shot of full heat.

Good Pizza Dough

Makes 2 pizzas

400g (14oz) strong white bread flour
1 teaspoon salt
1 sachet (7g/¼oz) easy-blend yeast
2 tablespoons extra virgin olive oil

Add oil and water to the flour.

1 Mix the flour with the salt and yeast and make a well in the centre. Add the oil and 150ml (5fl oz) water. Start mixing, first with the blade of a palette knife or a round-ended table knife, and then with your hands. Gradually add enough extra water to make a soft, slightly sticky dough.

2 Knead for a good 5–10 minutes until smooth and elastic. Rinse the mixing bowl out and dry, then return the dough to it. Cover the bowl tightly with clingfilm and leave to rise in a warm place, until doubled in bulk.

3 Knock the dough back (literally punch it, to deflate it), then gather it all up into a ball and knead again, for a mere 3–4 minutes this time. Now the dough is ready to use. See opposite for rolling and baking instructions.

Mix with a palette knife...

to a slightly sticky dough.

Knead...

until smooth and elastic.

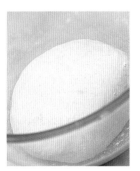

Leave to rise...

until doubled in size.

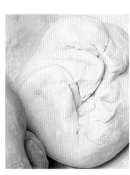

Knock back and knead again.

Rolling out.

Tomato Sauce for Pizza

Most pizzas are smeared with a thick tomato sauce before any other toppings are added. I really do mean smeared – too much sauce makes for a soggy base, and overwhelms the rest of the ingredients. In the height of summer, when tomatoes are at their most sumptuous, they are fabulous baked raw on to the pizza base (see Pizza alla Marinara on page 82), but throughout the rest of the year, it is better to make a simple, thick sauce from canned tomatoes. This is the one I use for pizzas.

Enough for 3–4 pizzas

1 x 400g can chopped tomatoes or 300ml (10fl oz) tomato passata
2 garlic cloves, peeled and crushed
1 tablespoon extra virgin olive oil
1 bouquet garni (1 bay leaf, 2 sprigs parsley, 1 sprig thyme)
salt and pepper

1 Put all the ingredients into a small saucepan. Simmer together slowly for about 20 minutes, stirring occasionally, until very thick. Discard the bouquet garni.
2 Taste and adjust seasoning and leave to cool.

Pizza Margherita

Serves 2

1 quantity Good Pizza Dough (see page 81)
½ quantity Tomato Sauce for Pizza (see above)
1½ x 150g (5oz) balls mozzarella (either di bufala, or cow's milk), cut in half, then sliced
black pepper
extra virgin olive oil
a handful of basil leaves

1 Preheat the oven to 230°C/450°F/Gas Mark 8. Roll the dough out (see page 78) and lay on two baking sheets.
2 Smear thinly with tomato sauce, leaving a 2.5cm (1in) bare border around the edge. Divide the mozzarella between the two pizzas, grind over some black pepper and trickle a little olive oil (roughly 1–1½ teaspoons per pizza) over each pizza.
3 Bake for approximately 15 minutes, until the edges are browned and puffed. Scatter fresh basil over each pizza and serve straightaway.

Pizza con Prosciutto e Olive

For a pizza with cured ham and olives, make as for **Pizza Margherita**, adding 2–3 strips of Parma ham on top of the tomato, and dotting a few black olives around the top. Instead of using basil, scatter dried oregano over the pizza before drizzling over the olive oil.

Pizza con Carciofi e Fontina

Fontina is a rich Italian cheese that melts to a creamy molten puddle. Some supermarkets sell it, but you may have to search for it at the local deli. Marinated baby artichokes are sold in glass jars and have a superb flavour. To make this pizza, prepare as for **Pizza Margherita**, but add around 60–85g (2–3oz) sliced fontina to each pizza and 2 marinated artichokes, cut into thin wedges. Sprinkle with oregano before drizzling with oil, and forget about the fresh basil.

Pizza Napoletana

From Naples, home of the pizza, comes this absolute classic. Make as for **Pizza Margherita**, adding half a dozen strips of tinned anchovy to each pizza and dotting each one with capers. Sprinkle with oregano before drizzling with oil. No basil.

Pizza al Formaggio di Capra e Salvia

To make a goat's cheese and sage pizza, add 85g (3oz) goat's cheese, rind removed, crumbled or sliced, to a **Pizza Margherita** as well as the mozzarella, and scatter with fresh sage leaves before drizzling with oil. A sprinkling of pine nuts makes it even more delicious. No need for basil.

Pizza al Quattro Formaggi

For a proper Italian-style four-cheese pizza, you will need (per pizza) around 60g (2oz) each of Gorgonzola, mozzarella and fontina cheeses, diced small, as well as roughly 30g (1oz) Parmesan that has been coarsely grated.

Roll out the dough and smear with tomato sauce, as for the **Pizza Margherita** (see page 80). Scatter the cheeses higgledy-piggledy over the pizza, then drizzle over 1–2 teaspoons extra virgin olive oil. Bake for 15 minutes as for the **Pizza Margherita**. Very rich, and very gorgeous.

There's no law dictating that only this quartet of cheeses may be used. Try replacing one or more of them with, say, goat's cheese or good Cheddar, or provolone, or…whatever takes your fancy. Choose cheeses with contrasting textures and flavours, some soft and creamy that will melt in an oozy way, others firmer and drier, some powerful and pungent, softened by milder, milkier cheese.

Pizza alla Marinara

A pizza for the summer tomato season. Extremely simple, so every element has to be good. For two pizzas, deseed and chop 450g (1lb) very ripe tomatoes. Mix with a teaspoon of salt and tip into a sieve. Leave to drain for half an hour.

Roll out the dough, and spread the drained, raw tomato pulp over the pizza bases. Sprinkle 1 garlic clove, finely chopped or thinly sliced, as you prefer, over each pizza. Scatter with a little dried oregano, season with salt and pepper, and then drizzle generously with extra virgin olive oil. Bake as for the **Pizza Margherita** (see page 80). I like to add a handful of fresh basil leaves after the pizzas come out of the oven, but this is not part of the authentic Neapolitan original.

A pizza con prosciutto e olive, ready to go!

Rice

Always have a stock of rice in the cupboard. Like pasta, it keeps for ages (as long as it is stashed in an airtight container once the packet is opened) and will provide you with the basis of a main course, or a super-efficient sauce-absorbing side dish.

Essential Rice Varieties

Long-grain Rice This is where you begin the rice journey, with a bag of a good-quality long-grain rice. This is the kind of rice that goes with a chicken stew, a curry or a stir-fry. It can be used to make a pilau (or pilaff, which is much the same thing), egg-fried rice, or to add substance to a soup. Choose either an all-purpose American long-grain white rice or, better still, wonderful basmati rice, with its curved grains and superior flavour. You may prefer to stock up on brown rice, which takes longer to cook, but is far more nutritious. It has a distinct nutty taste, and is chewier than white rice.

Risotto Rice If you love risottos, and want to master the art of making them yourself, then you absolutely must have a bag of risotto rice of one sort or another. No other rice will produce a decent risotto. Why not? Because short-grained risotto rice has the capacity to absorb a phenomenal amount of liquid, without going mushy, and is also blessed with a considerable helping of starch, which is what gives a risotto its creamy consistency (aided and abetted, it's true, by oodles of butter and Parmesan). The best-known risotto rice is arborio rice, but you may come across others, such as carnaroli, or my favourite, vialone nano.

Pudding Rice Like risotto rice, pudding rice has short, stubby grains that absorb large quantities of liquid, but pudding rice softens to a fabulous tenderness, which is what makes rice pudding such divine comfort food (turn to page 217 for the recipe for an old-fashioned baked rice pudding).

Just for Fun **Jasmine (a.k.a. Thai or fragrant) rice** This is the correct rice to use as an accompaniment to Thai food. It has a distinctive scent, and is slightly sticky, so don't expect to end up with separate clearly defined grains once cooked.

Wild rice The seeds of a grass rather than a true rice, this tastes more like a superior brown rice, and takes almost the same amount of time to cook. As the slender, brown-black grains simmer, they burst open in a rather fetching manner. Looks good mixed with long-grain white rice.

Quantities

Some people love rice and will eat huge quantities of it, whilst others are noticeably more restrained. This makes judging quantities somewhat tricky. I usually allow somewhere between 60g (2 oz) and 100g (3½ oz) per person depending on how well I know them, and how much else I am proposing to serve with the rice. It is probably best to err on the side of generosity.

Cooking Rice

There are two standard methods for cooking plain rice.

Method One (the startlingly obvious one)

1 Bring a large pan of salted water to the boil.

2 While it heats up, tip the rice into a sieve and run under the cold tap, to remove any starch. Leave to drain.

3 Once the water has reached a rolling boil, tip in the rice, and cook until just tender (check packet for timing guidelines). Drain thoroughly.

4 If you have to hold it for a short time before eating, tip into a warm serving bowl, dot with butter (nice but not essential), cover with foil and leave in the oven, set to a low temperature, for up to 20 minutes. Fluff up the grains with a fork.

Method Two (the pilau or absorption method)

This is more complicated, but guarantees the most perfect and delicious rice, especially when cooking basmati rice (as in the photographs overleaf).

Rinse under cold tap water.

1 First measure out the volume of your rice in a measuring jug. Now tip into a sieve and run under the cold tap to remove starch. Leave to drain, preferably for a good 15 minutes.

2 Measure out double the volume of water, as you had rice. Take a heavy-based, medium pan and add just enough sunflower or vegetable oil to cover the base, but no more. Heat over a moderate heat, then tip in the rice. Stir about for some 30–60 seconds, until every grain is coated in oil, and the rice is beginning to lose its glassy look. Add the water and season with salt. Bring up to the boil, and as soon as it starts to bubble, clamp on a tight-fitting lid, and turn the heat down as low as it will go. Set the timer for 10 minutes and then ignore the pan completely. Don't be tempted to stir.

Stir until the rice is beginning to lose its glassy look (left); perfectly cooked rice, pitted with little holes (right).

3 As soon as the timer rings, take the pan off the heat and remove the lid. Inside you will see a flat expanse of perfectly cooked rice, pitted with little holes. Give it a stir, just to check that there isn't a little pool of water at the bottom (there shouldn't be, but occasionally things don't go quite according to plan). Either drain off excess water if there is any, or return the pan to the heat, uncovered, for a few minutes.

4 Tip the rice into a warm serving dish, fluff up with a fork, and serve. If not eating immediately, keep warm as for Method One.

Rice for a Rice Salad

If you are cooking rice for a rice salad or indeed to make egg-fried rice (see page 91), use Method One on page 85. Once cooked, tip the rice into a sieve to drain, run under the cold tap, then set the sieve over the saucepan. Make half a dozen holes in the rice to allow steam to escape, then leave to finish draining and drying. When cool, transfer to a dish, cover with clingfilm and store in the fridge until needed.

Storing Cooked Rice

Cooked rice does not have a long shelf life, especially in hot weather, so get it into the fridge as soon as it is cool. A rice salad should be eaten on the day it is made, and not left standing around in a warm room for hours. Badly stored cooked rice can deliver an unpleasant bout of food poisoning, so never ever use stored cooked rice if it smells at all funny or off.

Cooking Risotto

Risotto, Italy's greatest rice dish, comes from the north of the country, where butter dominates rather than olive oil. A real risotto has a magnificent, rich, creamy texture, formed in part by liberal application of butter and cheese, allied with the natural starchiness of risotto rice. This is not, and never can be, a dish for dieters.

Essential Ingredients

Risotto rice You cannot make a risotto with anything but proper Italian risotto rice. It is a short-grained rice, stubby with an almost square cross-section. It is high in starch, which contributes to the creamy finish of a risotto, and absorbs massive amounts of liquid without collapsing. Look out for varieties like arborio (the most common), vialone nano (the finest, in my experience), and carnaroli. Store it, like any rice, in an airtight tin once the packet has been opened. **Wine** Most risottos contain a glassful of wine, usually white, occasionally red. This must be decent, drinkable wine. Cheapest plonk will leave a nasty taste in the rice. **Stock** You can make tolerable risottos with diluted stock cubes (use twice as much water as recommended), but you will need to have plenty of punchy ingredients to distract from the packet taste. To get a risotto that will make you sigh with pleasure, you must use a good home-made stock. I use chicken stock or vegetable stock most of the time (see pages 15–17). **Butter** Butter is used both at the beginning for frying and, perhaps even more importantly, at the end of the cooking time, where it enriches the sauce. Use a good-quality unsalted or lightly salted butter. **Parmesan** Freshly grated Parmesan is the second essential finishing component in most risottos. It harmonises all the other elements, and enriches the risotto at the same time. You cannot substitute lesser cheeses – they just won't do the job properly.

Method Highlights

Frying the rice Once the rice has been added to the pan, it needs to be stirred around over a low heat for about a minute. This ensures that each grain is coated in the buttery juices, giving it a decent send-off down the road to risottodom. **Adding the stock** In a risotto the liquid, usually hot stock, is added a little at a time, then stirred with the rice until it has all been absorbed or evaporated. Another ladleful of stock goes in, the stirring starts again and continues until the liquid has once again virtually disappeared. And so it goes on, stirring all the time, until the rice reaches very nearly the ideal state – just a thread less than al dente, or in other words, almost cooked to the state where it is tender but still slightly resistant to the bite. At this point, the consistency of the risotto needs to be roughly right. In some parts of northern Italy, this means pretty thick and almost gloopy, whilst in others it means much wetter, verging on soupy. Which camp you belong to is a matter of personal preference. Just add more liquid if you want it wetter, or cook for a minute or so longer to thicken it up. Incidentally, if you think this all sounds too tediously laborious, and decide to tip all the stock in at once and skip the stirring, you may end up with a pleasing enough result, but it will not develop the consistency of a true risotto. **Finishing a risotto** The last step is to stir in a final, generous knob of butter and a big handful of freshly grated Parmesan, then taste and adjust the seasoning. **Serving** Risotto must always be served as soon as it has been cooked, as it loathes hanging around. Risotto that has been kept hot soon goes mushy and gluey. Not a good thing, especially when you have just spent the last 15–20 minutes stirring it constantly.

Courgette and Pancetta Risotto

This is a fresh and vivid summer risotto to be made with the finest small courgettes.

Serves 6 as a starter, 4 as a main course

500g (18oz) courgettes
60g (2oz) butter
1 tablespoon extra virgin olive oil
900ml–1.2 litres (1½–2 pints) Chicken or
    Vegetable Stock (see pages 15–17)
1 onion, peeled and chopped
6 thin slices pancetta, cut into narrow, short
    strips
225g (8oz) arborio or other Italian risotto rice
150ml (5fl oz) dry white wine
2 tablespoons chopped parsley
salt and pepper
a small handful of basil leaves
30g (1oz) Parmesan, freshly grated or shaved

1 Wash, top and tail the courgettes. Take roughly a third of them and grate coarsely. Dice the remaining courgettes.

2 Heat 15g (½oz) of the butter and the olive oil in a frying pan, and sauté the diced courgette over a high heat, until tender and patched with brown. Reserve.

3 Pour the stock into a pan and bring gently up to the boil, then turn the heat down as low as it will go, to keep the stock hot, but not boiling.

4 Heat a further 30g (1oz) of the butter in a wide pan over a low to moderate heat. Add the onion, grated courgette and pancetta, and fry gently until the onion is tender, without browning. Now add the rice, and stir for about 1 minute until it turns opaque. Pour in the white wine, add the parsley, season with salt and pepper, and stir until the wine has almost all evaporated.

5 Next add a ladleful of the hot stock, and keep stirring until that has been absorbed. Keep adding the stock in the same way, a ladleful at a time, until the rice is al dente. Should you run out of stock before that, just start adding hot water. At this point, the risotto should still be fairly wet and moist, but not swimming about in a lake of liquid.

6 Stir in the fried courgettes and cook for a further 1–2 minutes to heat through. Now draw the pan off the heat and stir in the basil, roughly torn up, the last of the butter and the Parmesan. Taste and adjust seasoning and serve.

Add a ladleful of stock and stir until it has been absorbed.

Egg-fried rice.

Egg-fried Rice

This is so easy when you've got some leftover rice, and you can adapt it endlessly to fit whatever you have lurking in the fridge. All kinds of cooked vegetables can go into the rice, as long as they are heated through really well. For a really special version add a good handful of cooked prawns too. And of course, if you have a taste for hot things, add one (or more) chopped, deseeded red chillies to the wok with the garlic and ginger.

Don't be tempted to season the rice in the wok with soy sauce; it just turns it a rather nasty, dirty-looking off-white which is not at all appealing. Use a little salt, and put the soy on the table for those that want it.

Serves 3–4

200g (7oz) long-grain rice
1 tablespoon sunflower or vegetable oil
1 garlic clove, peeled and chopped
1cm (½in) piece fresh root ginger, peeled
    and finely chopped
4 spring onions, chopped
1 egg, beaten
6–8 cooked shelled prawns
about 60g (2oz) cooked ham, diced
about 60g (2oz) peas and/or sweetcorn,
    thawed if frozen
1 tomato, deseeded (see page 8) and diced
salt

1 Cook the rice in lots of salted boiling water until just tender (see page 85). Drain in a sieve. Using a chopstick, or the handle of a spoon, make half a dozen holes in the steaming rice as it sits in the sieve. Leave to cool in the sieve.

2 Prepare all the remaining ingredients and arrange them right beside the hob.

3 Heat the wok over a high flame until it begins to smoke. From now on, it's all systems go. Add the oil, swirl around then add the garlic, ginger and half the spring onions. Stir-fry for 20 seconds.

4 Next add the beaten egg, and stir-fry and scramble for 10–20 seconds. Then quickly tip in the rice, and stir-fry, really making sure that you slide the spatula or fish slice right down under the rice, scraping all the egg from the sides of the wok.

5 Add the prawns, ham, peas (or sweetcorn) and tomato, and carry on stir-frying until everything is steamingly hot. Season with salt. Serve immediately, scattered with the remaining spring onion.

chapter three

Meat and Poultry

It is not easy to encapsulate the art of cooking meat and poultry in a few lines. Probably best not to try, you may say. So I won't. Suffice it to say that this is an area that can produce some sublime meals or nose-dive into the positively inedible. The point of this chapter is to avoid the latter, and aim towards the former, making it the stuff of everyday living. Cooking meat well is not necessarily tricky, but it does depend largely on two things: the first is the use of high-quality meat and the second is experience.

Buying Meat

Half the battle is won in the shop – when you start with good meat you are likely to end up with a good meal on your plate. This is as true for the expensive cuts like steak as it is for the cheap cuts that make the succulent stews.

Good meat is dependent on a multitude of things such as breed, husbandry, feed, butchery, hygienic handling, hanging and storage. These are all factors that your retailer will be aware of, whether you are buying from a supermarket or an independent butcher. The big difference is the customers' access to information.

The advantage of shopping for meat in a supermarket is that it all comes ready-prepared and packed in airtight plastic. You don't have the choice that you will get in a good butcher's shop, but it's quick and less intimidating. But you can't get answers to questions like: How should I cook this cut? Can you slice me a steak 3cm thick? What is the best cut for a stew? Why is this meat darker than that? How far did the live animals have to travel to the abattoir? How long was the meat hung for? Good butchers (these days bad ones rarely stay in business) will happily supply answers to all these questions and more. That's their job, and they'll be delighted to introduce new customers to the joys of gorgeous meat.

For some of the very best meat in the country, often at brilliant prices, make a beeline for the nearest farmers' market. Here you will be able to buy meat of all kinds direct from the producers themselves. This is your chance to discover every last detail of the beast's life, if you are interested, or just to get a superb bargain, if you aren't.

Wherever you shop, there are some fundamentals to bear in mind. The first is that free-range meat nearly always tastes better than intensively reared – or in other words, you get what you pay for. The second is that hanging makes a massive difference to the taste and texture of meat. Hanging in controlled temperatures renders meat (from beef to chicken) more tender and enhances the flavour. The longer the meat is hung the darker the colour, especially with beef or lamb. So, bright red beef will not taste half as good as dark brown-red beef that has been hung for a longer time. Colour can be deceptive.

But not always. Meat tainted with a miserable grey tinge is invariably on its way out. Even if it is within its sell-by date, do not be tempted. Whilst you may not actually be poisoned by it, you certainly won't get any satisfaction either.

Storing Meat

Keep raw meat in the fridge, sitting in a shallow dish, wrapped loosely in greaseproof paper. Make sure that it cannot possibly drip on to other foods, especially those that may be eaten raw. Observe use-by dates strictly, but be aware that it is possible for meat to go off before the stipulated date, if for instance, your fridge is a few degrees warmer than the ideal 4°C or if it sat in the back of your bike/car for a couple of hours on a warm day. Meat bought from the butcher's or farmers' market probably won't be graced by a use-by date, so use your common sense instead. Cook and eat it within three or four days at the outside, and be guided by the smell. Your nose is an invaluable diagnostic tool. If the meat has the merest hint of a nasty niff to it, chuck it straight in the bin. It's not worth the risk.

Resting Meat

Why, you may well ask, am I putting a process that happens after cooking, right at the head of the cooking methods? Because it is just too important for me to risk leaving it to the end, where you will probably miss it altogether. So please don't skip on to the next section.

Every single piece of meat will taste far better if it is adequately rested after cooking, before hitting the plate. Resting just means leaving it alone in a warm place (e.g. on top of the stove, or in the oven, turned off, but still warm from the cooking, with the door ajar). During this time something nigh on magic happens.

Effectively, the meat seems to re-absorb its juices, spreading them evenly around. Once this is sorted, you will find that less liquid oozes out as you cut or carve the cooked meat, and that every mouthful tastes juicier and more succulent.

Quite how long the meat needs to rest depends on size. A small steak or chop needs only 4 or 5 minutes, which may well be just the time it takes to get everything on the table. Larger joints, such as a whole chicken, benefit from a 20-minute rest, whilst a dense chunk of grand roast beef may require a full 30 minutes. Use this time to your advantage to finish off vegetables and/or gravy, grab another glass of wine, gather those who are eating, etc.

Grilling and Barbecuing

Healthy and oh so good, grilled or barbecued meat is the ultimate treat. As long as you get it right. Which means the more expensive, more tender cuts, cooked under or over a belting heat. Under these circumstances the end result, crusted brown on the outside, tender and juicy inside, is virtually a guaranteed winner. Marinating adds an extra nuance of flavour, and will tenderise the meat to some small extent.

So, remember to get the grill going at full tilt at least 10 minutes before sliding the meat under it, and make sure that the charcoal has reached the requisite white heat (which can take 40 minutes) before the meat is slapped on the rack above it. Whichever system you use, ensure that the meat is close to the heat source, at least in the early stages of cooking. With the grill, I reckon you want to get it around 5–7.5cm (2–3in) away; with the barbie, around 10cm (4in). With thicker pieces (particularly chicken), you can increase the distance from the heat source once the exterior is lightly browned, so that the meat cooks adequately without burning.

When the meat has not been marinated, brush lightly with oil before grilling to help keep it moist and to prevent sticking to the rack.

Cuts for Grilling/ Barbecuing

Beef: steaks (rump, sirloin, fillet, T-bone, porterhouse). **Lamb:** chops (chump or loin), cutlets, leg or shoulder steaks, butterflied leg of lamb. **Pork:** loin chops, chump steaks, leg steaks. **Chicken:** drumsticks, breasts, boned thigh, chicken portions, spatchcocked chicken.

Grilled Steak

A plump, well-hung steak needs very little in terms of improvement. I usually grill steak as it is, seasoning after cooking, then serve with either a few pats of a flavoured butter or a simple sauce. Add some crisp potato wedges or a few new potatoes, a big green salad, and who needs more?

For grilling, a steak needs to be cut between 2 and 2.5cm (¾–1in) thick. Sirloin has what is considered by many to be the optimum combination of flavour and texture, though I really like the marginally chewier texture of rump, with its rich, savoury taste. Fillet is phenomenally expensive, as soft as butter, and light on flavour.

Take the meat out of the fridge at least half an hour before cooking so that it can come up to room temperature. Preheat the grill really thoroughly – in other words give it a good 10 minutes to heat up. Brush the steak lightly with oil and grill close to the grill until browned, then, if it needs more time, either reduce the heat of the grill a little or move the rack further away from the grill.

Approximate timings for steaks are:
Blue (i.e. barely cooked at all on the inside): 1–2 minutes per side
Rare: 2–3 minutes per side
Medium rare: 3–4 minutes per side
Medium: 3–5 minutes per side
Well done: the ruination of a good steak. Work it out for yourself.

As you can tell, times are only approximate. You need a second method for judging the degree of cooking achieved. You could just cut straight into the centre and have a look, but I have recently been introduced to a much cleverer trick. Touch the tip of your thumb and first finger together lightly, then prod the bulge of flesh just below your thumb with your other forefinger. This is what a rare steak feels like. Now touch the tips of your thumb and second finger together, and again prod the bulge of flesh – this is what a medium-rare steak feels like. Then it's thumb and ring finger for medium, and finally thumb and little finger for well-done. As you move from one finger to the next the firmness of the bulge increases, just as the firmness of a steak increases as it is cooked. Neat or what?

Once the steak is cooked, season with salt and pepper and let it rest for a few minutes before serving.

Griddled steak with roast potato wedges (see page 174), salad and some rosemary and garlic butter (see page 103).

Lamb Burgers with Minted Yoghurt

The combination of hot grilled lamb burgers and cool minty yoghurt is a real winner. Serve the burgers with a mound of couscous or roast new potatoes, and roast tomatoes or hot green beans, or in a ciabatta roll, perhaps with watercress and tomato, with roast potato wedges or chips on the side.

The minted yoghurt goes very nicely with grilled lamb chops, as well.

Serves 4

500g (18oz) minced lamb
2 teaspoons very finely chopped rosemary
1 garlic clove, peeled and crushed
1 shallot, peeled and very finely chopped
1 red chilli, deseeded and finely chopped
salt and pepper
1 egg, lightly beaten
a little sunflower or olive oil
lemon wedges, to serve

MINTED YOGHURT

150g (5oz) Greek-style yoghurt
a big handful of mint leaves, chopped
1 garlic clove, peeled and crushed

1 To make the minted yoghurt, just mix all the ingredients together, seasoning with salt, then cover and leave until needed (in the fridge if we are talking more than an hour, but bring back to room temperature before serving). Making it first allows enough time for the flavour of the mint to develop.

2 Mix the minced lamb with the rosemary, garlic, shallot, chilli, salt and pepper and just enough of the beaten egg to bind without making the mixture sloppy. Divide into four and shape into round burgers about 2.5cm (1in) thick. If you're not too pushed for time, chill the burgers in the fridge, covered loosely with clingfilm, for 30–60 minutes, or longer.

3 Preheat the grill thoroughly. Brush the lamb burgers with a little oil on each side and grill, close to the heat, for about 4–5 minutes on each side until nicely browned. Serve hot, with the minted yoghurt.

Lamb Burgers with Cheese and Apple

For a completely different meal, top each lamb burger, once cooked, with a slice of Wensleydale or Lancashire cheese, and return to the grill until melting. Then lay a ring of apple that has been swiftly fried in a little oil, on the melted cheese and clamp the whole thing between two halves of a toasted roll. Fancy finger food…

A lamb burger in a hot bun with salad leaves, with minted yoghurt to the side.

Grilled Lamb Chops

Choose plump lamb chops, cut about 2cm (¾in) thick. Using a sharp knife, make small incisions at 1cm (½in) intervals all along the border of fat that edges the meat.

Time permitting, make a marinade (see suggestions on page 102) for the chops to give extra flavour and ensure maximum tenderness. Not essential, but a pleasing touch. Arrange the chops in a shallow, close-fitting dish and pour the marinade over them. Turn the chops so that they are nicely coated. Cover the dish with clingfilm and leave to marinate at room temperature for up to an hour, or in the fridge for up to 48 hours. Turn the chops occasionally, so that they soak up the marinade evenly.

Preheat the grill thoroughly, letting it heat up for at least 5 minutes. Take the chops out of the marinade, shake off excess, and then grill fairly close to the heat until browned. This should take about 4–5 minutes. Turn the chops and cook the other side in the same way, for a further 4 minutes or so. Let the chops rest in a warm place for a few minutes and serve swiftly, together with plentiful green vegetables (French beans or runner beans, perhaps), grilled or roast tomatoes, and new potatoes.

Grilled Chicken

Grilling chicken is much trickier than grilling steaks or chops, which are the same thickness from one end to the other. Everyone has come across the burnt-outside-raw-inside chicken portion of barbecue fame. All too easy to achieve, under the grill as well as on the barbecue. The key to grilling chicken, which has a dense flesh of uneven thickness, is mandatory marination, to preserve succulence, and lots of attention as it cooks. On the whole, I'd suggest that it is more effective and more successful to roast chicken and chicken portions in a hot oven than to grill them. Chicken breasts, as long as they have languished for a few hours in a marinade beforehand, are the best bet under the grill.

As with all grilling, make sure that the grill is thoroughly preheated before use –

allow some 5–10 minutes for this. Adjust the grill rack so that the upper surface of the chicken will be about 7.5cm (3in) from the heat source. Lay the chicken on the rack, skin-side up, and grill until browned. Turn over and grill the other side until lightly browned. Baste the chicken with any marinade left in the dish and turn again. Now move the rack a couple of inches lower, so that the meat cooks more gently, allowing time for the heat to penetrate right the way through to the centre, hopefully without singeing the exterior.

Grilled Pork Chops

Pork needs to be cooked at a gentler heat than steak, lamb or chicken. This can be taxing to achieve under a grill. Marinating the meat before it is cooked helps to prevent it drying out.

Snip the fat around the edge of the chops at 1cm (½in) intervals to prevent it curling up. Arrange the grill rack so that the meat is 10cm (4in) or so from the grill. Grill the chops slowly, allowing about 6 minutes on each side, until lightly browned and cooked right through.

Marinades and Accompaniments

Marinades are an easy way to bring more flavour to meats, particularly those that are going to be exposed directly to the heat of, say, a grill or barbecue. The marinade will also offer some protection, helping to keep the inside moist as it cooks. Add a simple sauce, or a pat of flavoured butter that will melt seductively, and suddenly you have an immaculately dressed main course of distinction.

Spiced Yoghurt Marinade

Although it tastes fine with chicken or pork, this is a marinade that matches lamb best of all. Process together 5 generous tablespoons natural whole milk yoghurt, 1–3 teaspoons curry paste, 1 small tomato, deseeded and roughly diced, and 2 peeled and finely chopped garlic cloves. If you don't have a processor, quarter the tomato, and grate the flesh of each quarter on the coarse side of your grater to give a tomato pulp, then mix with the other ingredients. Add salt and pepper, and then spoon over up to six lamb chops. Serve the grilled chops with wedges of lime, and a scattering of fresh coriander leaves.

Balsamic Vinegar and Tarragon Marinade

A superb marinade that marries the natural sweetness of balsamic vinegar with the gentle aniseed scent of tarragon. As well as being a gem with lamb, it also tastes good on chicken and pork. Mix together 2 crushed garlic cloves, the finely chopped leaves of 1 large sprig of tarragon, 1 shallot, finely chopped, 1 teaspoon paprika (or better still, Spanish smoked pimentón, available from the spice racks of larger supermarkets), 1 teaspoon tomato purée, 2 tablespoons balsamic vinegar, 4 tablespoons extra virgin olive oil, and some salt and pepper. There's enough marinade here for either four to six lamb chops, or three to four chicken breasts.

Mediterranean Marinade

This is one of the simplest of all marinades and one of the best. Not only is it fabulous with lamb, but it also works well with chicken, pork and meaty fish like tuna.

Mix together the juice of 1 large lemon, a good tablespoon of dried oregano, 2 peeled and crushed garlic cloves, and 5 tablespoons extra virgin olive oil. Season with salt and pepper. Enough for four to six lamb chops and three to four chicken breasts.

Maître d'Hôtel Butter (a.k.a. Lemon and Parsley Butter)

This butter is very good with steak, chicken, or on vegetables, and makes enough for up to six servings. Either process together, or mash with a fork 110g (4oz) softened butter, 1 teaspoon finely grated lemon zest, 1½ tablespoons lemon juice, 3 tablespoons finely chopped parsley, and some freshly ground black pepper. Once smoothly mixed, scoop on to a sheet of greaseproof paper or foil, form into a cylinder and roll up. Chill in the fridge until firm. Lay two or three slices on top of each steak when serving.

Blue Cheese Butter

Blue cheese butter is devastatingly good on steak and baked potatoes and can be tossed into pasta to good effect. It makes enough for up to eight servings. Either process together, or mash together thoroughly 110g (4oz) lightly salted butter and the same amount of blue cheese (e.g. Stilton, Roquefort or Gorgonzola), adding 2 tablespoons finely chopped parsley and 1 tablespoon finely chopped chives. Shape into a cylinder and chill as for **Maître d'Hôtel Butter**.

Rosemary and Garlic Butter

This is excellent with steak and grilled lamb chops, and makes enough for up to six servings. Strip fresh rosemary leaves off several sprigs of rosemary and chop finely. Measure out 1 tablespoonful. Mix with 2 garlic cloves, finely chopped, and the finely grated zest of 1 lemon. Chop this mixture together until incredibly finely chopped, then mash with 110g (4oz) softened butter and 1½ tablespoons lemon juice, as well as plenty of freshly ground black pepper. Form into a cylinder and chill as for **Maître d'Hôtel Butter**.

Salsa Verde

Italian salsa verde is one of the all-time great sauces that goes brilliantly with almost any grilled meats. It can be made very swiftly in a processor, but if you don't have one, it still won't take too long to chop the ingredients finely by hand.

Serves 5–6

45g (1½oz) curly or flat-leaf parsley leaves
15g (½oz) basil leaves
3 canned anchovy fillets
1 tablespoon rinsed capers
1 tablespoon white wine vinegar
½ slice white bread (crusts removed)
1 small garlic clove, peeled and chopped
salt and pepper
150ml (5fl oz) extra virgin olive oil

1 To make in a processor, pile in all the ingredients except the oil. Whirr until very finely chopped; scrape down the sides.
2 Set the blades running again and gradually trickle in enough oil to give a creamy sauce. Taste and adjust seasoning (easy on the salt if you used salted capers).
3 To make by hand, pile all the ingredients except the oil up on a wide chopping board. Using a large sharp knife, chop them all together until very, very finely chopped. Tip into a bowl and mix in enough oil to give a sauce-like consistency. Store in the fridge, covered, for up to three days.

Variations

Parsley and mint salsa verde Replace the basil with mint leaves.

Coriander Use 45g (1½oz) coriander leaves and 15g (½oz) parsley leaves. No basil.

Frying

Frying is a great way of cooking thin cuts of tenderest meat. It is also used to colour tougher cuts of meat for a stew. The trick with frying is to make sure that the fat in the frying pan is thoroughly heated through before adding the meat. Just before the meat goes into the frying pan, pat it dry with kitchen paper so that it doesn't spit too violently in the fat, and to reduce the chances of stewing in its own juices, which is not at all the aim. The second critical tip is to leave the meat alone for at least 2 minutes, if not 3, once it is in the pan. During this time it will brown underneath, forming its own non-stick layer. Meat sticks to the surface of the pan only when a) the fat was not hot enough, and b) you jiggle it around before it has browned. Don't say I didn't warn you.

(Stir-frying gets its own special section on page 134.)

Cuts for Frying **Beef:** steaks (rump, sirloin, fillet, T-bone, porterhouse, as well as flash-fry steaks and minute steaks). **Lamb:** chops (chump or loin), cutlets, leg or shoulder steaks, noisettes of lamb, lamb fillet. **Pork:** loin chops, chump steaks, leg steaks, pork fillet (a.k.a. tenderloin). **Chicken:** breast escalopes or slices, boned thigh.

Steak Teriyaki

Steak gets the Japanese treatment with this dark, sticky, salty glaze of a sauce. You can buy ready-mixed teriyaki sauce, but it is easy enough to make a passable replica yourself if you have a bottle of soy sauce, some dry sherry or white wine (or better still, Japanese saké) and a shake or two of caster sugar.

Serves 2

sunflower or vegetable oil
2 sirloin steaks, cut about 2.5cm (1in) thick
4 tablespoons dry white wine, or dry sherry, or saké
2 tablespoons dark soy sauce
2 tablespoons caster sugar

1 Cover the base of a heavy frying pan with a very thin film of oil. Place over a high heat and leave for 3 minutes to heat through thoroughly.

2 Lay the steaks in the pan and fry for 3 minutes. Turn over and cook for 1 more minute.

3 Spoon over 2 tablespoons of the dry white wine or sherry. It will sizzle madly and smoke. Cover the pan tightly and cook for another 2 minutes. Transfer the steaks to a heated plate and keep warm.

4 Add all the remaining ingredients to the pan and stir and scrape all the residues from cooking the meat into the liquids. As soon as the sauce has thickened, return the steaks to the pan with any juices that have seeped out, and cook for a final minute, turning once so that they are glazed in the sauce. Serve immediately.

Chicken Escalopes with Mustard and Crème Fraîche

A whole chicken breast is a chunky piece of meat and has a tendency to be dry if fried as is. Transform it into a thin escalope, however, and it cooks in a matter of minutes, remaining moist and tender. Here it is finished quickly with a mustard cream sauce, to make a speedy supper dish that is good served with broccoli and noodles, or new potatoes. (Do the same with pork fillet.)

Serves 2

2 chicken breasts
15g (½oz) butter
1 tablespoon sunflower oil
salt and pepper
4 generous tablespoons crème fraîche
1 tablespoon Dijon mustard
1 teaspoon chopped chives

1 Place one of the chicken breasts on the chopping board. Using a sharp knife, cut it in half horizontally, slicing almost, but not quite right through to the other side. The two halves should still be attached, so that you can open them out like a newspaper. Don't worry if the small fillet of chicken underneath becomes detached – just lay it back in place and carry on regardless. Repeat with the other chicken breast.

2 One at a time, sandwich the opened chicken breasts between two sheets of greaseproof paper or clingfilm. Using either the bottom of a heavy pan, or a rolling pin or perhaps even a real meat mallet, bash the chicken out flatter and flatter, until it is spread out very thinly. Don't get too carried away, though – you are not aiming to make lace out of it.

Open out the chicken breasts...   and flatten between sheets of clingfilm.

Chicken escalopes with mustard and crème fraîche, served with noodles and broccoli.

3 Heat the butter and oil in a wide frying pan over a medium heat. Once the butter is frothing away, lay the chicken escalopes in the pan, overlapping as little as possible. Fry for 1–2 minutes, then turn and repeat on the other side. Lift out on to a plate, season lightly with salt and pepper, and keep warm.

4 Add the crème fraîche and mustard to the pan, together with a little salt and pepper. Heat up and mix together thoroughly, then let the sauce simmer for a minute or so to thicken. Taste and adjust seasonings.

5 Return the chicken escalopes to the pan, with any juices that have gathered under them. Turn to coat in the sauce, then lift out on to a serving dish and pour the remaining sauce over them. Scatter with chives and serve.

Chicken Fajitas

The thing I like about this sort of Tex-Mex dish is that it is such fun. Lots of bowls of this and that on the table, warm tortillas and a big plate of spiced chicken and peppers, and everyone digs in and makes up their own combination. All that passing of bowls is virtually guaranteed to generate a lively atmosphere. And then there's the taste, every mouthful slightly different as you work your way down the folded tortilla. It's a potentially messy business, but that's all part of the enjoyment.

Serves 4

4 skinned and boned chicken breasts
2 tablespoons sunflower or olive oil
1 onion, peeled, halved and thinly sliced
2 red peppers, deseeded and cut into strips
juice of 1 lime
4 tablespoons roughly chopped coriander

MARINADE
1 tablespoon cumin seeds
1 tablespoon coriander seeds
1 teaspoon dried oregano
1 dried chilli, crumbled
juice of 1 lime
1 garlic clove, peeled and crushed
salt and pepper

TO SERVE
8 flour or corn tortillas
soured cream or crème fraîche
Guacamole (see page 40)
pickled sliced jalapeño chillies
150g (5oz) cherry tomatoes, quartered
medium Cheddar, grated (optional)

1 To make the marinade, heat a small frying pan over a moderate heat. Add the cumin and coriander seeds and shake for a few minutes to toast them. They are ready when you can smell a tantalising spicy scent wafting from them, and they turn a shade darker. Immediately tip into a bowl. Cool, then grind to a coarse powder. Mix with the remaining marinade ingredients.

2 Slice the chicken thinly into strips, place in a bowl and then pour over the marinade. Turn, cover with clingfilm and leave to marinate at room temperature for up to half an hour, or in the fridge for up to 24 hours. Bring back to room temperature before cooking.

3 Preheat the oven to 180°C/350°F/Gas Mark 4. Put the soured cream, guacamole, chillies, tomatoes and cheese (if using) into separate bowls and arrange on the table. About 20 minutes before serving, wrap the tortillas in silver foil and slide into the oven to heat through.

4 Heat a wide frying pan over a high heat. Add half the oil and then sauté the onion and peppers briskly until they are soft and tinged with brown here and there. Tip into a bowl.

5 Add the remaining oil to the pan. Heat through, then place the chicken in the frying pan. Stir-fry for 3–4 minutes, until just cooked through. Now return the vegetables to the pan, and season with salt and pepper. Fry for about 2 more minutes, tossing and turning to mix everything together well. When steaming and hot, stir in the lime juice and the coriander, then tip into a warm serving bowl.

Chicken fajitas.

6 Place on the table, along with the tortillas, and let everyone help themselves to whatever they want, making up their own mix of the chicken and peppers with all the other bits and pieces. Just remind them not to over-fill each tortilla, or else it is impossible to wrap up neatly!

Roasting

Roasting is best suited to bigger hunks of meat, cooked over a longer period of time. Naturally there are exceptions to this rule (e.g. rack of lamb or fillet), but that's another story. Roasting is both one of the most convenient ways of cooking meat and one of the most daunting. Do you worry about producing a Sunday roast worthy of your or somebody else's Mum (or Dad, let's not be sexist)? Well stop it, right now. There really isn't much more to the business than buying a decent joint of meat, shoving it in a hot oven, and leaving it there for an hour or more. Sure, you can make endless refinements and variations by working marinades and so on into the equation, but the three fundamentals are a) buying the right kind of joint, b) basting it every now and then as it cooks, and c) not over-cooking it.

Let's begin with the joint itself. A roasting joint needs to be tender, prime meat, which on the whole means those cuts from the upper back and rump area of the animal. These are the parts that do least work when the beast is alive. Legs and forequarters are tougher because that's where all the action took place as the animals were wandering around grazing. The second criterion is that the meat should be marbled with fat. This is essential both for flavour and for moistness. Think of it as an inner marinade, if you like. So, if you value the taste of your Sunday joint, don't go for the leanest piece of meat, as you will only be disappointed.

With pork the layer of fat under the skin is critical, too. If it is so thin as to be almost negligible, your crackling won't crackle, and the meat itself is likely to be chewy and stringy. If all this talk of fat makes you concerned for your health, remind yourself that much of this fat, once it has done its work, will drip down into the roasting tin. Perfect for roasting potatoes...or throwing out.

Basting means spooning hot cooking juices back over the joint of meat as it cooks to keep it moist and juicy inside, and enhance the taste. In an ideal world this should be done every 20–30 minutes, but it won't be an utter disaster if you stretch it out to every 40–60 minutes with a larger piece of meat. To baste, lift the joint in its pan out of the oven and sit on the hob. Close the oven door (so that you don't lose too much heat), then either tilt the pan and spoon up the juices with the largest spoon you own, or easier still use a basting bulb. (These are sold in most cookware shops but do make sure that you buy a glass or toughened plastic one.) Pour the juices over the top of the joint, making sure that it is all moistened. Then quickly return the joint to the oven to carry on cooking. Pork is one of the few meats that doesn't need basting – you don't want to soften the crackling.

Over-cooking is fairly easily avoided. Calculate the cooking time of your joint carefully (see below). Weigh your joint, complete with stuffing if using, once it is oven-ready. If necessary, use the bathroom scales. Then look at the chart below to work out the cooking times. Write down the result. And make a note of the time the joint goes into the oven, and the time it should come out. I say 'should' here quite deliberately, as no two ovens are ever quite the same, so this spot of mathematics you've undertaken is to be used only as a rough guide to cooking time.

The best way to get an accurate idea of when a joint of meat is done to your liking, is to buy a meat thermometer and plunge it into the heart of the joint before it goes into the oven. Then it is easy to gauge the state of play in the middle of the meat. A second less high-tech method is to plunge a skewer into the centre of the joint (but not up against any bone) and keep it there for 30 seconds. Take it out and lay the tip on the inside of your wrist. If cold, the meat is not yet done. When warm, the meat is rare, when fairly hot, medium and when very hot, well done.

When roasting beef or lamb, you should aim either for rare or medium, for well-done beef or lamb is actually over-cooked, tough and a crying shame. Pork, on the other hand, should be cooked right through, i.e. well done.

Roasting Chart

	Mins per kg	Mins per lb	Oven temperature
Beef: Rare	26-30	12-14	240°C/475°F/Gas Mark 9 for first 20 mins, then 190°C/375°F/Gas Mark 5
Medium rare	40-44	18-20	
Lamb: Pink	36	16	230°C/450°F/Gas Mark 8 for first 15 mins, then 200°C/400°F/Gas Mark 6
Pork: Well done	66-70	33-35	230°C/450°F/Gas Mark 8 for first 15 mins, then 180°C/350°F/Gas Mark 4

Cuts for Roasting   **Beef:** rib roast, sirloin, fillet (topside and silverside can be roasted but need extra attention as they are so lean). **Lamb:** leg, shoulder, loin, rack, saddle, boned, rolled breast. **Pork:** leg, knuckle, loin, fillet, belly pork, blade, spare ribs (best blanched first, see below). **Chicken** gets its own roasting section all to itself on page 116 .

Sticky Spare Ribs

The meat nearest the bone is always said to be the best, and spare ribs prove it! I love being able to give up on table manners, grasp a bone in my fingers and gnaw off the flesh, permeated with its sticky coating. I guess spare ribs bring out the caveman in all of us.

It is really worth taking time to blanch them in water first as this makes the meat more tender. Don't waste the cooking water, either, as it makes a good stock for soup.

Serves 4

2 racks of spare ribs, or about 1.25 kg (2½lb)

MARINADE
2 tablespoons runny honey
2 tablespoons tomato ketchup
2 tablespoons soy sauce
2 tablespoon English or Dijon mustard
2 tablespoons sunflower or vegetable oil
½–1 tablespoon chilli sauce (optional)
2 tablespoons light muscovado sugar
1cm (½in) piece fresh root ginger, grated

1 Bring a large pan of lightly salted water to the boil. Slide in the spare ribs, bring back to the boil, then reduce the heat and simmer for 20 minutes. Drain.

2 Preheat the oven to 200°C/400°F/Gas Mark 6.

3 Mix all the marinade ingredients together. Line a roasting tin with silver foil, then lay a wire rack on top. Arrange the spare ribs on top, and brush the marinade over thickly. Turn over and brush the other side with the marinade, too. Be generous with it.

4 Roast for 20 minutes, then turn and brush again with any remaining marinade. Return to the oven for a further 20–25 minutes or so, until dark and sticky and just beginning to catch in the heat here and there.

5 Serve, get sticky, provide generous quantities of napkins and finger bowls.

Roast Rack of Lamb with Parsley and Orange Crust

For a special treat for two, there is no doubt that the best joint is a rack of lamb. The sweet tender meat cooks quickly and tastes very good. If I'm short on time, I just smear some mustard, or a little oil and crushed garlic, over the outside before popping it into the oven. When I'm not quite so pushed, I make a buttery crisp crust speckled with herbs.

Incidentally, French trimmed is how a rack of lamb is usually sold. It just means that the excess fat and scraps of meat have been cleaned off the long bones, to make the rack look more sightly.

Serves 2

1 French-trimmed rack of lamb
30g (1oz) slightly stale breadcrumbs
20g (a generous ½oz) butter, melted
1½ tablespoons chopped parsley
finely grated zest of ½ orange
salt and pepper

1 Preheat the oven to 230°C/450°F/Gas Mark 8.

2 Mix the breadcrumbs with the melted butter, parsley, orange zest and some salt and pepper. Use your hands to turn and mix until the breadcrumbs have soaked up the butter evenly.

3 Place the rack of lamb, curved outer side upwards, in a baking dish or small roasting tin. Pat the breadcrumb mixture evenly over the upper surface.

4 Roast for 23–25 minutes for pink meat, another 4 or 5 minutes if you must have it well done. Either way, check the crust after about 18 minutes and cover loosely with silver foil if necessary to prevent burning.

5 Rest the meat for 5–10 minutes, then use a sharp knife to slice down between the bones, releasing individual cutlets.

Patting the mixture over the rack, and resting the meat after roasting.

Roast Leg of Lamb

An absolute classic for Sunday lunch. A roast leg of lamb looks magnificent when set on the table, and other than over-cooking, it's hard to go wrong with it. Serve with a potato gratin, or roast potatoes, carrots and green veg.

Incidentally, a parsley and mint salsa verde (see page 104) goes very well with roast lamb, and makes a change from over-sharp mint sauce. Don't forget the jar of redcurrant jelly, either.

Serves 6–8

1 leg of lamb, weighing about 2.75kg (6lb)
2–3 garlic cloves, peeled and cut lengthways into thin slivers
leaves from 2 sprigs rosemary
2–3 tablespoons extra virgin olive oil
salt and pepper
300ml (10fl oz) white wine

1 Preheat the oven to 230°C/450°F/Gas Mark 8.

2 Using a small narrow-bladed knife, make a small slit in the meat. Push a sliver of garlic and a few leaves of rosemary down into the slit (I use the handle of a teaspoon to help push them in). Repeat all over the lamb, then rub with olive oil and season with salt and pepper.

3 Place in a roasting tin, and pour the wine around it. Slide into the oven and cook for 1 hour, 40 minutes if you like your lamb cooked medium (i.e. pink), or 2–2¼ hours for well done. After the first 15 minutes, reduce the heat to 200°C/400°F/Gas Mark 6.

4 Baste with its own juices every 20–30 minutes as it cooks. Add a little water to the pan if the juices threaten to dry up.

5 When cooked, transfer the meat to a warm place to rest for 25–30 minutes before carving. Skim the fat from the juices in the pan and pour the juices into a jug to serve as a thin gravy, or make a gravy proper in the roasting tin (see page 120).

Make slits in a leg of lamb and insert slivers of garlic and tiny sprigs of rosemary.

Roast Chicken   Some people dream of caviar and lobster, but if you ask me, there's little to beat a perfect roast chicken. Just imagine the sight and smell of it, all crisp glistening brown skin, tender flesh, rich beckoning scent wafting from the kitchen.

Pickin' a chicken   First and foremost, you must consider the bird itself. Frankly, you get what you pay for, and with chicken the differences really show. The cheapest broiler chicken has led a sad short life, cooped up in a dismayingly small cage. This means it has had little or no exercise and as a result will have little flavour, and a damp cotton-wool texture. Free-range and organic birds are more expensive, but by law must have had access to more space, and been free to move around and peck at the ground. Their degree of freedom will be reflected in their improved taste and firmer texture. Most supermarkets now stock free-range chickens, but best buys are to be found at farmers' markets and farm shops, as well as good butchers, where the seller will be able to tell you a little about how the birds are reared if you are interested. Prices may well be cheaper than in supermarkets, too.

Keep it clean   Scrupulous and military adherence to hygiene principles is critical when it comes to handling chickens. Uncooked chicken can be contaminated with salmonella, which gives humans an extremely unpleasant dose of food poisoning. This is undoubtedly something to avoid. So, first of all wrap the chicken in an extra plastic bag at the check-out to avoid it dripping on the way home.

Get it into your fridge a.s.a.p., and make sure that cannot possibly come into contact or ooze on to anything else, especially things that are likely to be eaten raw.

When you get to cooking, make sure that you wash your hands, knives, chopping boards and any other items that have come into contact with the bird or its juices as soon as you have finished preparation, and before you move on to any thing else. Use hot soapy water and give the whole works a good going over.

To truss or not to truss?   These days birds arrive snugly trussed, in other words tied up with elastic string to prevent the odd thigh waving about provocatively. The theory is that a trussed bird cooks more neatly, but that's a bit of an old-fashioned concept. It's fairly obvious that with string removed and legs akimbo, the hot air of the oven can circulate more freely around an untrussed bird, which means more successful and even cooking.

If you honestly believe that the cooked bird looks better trussed, that's fine, but just take extra care to test that it is really cooked through when served.

A trussed chicken.

An untrussed chicken.

Basting a roast chicken.

Basting Basting means spooning hot juices (usually those in the roasting tin) over the bird two or three times during the cooking period. This makes for moister flesh and oddly enough helps to crisp the skin (because of the fat melted into the juice). When you baste, lift the roasting tin out of the oven, close the door so that you don't lose too much heat, then use a large spoon or a basting bulb (available from cookware shops) to spoon the juice over the breast area in particular, and swiftly return the whole lot to the oven to carry on cooking.

To test whether a roast chicken is done, poke a skewer or the tip of a knife into the flesh at the thickest part of the thigh.

Is it done? Everyone knows that under-cooked chicken carries a risk of salmonella taint, so it is absolutely critical to make sure that it is cooked properly. Two tests. First of all, give the thigh a quick wiggle. If it moves loosely, then it is probably done to a 'T'. Next, poke a skewer or the tip of a knife right down into the flesh at the thickest part of the thigh. If the liquid that oozes out is clear, then it's cooked. If it looks at all pink or bloody, put the bird back into the oven for a further 10–15 minutes.

By the way, before you start cooking the chicken, please make sure that it is at room temperature and not straight out of the fridge. It will cook through much more efficiently, reducing the risk of food poisoning.

Resting and Relaxing   See pages 94-95.

Carving   An extraordinary mystique has grown up around the skill of carving, which is really quite unfounded. The one and only matter of absolute, critical import is the knife. It must be a) big enough, and b) sharp, sharp, sharp.

Once that is sorted, here's how you carve a chicken (after it has rested, see page 94). First, pull back each leg until the joint snaps free, then cut it off close to the body (photos 1 and 2). You may want to remove the wishbone (situated at the back of the wing end of the body) - this does make carving somewhat easier. You may have to do a little probing here, but the idea is to find the point where the breastbone ends, and to cut down at an angle, lifting the wishbone off, embedded in lots of white meat. Now all you have to do is cut nice neat slices of breast, slicing down parallel to the breastbone, angling the knife slightly outwards as you cut down (photos 3 and 4). Oh, and one very final thing – don't forget the 'oysters', considered by many to be the choicest nugget of flesh – on either side of the backbone, just where the thigh was joined on.

But if you hate the thought of carving, go for the more casual hacked-up look, possibly best done privately in the kitchen rather than at table. Using a strong pair of scissors, or a big sharp knife, cut the bird in half from head to tail. Cut each half in half again, quite close to the thigh, so that the person getting the wing side has more of the breast. Pile in a warm serving dish, spoon a little of the pan juices or gravy over the chicken, and serve while still warm.

Carving

The Best Easy Roast Chicken

Try this most elementary of roast chickens first – the combination of olive oil and lemon keeps the flesh moist and turns the skin divinely crisp. However, if you don't have any olive oil to hand, a generous knob of butter will do nicely instead.

Serves 4

1 x 1.5–1.8kg (3lb 5oz–4lb) chicken
1 onion, peeled and quartered
1 large carrot, peeled and cut into chunks
 (optional)
a couple of sprigs of parsley (optional)
½ lemon
2 tablespoons olive or sunflower oil, or
 30g (1 oz) butter
salt and pepper

1 At least half an hour in advance, take the chicken out of the fridge, remove its clingfilm, and let it come back to room temperature. Preheat the oven to 200°C/400°F/Gas Mark 6.

2 Snip the string that holds the legs close to the body, and remove it altogether. Slip two quarters of the onion inside the chicken. Slice the remaining onion and spread out in a roasting tin. Add the carrot and parsley if using. Sit the chicken squarely on top.

3 Squeeze the juice of the lemon all over the chicken, then drizzle over the olive oil (or smear the butter over the breast and thighs). Season generously with salt and pepper and then rub the whole lot into the skin of the chicken.

4 Pour 250ml (8fl oz) water around the chicken. Place in the oven and roast for 1¼–1½ hours. After about half an hour, baste the chicken with the juices in the pan. Repeat after another 20 minutes or so.

5 Check that the chicken is cooked through (see page 117).

6 Transfer the chicken to a serving dish, and leave in a warm place – either on top of the stove, or even in the oven, heat turned off and door left ajar. Leave for 15 minutes to rest, before serving, either with the pan juices just as they are, or with gravy (see overleaf).

need to know

GRAVY To make gravy you will also need 1 tablespoon plain flour and 300ml (10fl oz) Chicken Stock (see pages 15–16) or water from cooking vegetables. Once your roast chicken is resting in the warmth somewhere, go back to its roasting tin. Take out the vegetables (I think they taste really good, so save them to eat with the bird), and pour off all but a tablespoon or two of the juices into a bowl. Put the roasting tin directly on the hob (over two burners if possible), and turn to a low to medium heat. Sprinkle the flour into the roasting tin, then stir and whisk with a small whisk until the liquid left in the pan has been absorbed and the resulting paste is beginning to brown. Now stir in the stock or vegetable water, a good splash at a time. Spoon the fat off the chicken juices, and add those too. Simmer for a few minutes, until slightly thickened. Season with salt and pepper. Taste and adjust the seasoning, then strain into a warm serving bowl, or jug.

Meat gravies are made in exactly the same way.

Sprinkle the flour into the tin.

Whisk until it starts to brown.

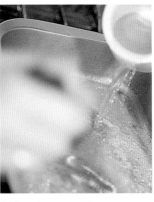
Add stock or vegetable water.

Add chicken juices.

Roast Chicken with Tarragon Cream Sauce

One of the great French Sunday lunch dishes is 'poulet à l'estragon', chicken with a tarragon cream sauce.

Follow the recipe for **Best Easy Roast Chicken**, using butter, not oil. Tuck 2 or 3 sprigs of fresh tarragon inside the chicken along with the onion quarters. Add only 150ml (5fl oz) of water to the pan, and top up with an equal quantity of white wine, or Noilly Prat (dry Vermouth). Roast in the same way, until cooked. Leave to rest in a warm place.

Chop the leaves only of another 2 sprigs of tarragon. Use a wide shallow spoon to skim as much fat as you can from the juices left in the roasting tin. Tilting the pan towards one corner will make it easier, then you can even blot a little more fat off by laying a sheet of kitchen paper on the surface of the juices and lifting it off swiftly. Place the roasting tin over two rings, set to medium blast, and stir the remaining juices around, scraping up all the nice gooey brown bits. Now stir in 1 small 200g (7oz) pot crème fraîche, or 150ml (5fl oz) double cream. Add the fresh tarragon, bring up to the boil and simmer until slightly thickened. Taste and adjust the seasoning.

Stuff it! Adding a vibrant stuffing is a doddle – everyone will love you for it, and you might even be able to stretch the bird around five people with a touch of clever carving. A stuffing will also help to keep the chicken moist as it cooks (a kind of internal basting) and its flavour will permeate lightly into the meat itself.

Parsley and Lemon Stuffing

1 small onion, peeled and chopped
60g (2oz) butter
1 garlic clove, peeled and chopped
110g (4oz) fresh white breadcrumbs
3 tablespoons chopped parsley
finely grated zest of ½ lemon
1 tablespoon lemon juice
salt and pepper

1 Fry the onion gently in the butter until soft, but not browned. Add the garlic and fry gently for another minute or so.

2 Mix with all the remaining ingredients to form a moist stuffing.

need to know

WHERE TO STUFF IT A chicken naturally has two handy pockets for stuffing. One is under the flap of skin that hangs loose at the neck end of the bird and the second is the comparatively hangar-like central cavity. Use both. First pack as much as will fit comfortably under the skin flap, and then put the rest, more loosely, into the central cavity. Don't over-load at either end, as the stuffing will swell a little as it cooks. If you wish you can close up gaps with an adroitly placed wooden cocktail stick, but this is not strictly necessary.

A stuffed bird will take longer to cook than an unstuffed one. Add an extra 20 minutes to the cooking time.

Stewing and Braising

There is something utterly, comfortingly, reassuringly and irresistibly enticing about a well-made stew or casserole. There are few people (vegetarians excluded) whose mouth doesn't water at the prospect of a lovingly cooked, dark-sauced, tender and savoury beef stew, spooned over a cushion of buttery mash.

Stewing, or in other words cooking meat (usually) with vegetables and aromatics in a liquid for a fairly lengthy amount of time, is easy but not quick. Despite this, I think of stews as remarkably convenient. You see, once you've browned the meat and got all the ingredients into your casserole, burbling away gently in or on the stove, you can wander off and get on with something completely different. An occasional stir is all that is required of you for some time to come. And there's more. Most stews actually benefit from being made in advance, then reheated, say, a day later. Finally, the added bonus is that it is often the cheaper cuts of meat (particularly beef or lamb) that make the best stews.

The Meat Getting the right cut of meat for a casserole makes a considerable difference to the final outcome. Not surprising really as it is the meat that brings the characteristically complex flavour to the sauce, which in turn suffuses all other ingredients that have been lobbed into the pot.

With one exception (chicken, but I'll come to that in a moment) you really should avoid the more expensive fancy cuts of meat. They just can't take the pace. So it's a big NO to pricey sirloin or rump steak, to boned leg of lamb and pork fillet. A resounding YES, on the other hand, to cheaper cuts. If you are a confirmed supermarket shopper, then you will have to settle for the anonymity of 'stewing steak' or 'cubed lamb', which will do a perfectly adequate job.

You would be better served, however, by heading off to a real butcher, who knows a bit about what she or he sells. Use her/his expertise to your advantage and never feel embarrassed that you don't know the names of every single cut of meat. That's her/his job, not yours. Farmers' markets are also a brilliant source of high-quality meat, and usually at a great price.

Either way, if it is a **beef stew** you've set your heart on, I reckon that shin of beef makes the very best of casseroles. It doesn't look too promising, with strange almost translucent lines running through it, which could be mistaken for gristle. Actually this is connective tissue, and during the long, slow cooking period, it will dissolve into the sauce to give a slightly sticky, velvety richness that is hard to beat. Almost as good are skirt steak, or chuck steak, both of which are full of flavour.

When you are out to produce a **lamb stew**, I'd suggest one of two options. The first is shoulder of lamb, which seems very fatty, but cooks to an excellent tenderness with oodles of flavour. The second, which looks less than sexy to be frank, is scrag or middle neck. This comes on the bone, so you need a fair amount of it to make decent helpings, but the bone itself gives the stew a particularly rounded flavour.

Practically all cuts of **pork** are tender, but for a stew avoid the fattiest, like belly pork. Pork needs less cooking than beef or lamb – one hour is usually enough.

Chicken is easy. Any parts will do, though if you cooked up nothing but chicken wings you wouldn't get a lot of meat. Ideally, you want a mix of breast, thigh and drumsticks; the leg portions yield up far more flavour to the stew than breast alone. I usually buy a whole chicken and cut it up into smaller portions, but if you buy your chicken from a butcher, she or he will willingly do this for you.

Preparation

With beef, lamb and pork, cut the meat up into cubes that are at least 3cm (1¼in) across. Bigger is fine, but no smaller, please. Smaller cubes tend to break down into a sludge. Try to keep the cubes roughly the same size, though there's no need to get out a ruler. As you cut the meat up, remove obvious bits of gristle and large chunks of fat. A good butcher will do this for you.

And the Rest of the Ingredients

Besides the meat, a stew is made up of a selection of vegetables and herbs or spices chosen to give a rounded background flavour – onion, sometimes carrot and celery, garlic, thyme, parsley, bay, rosemary, chilli, ginger, cumin, coriander and so on. Bacon, pancetta or lardons (cubes of bacon) may also be included in this cluster of ingredients. The other essential element is some sort of liquid, or maybe liquids, to form the sauce. In the simplest stew this will be water. Often some or all of the water is replaced by wine, brandy, beer, lager, stock or even coconut milk. Last but not by any means least are the club of ingredients that add to the substance of the stew – vegetables such as carrots or parsnips or peppers, cut into largish chunks, mushrooms, pulses such as cannellini beans or butter beans, and so on.

Seasoned Flour

This is often used to coat meat before frying, helping to form a brown crust, as well as helping to thicken the stew. It is simply plain flour, mixed with a generous shot of salt and pepper. If you fancy a hint of something livelier in there, you could also add cayenne pepper or ground spices such as nutmeg, cumin or cinnamon. The meat should only be tossed in the flour just before cooking, otherwise it turns gluey.

Casserole Dish   When buying a casserole dish, look for one that is thick and heavy. Pottery or china casseroles are a good option, but cannot be used on top of the stove. Enamelled cast-iron is the favourite, as it can be used both on the hob and in the oven, as well as holding the heat well. Your stew is also less likely to burn, as the heat will be more evenly distributed than in a cheaper, thinner-based pan. The price is frightening, but a good-quality cast-iron casserole will last you for ever.

Make sure that the lid fits snugly. It makes sense to opt for a fairly large, deep casserole – you can cook a small quantity of stew in a roomy dish, but there's no way you can squeeze enough for six into a dish designed to feed three.

Cooking   **Browning the meat** The first major step in making most stews is browning the meat in hot fat. This is sometimes called 'sealing', a misleading term as nothing is sealed in or out at all. The purpose of this process is three-fold: to give colour to the meat to make it look more appealing, to develop a rich colour for the sauce, and to bring extra flavour to the stew.

You can brown the meat directly in a casserole dish that can be used on the hob, but I prefer to do it in a wide frying pan, where it is easier to control (and which is easier to wash if you burn anything by mistake). Heat the oil or butter and oil in the frying pan over a medium heat. If the meat has been coated in flour, shake off excess, and add only enough pieces to the pan to fill it in a single layer, allowing a little space between pieces. If you over-crowd the pan, the meat will stew in its own juices. Far better to cook the meat in two to three batches.

Once the meat is in the pan, leave it alone for 2–3 minutes or longer before turning – the underneath should be richly browned, not just a marginally deeper colour. Keep turning the meat until it is really well browned on all sides. As the pieces are done, transfer them to a plate. Cook the second batch in the same way.

Deglazing To get every last drop of flavour from the frying process, it is usual to 'deglaze' the pan. To do this, a glass or so of liquid, usually alcoholic, is poured into the hot pan. As it comes up to the boil, the liquid is stirred and all the brown goo left from frying is scraped up and dissolved into the liquid. Once the liquid has boiled for a few seconds, it is poured over the meat in the casserole.

Oven or hob? Once all the ingredients have been incorporated into the casserole, it can be left to burble very gently until the meat is tender. This can be done on the hob (for quicker cooking meats, such as chicken, this is often the best option) or in the oven, set to around 150°C/300°F/Gas Mark 2, for meats that take longer to cook. The advantage of the oven is that the stew is unlikely to catch on the bottom of the pan and needs little attention while it simmers. The hob is more economical, and a stove-top stew is easily checked.

How long? Never rush a stew. Chicken will need no more than 35–40 minutes to cook through, lamb will take between 1 and 2 hours, while beef may require anything from 2–3 hours to cook to a melting tenderness. Pork needs somewhere between 30 and 60 minutes.

Thickening/thinning No recipe is ever perfect, and it may well come to pass that at the end of the recommended cooking time your stew is either too thick or too thin. Both are easily corrected. If the sauce is too thick and gluey, just stir in a little water or sauce to correct the consistency. If it is too thin, you are faced with several options. The first is simply to ladle off as much of the sauce as you can into a frying pan and boil it down hard to reduce and thicken, before stirring back into the stew. Alternatively, you could sieve a few ladlefuls of sauce with some of the softened vegetables, rubbing them both through a sieve to form a purée. Stir this back into the stew to thicken. And thirdly, you can use a 'beurre manié'. This is a straightforward mixture of equal quantities of softened butter and flour, mashed together thoroughly to form a paste. Turn the heat under the stew down very low, and dot small blobs of the beurre manié on to the stew. Stir, then shake the pan gently until the beurre manié has disappeared into the sauce. Cook over a gentle heat for 3–4 minutes until the sauce has thickened sufficiently.

Reheating The vast majority of stews benefit from being made in advance, then reheated before serving. Cool the stew rapidly, once cooked, by standing the casserole in a sink of cold water. As soon as it has cooled down, cover and store in the fridge for up to 48 hours. Before reheating, lift off and discard the crust of fat that may have formed on the surface. Reheat the stew thoroughly, adding a glass or so of water if the sauce seems overly thick. Make sure that the stew bubbles for at least 4 minutes, to kill off any unwanted bacteria. Serve as normal.

Cuts for stews   **Beef:** shin, brisket, thin flank, chuck and blade, skirt. **Lamb:** practically any cut, but shoulder is good value and has an excellent flavour. **Pork:** any bit, though belly is very fatty. **Chicken:** breasts, thighs, drumsticks, chicken portions; in fact, any part.

Beef Stew with Mushrooms and Guinness

Here it is: an absolute cracker of a beef stew with a deep, dark savour that comes from the lengthy communion of beef, mushrooms and inky-black Guinness in a warm oven. Serve with mash (lots of it, see page 173) and carrots.

Serves 4

1kg (2¼lb) shin of beef, or stewing steak
seasoned flour (see page 123), for dusting
3–4 tablespoons sunflower oil
4 rashers back bacon, cut into short strips
2 onions, peeled and roughly chopped
1 bouquet garni (2 sprigs parsley, 1 bay leaf,
  2 sprigs thyme)
salt and pepper
350ml (12fl oz) Guinness, or Murphy's or any
  other stout
2 tablespoons tomato purée
½ tablespoon caster or granulated sugar
250g (9oz) button mushrooms
15g (½oz) butter

1 Trim excess fat or gristle off the meat and cut into 3–4cm (1–1½in) cubes, if this hasn't already been done. Pat dry on kitchen paper. Put the seasoned flour in a plastic bag, and add the beef. Toss it around in the bag to coat evenly in flour, then tip out on to a plate.

2 Preheat the oven to 150°C/300°F/Gas Mark 2.

3 Heat 2 tablespoons of the oil in a wide frying pan over a moderate heat. Add half the beef and brown on all sides. Take the first batch out, and place in a casserole. Repeat with the remaining beef, adding a little more oil when necessary .

4 Fry the bacon and onions gently in the pan, stirring and scraping up brown bits, until the onions are tender and translucent and the bacon is cooked. Tip them over the meat in the casserole. Tuck the bouquet garni in amongst the meat, and season with salt and pepper.

5 Return the pan to the heat and add the Guinness or stout. Bring up to the boil, scraping up the tasty brown residues stuck to the base of the frying pan. When it is boiling, stir in the tomato purée and sugar, then pour over the contents of the casserole.

6 Add enough boiling water to cover the meat. Stir, then cover with a lid and transfer the casserole dish to the oven. Leave to cook for 2–3 hours, stirring occasionally, until the meat is very tender.

7 Scrub the mushrooms clean and cut in half. Melt the butter in a frying pan

Brown the meat on
all sides.

Beef stew with mushrooms and Guinness.

Adjust seasoning and serve.

over a moderate heat. When it is foaming add the mushrooms and fry until patched with brown and tender. Stir into the casserole once the meat is tender, then return to the oven, without the lid, for a further 15 minutes. Taste and adjust seasoning, adding more salt and pepper if needed.

8 Serve right then and there, or leave to cool and store in the fridge for up to 24 hours. Reheat thoroughly on the hob, allowing the stew to bubble for a good 4–5 minutes (add a little extra water if necessary) before serving.

Daube de Bœuf

This is the south of France's version of a beef stew. It comes in many different forms, but one of the finest is made with red wine, tomatoes, rosemary and a strip of dried orange peel (just peel off a strip of orange zest with a vegetable peeler, and leave to dry on the radiator). Follow the **Beef Stew** recipe on page 126 but leave out the mushrooms and the butter they fry in. Replace 1 of the onions with a large carrot, diced small, and a stick of celery, sliced, frying them all with the remaining chopped onion after the meat has been browned. Replace the Guinness with about 250–300ml (9–10fl oz) red wine. Add 2 tomatoes, skinned, deseeded and roughly chopped, to the casserole with a bouquet garni made of 2 sprigs of rosemary, 1 of thyme, 2 of parsley and that strip of dried orange peel. Serve the stew either with mash, or better still with tagliatelle that has been tossed with butter and chopped fresh parsley.

Or, for a daube 'aux olives', stir in 85g (3oz) small black olives with stones in, about 5 minutes before the stew is ready to serve. This one should definitely be served with buttered noodles.

Beef with Carrots

Make as for the **Beef Stew** on page 126, but forget the mushrooms and the butter. Replace the Guinness with either lager or wine. Thickly slice 675g (1½lb) carrots, and add half to the casserole along with the onions and bacon. Stir the remainder in about half an hour before the stew is cooked.

Jamaican Beef Stew with Butter Beans and Coconut

Cook as for the **Beef Stew** on page 126, making the following adjustments. Forget about the bacon, but fry 1 hot chilli, deseeded and sliced, with the onions. When they are almost done, sprinkle over 1 heaped teaspoon ground allspice and cook for another minute or so. Replace the Guinness with 500ml (18fl oz) canned coconut milk, and replace the bouquet garni with 8 sprigs thyme, tied together with string. Half an hour before the stew is cooked, stir in 500g (18oz) cooked butter beans.

Rich Chicken Casserole with White Wine, Leeks and Peas

This is a really classy chicken stew, with a creamy white wine sauce. Serve it either with rice or boiled new or salad potatoes and a few carrots or a crisp green salad.

If you use frozen peas, let them thaw before adding to the casserole, 5 minutes after adding the leeks.

Serves 4

30g (1oz) butter
1 chicken, cut into 4, or 4 chicken portions
1 onion, peeled and chopped
2 garlic cloves, peeled and chopped
1 bay leaf
about 150ml (5 fl oz) white wine
600ml (1 pint) Chicken Stock (see pages 15–16)
salt and pepper
400g (14oz) leeks
200g (7oz) podded peas
100ml (3½fl oz) whipping or double cream

BEURRE MANIÉ
30g (1oz) softened butter
30g (1oz) plain flour

1 Melt the butter over a medium heat in a wide, deep frying pan, or shallow casserole dish. When it is foaming, add the chicken pieces and leave them to sizzle until golden brown underneath. Turn over and brown the other side. Take out, and reserve. Ideally, the heat should be low enough to prevent the butter burning, but high enough to colour the meat. If by any awful chance your butter has blackened (a nice hazelnut brown is fine), wipe out the pan and add a new knob of butter to cook the onions in.

2 Add the onion and garlic to the pan and cook gently until tender and translucent. Return the chicken to the pan, along with the bay leaf. Pour in the wine and let it all come up to the boil and bubble hard for about 30 seconds .

3 Next add the stock and salt and pepper. Bring up to the boil, then reduce the heat to a lazy simmer. Cover the pan, and leave to cook gently for 30 minutes, turning the chicken portions every 10 minutes, so that they cook evenly.

4 While the chicken is cooking, clean and prepare the leeks. Trim off the top part of the dark green leaves (good for stock, as long as you rinse off all the earth) and the root end. Using a sharp knife, make a cut about 5cm (2in) deep, down through the centre of the upper part of the leek, and then make a second cut, to the same depth, at right angles. Splay the leaves out under the tap, letting the running water wash away any dirt and grit. Shake off excess water. Now, slice the leek into 1cm (½in) rings.

5 Add the leeks and peas to the chicken, stirring them in as

Brown the chicken pieces.

best you can. As they cook, they will shrink down, so don't worry if the quantity seems overwhelming at first. Cover again and leave to simmer for another 10 minutes.

6 To make the beurre manié, mash the butter and flour together until evenly mixed.

7 When the leeks and peas are done, remove the lid and stir in the cream. Turn the heat under the casserole down low and start adding small lumps of the beurre manié, dotting them around the casserole. Initially, use just half of the beurre manié. Stir it in, and shake the pan gently over the heat. Let it cook for about ½–1 minute. If you feel that you would like the sauce a little thicker, add more beurre manié, in the same way, until you get a pleasing consistency. I find that I usually need about three-quarters of the amount made.

8 Finally, taste and adjust the seasoning, then serve.

Add wine and stock and allow to simmer.

Add small lumps of beurre manié.

Tagine of Lamb with Apricots and Almonds

A tagine is a Moroccan casserole, both an earthenware dish itself and the stew that is cooked inside it. They are beautiful objects with their high, conical lids, designed to gather condensing steam and let it drip back down into the food. Don't despair if you don't own a proper tagine. This warmly spiced stew of lamb with apricots and almonds can be cooked in any wide casserole, or a big sauté pan.

The grated onion and carrot help to thicken the sauce. Serve the tagine with couscous or rice.

Serves 4

1kg (2¼lb) shoulder of lamb, trimmed
2 teaspoons ground cumin
¼ teaspoon freshly ground black pepper
1 teaspoon ground cinnamon
a good pinch of saffron
2 tablespoons olive oil
1 onion, peeled and grated
1 large carrot, peeled and grated
2 garlic cloves, peeled and chopped
2 tablespoons clear honey
salt and pepper
150g (5oz) ready-to-eat dried apricots, halved
60g (2oz) flaked almonds
3 tablespoons chopped parsley

1 Trim any gristle and large gobbets of fat from the lamb. Cut into 4cm (1½in) cubes – consider this measurement a rough, amiable guide, rather than an autocratic command. Toss the cubes with the cumin, pepper and cinnamon.

2 Put the saffron into a small bowl and pour over just enough hot water to cover. Set aside.

3 Heat the oil in a wide casserole or sauté pan or saucepan over a moderate heat. Add the lamb, and turn the pieces in the hot oil. For once, you don't have to brown the meat evenly. The idea here is to develop the aromas of the spices, so keep turning the chunks of lamb for about 2 minutes.

4 Now add the grated onion, carrot and garlic and stir around to mix in evenly. Pour in enough water to just barely cover the lamb, then add the honey and salt. Bring up to the boil, lower the heat, cover and leave to simmer for 40 minutes.

5 Remove the lid and stir in the apricots. Cook, uncovered, for a further 15–20 minutes until the meat is very tender and the sauce has reduced down to a pleasing thickness. Stir in the saffron and cook for another minute or two.

6 Meanwhile, toast the almonds (see page 156 for various options).

7 When the tagine is done, spoon into a warm serving dish (unless your pan is handsome enough to place straight on the table) and scatter over the almonds and parsley. Serve immediately.

Stir-frying

We all ought to stir-fry more often. It is a method of cooking meat, vegetables and noodles that fits 100 per cent into busy modern lives. There's a fair bit of chopping to be done (perfect for releasing tension after a trying day), the cooking part itself is swift, extreme and furious (ditto), it brings out all that is best in the ingredients and, wonders will never cease, it also happens to be terrifically healthy. You could almost re-brand stir-frying as modern lifestyle convenience cooking, if it weren't for the fact that the phrase sounds so utterly tedious.

Equipment

You cannot stir-fry properly without a wok. Whatever anyone says, even the swankiest frying pan in Christendom will not do the job properly. The good news is that a fine wok costs very little. In fact, I would even go as far as to say that spending huge amounts of dosh on an expensive wok is a ridiculous waste of money.

The best place to buy a wok is a Chinese supermarket. Choose one that has two wooden handles, on opposite sides, so that the wok is balanced. A one-handled wok has a tendency to tip over at just the wrong moment. Buy a big wok. Stir-frying demands plenty of space for movement and plenty of hot surface area for evaporation; you can cook enough for one or four in a large wok, but a small wok is suitable for no more than one or two. When you are buying the wok, make sure that it comes with instructions for seasoning it (getting it ready for use), or else ask the assistants and write down their advice. Then follow it religiously when you get home. You can buy pre-seasoned woks, and this is the only 'extra' worth paying for, though it is not strictly necessary. While you are at the Chinese supermarket pick up a metal stir-frying spatula, too.

Do not believe the myth that a wok should never be washed, but never leave it to soak, either. A quick dip in warm soapy water, and a quick going over with a washing-up brush to remove stuck-on residues is all it needs. Do not scour it clean. A wok improves with use, developing a perfect, black, virtually non-stick surface all of its own. The seasoning process is what starts this off. As soon as it has been washed, dry it thoroughly. Never tuck a damp wok away in the cupboard – it will be rusty by the time you next get it out.

A final word on the subject of woks. I bought my very cheap, thin-sided wok when I was a student, almost quarter of a century ago (frightening) in Manchester's Chinatown. It is still in perfect condition, having developed a superb non-stick surface. I still use it and fully intend to carry on using it until I am old and grey.

Preparation of Ingredients

You will probably spend more time preparing the ingredients for stir-frying than actually cooking them. Each of the main elements needs to be cut into small pieces that will cook evenly and adequately in the spanking heat of the wok. Meat, poultry and seafood should all be cut into thin short strips of equal size, give or take a few millimetres, so that they are cooked through in minutes, if not seconds. Vegetables also need to be cut into small strips or squares of equal size as appropriate. Cut denser veg, such as carrots, extra thin so that they do not take an age to cook. With awkwardly shaped vegetables like broccoli or cauliflower, break the tops into very small florets (about 1 cm/½in) across at most, and slice the stems thinly. Garlic, chilli, and ginger may be finely chopped, or cut into extremely slender matchsticks.

There are many forms of noodle for stir-frying, from dried Chinese egg noodles that come in flat slabs and are available in any decent supermarket, to the delightfully slippery fresh oil noodles from the chilled shelves of Oriental supermarkets. More recent innovations have been the new 'ready-to-stir-fry' noodles in ambient packaging, which save no more than a few minutes, so are hardly worth the extra pennies, and the wider availability of silky, slithery rice noodles in dried form. I love these, and usually they are rehydrated in a matter of 3 or 4 minutes in a pan of boiling water. Whichever you choose, rehydrate them according to the instructions on the packet.

Mini-Compendium of Oriental Condiments and Sauces

Soy sauce   There should be a bottle in every kitchen cupboard, as soy sauce is fantastic for adding a salty depth of flavour and colour to all kinds of marinades and sauces. I often add a tablespoon or two to beef stews, or to salad dressings. It is made from naturally fermented soya beans, aged for up to two years. Chinese light soy sauce has, as you might expect, a lighter, more subtle flavour that of the thicker, butch-er dark soy sauce.

Japanese soy sauce (shoyu) is a touch sweeter and less salty than Chinese dark soy sauce, so you may need a little more to achieve the same degree of seasoning.

Indonesian sweet soy sauce (ketjap manis) is made of soy sauce sweetened with palm sugar and seasoned with garlic and other spices. It is a fantastic creation, excellent in marinades and dressings, but should not be substituted for standard soy sauce in recipes because of its sweetness.

Fish sauce This is the South East Asian equivalent of soy sauce, made from fermented small fish, so is not suitable for vegetarians. It is used to salt most savoury dishes from this area. It smells atrocious, but luckily tastes quite different! It does not have an obviously fishy taste, so doesn't clash with chicken or meat. If you are making a Thai dish, but have no fish sauce, substitute light soy sauce – not quite the same, but a tolerable approximation. Thai fish sauce (nam pla) and Vietnamese fish sauce (nuoc mam) differ marginally in taste, but can be used interchangeably.

Sesame oil This is an amber oil with a divinely nutty, toasty scent and flavour. The oil is extracted from roasted sesame seeds. It is used as a condiment, sprinkled over food that has just been cooked. It is almost never used as a cooking oil, as it loses much of its aroma when heated and burns far more easily than straightforward vegetable or sunflower oil. It is delicious used in Western-style salad dressings, softened with double its volume of bland sunflower or grapeseed oil. Always buy in small quantities, as it turns rancid fairly quickly (within about three months), especially if left out in the light.

Black bean sauce This is made from fermented soya beans, crushed and mixed with other aromatics to make a salty, almost winey sauce, that can be tossed into stir-fried foods at the last minute. The jar will keep for months in the fridge.

Oyster sauce The genuine article is made from oysters, water, salt, caramel (for colouring) and thickened with cornflour. As a rough guide, the more expensive the sauce is the more oysters it actually contains, therefore the better the flavour. You don't have to be partial to oysters to appreciate the taste of oyster sauce, however, as the two taste very different. Like black bean sauce, it is added to the stir-fried food at the last minute, to impart its unique flavour. Delicious and quite unlike anything else.

Chilli sauces and pastes There are literally hundreds of these to choose from, so it has to be largely a matter of trial and error, until you find one that you like. Chilli sauces are brewed up from terrifyingly hot chillies, aided and abetted by a large range of spices and herbs. Many are softened by the inclusion of sugar, which is good for some dishes, but inappropriate in others. It makes sense to use an Oriental chilli sauce for oriental dishes, but something like old-fashioned, long-lived Tabasco is a great all-rounder.

Rice wines These are many and various, but the principal ones used in Oriental cooking are Chinese shaoxing wine, and Japanese mirin.

Shaoxing wine is amber-coloured and dry with a taste that is reminiscent of dry sherry (it is also as potent, with an alcohol content of 18 per cent), which can be substituted for it. At a pinch you could use dry white wine, but that's straying further away from the original.

Mirin is a sweetened rice wine used in many Japanese dishes, especially in a teriyaki sauce. You can replace it with a mixture of dry sherry and sugar.

How to Stir-fry

Stir-frying is an exceptionally quick way of cooking meat, vegetables and noodles and demands undivided attention once you get going. So you absolutely must make sure that you have every ingredient prepared and ready to go into the wok. Measure out sauces and oils, but keep the bottles nearby as well, in case you need to add more in a hurry. If you are really efficient, you will read your recipe carefully and have the items that go into the wok at the same time already mixed on one plate, or in a small bowl, as appropriate. Arrange everything right beside the hob so that you can grab it easily. That includes serving bowls and/or plates.

Because stir-frying is inevitably a last-minute process, I wouldn't advise attempting more than two stir-fried dishes for one meal, and one of those should be hyper-quick. Stir-fried food does not improve with hanging around in a warm oven, so cook the slowest one first, and the quickest one second. Have rice and any other elements of the meal already cooked and ready to serve.

Stir-frying is more successful on a gas hob than on an electric one as you can achieve a higher heat. If you do cook with electricity, make sure the ring is thoroughly preheated before sitting the wok on it. With gas, turn the largest ring to maximum heat and just sit the wok straight on it. Whichever you cook on, the heat should be left at its highest setting throughout the cooking time, unless the recipe clearly states otherwise. Stir-frying demands a bit of nerve, but reassure yourself that the heat in your kitchen is pathetic compared to that used in a Chinese restaurant kitchen.

Let the empty wok heat up until it smokes; this usually takes no more than a minute or so. Now start stir-frying. In other words, add the oil, swirl it around briefly to heat through and then begin adding the ingredients in the order given in the recipe. The idea of stir-frying is to keep the contents of the pan in constant motion, so from the minute the first solids (probably garlic and ginger) go in, start wielding your spatula – either a metal or a wooden one. Slide the spatula down the side of the wok, right under the ingredients, then lift them swiftly up and over, keeping everything on the move, tossing and turning all the time. This is stir-frying.

Keep on stir-frying, adding more ingredients as the recipe demands, until everything is cooked perfectly. With meat this means just nicely cooked through whilst with noodles, that are already cooked, it just means heated right through. But with vegetables it means cooked to a crisp-tender state, patched here and there with brown. No other cooking method achieves this gorgeous amalgam of juiciness and tenderness with a hint of crunch. Savour it.

Incidentally, when stir-frying noodles I find it easiest and most effective to lift and turn them with a pair of forks, one in each hand.

Flavourings such as soy sauce or rice wine are usually added at the end of the cooking time.

Use two forks when stir-frying noodles.

Stir-fried Ginger Pork with Mangetouts and Cashew Nuts

Just 10 minutes to prepare and at most 8 minutes to cook – not bad for a supper dish as good as this. Just remember to get the rice going before you start to stir-fry. Chicken (one large or two small breasts), beef (one sirloin steak) or lamb (two chump chops) can be substituted for the pork if you prefer.

Serves 2

2 boneless pork steaks
2 tablespoons sunflower oil
1cm (½in) piece fresh root ginger, peeled and grated
1 garlic clove, peeled and finely chopped
½ red chilli, deseeded and cut into thin strips (optional)
110g (4oz) mangetout peas
60g (2oz) unsalted cashew nuts
2 tablespoons dark soy sauce
1 tablespoon dry white wine, rice wine or dry sherry
1 teaspoon caster sugar
freshly ground black pepper
1 teaspoon sesame oil

1 Cut the pork steaks into thin strips. Measure and prepare all the remaining ingredients and arrange them close to the hob.

2 Set the wok over a high heat, and heat up until smoking. Add half the sunflower oil and swirl around once or twice to heat through.

3 Add the ginger, garlic and chilli, and stir-fry for 10–20 seconds until beginning to colour. Quickly add the pork pieces and continue to stir-fry for 2–3 minutes until just cooked through. Transfer to a plate.

4 Return the wok to the heat and add the remaining sunflower oil. Swirl again to heat through, then add the mangetouts. Stir-fry for 2–3 minutes until crisp-tender and beginning to catch the odd patch of brown. Next add the cashew nuts and stir-fry for another 30 seconds.

5 Now return the pork to the pan, and add all the remaining ingredients except the sesame oil. Stir-fry for a final minute. Add the sesame oil and toss to mix. Serve immediately.

Stir-frying the strips of pork.

Thai Stir-Fried Noodles (Pad Thai)

This is a simplified version of pad thai, the standard Thai fried noodles served on every other street corner throughout the land. Thais eat this for breakfast, lunch and supper as the mood takes them. I'm with them on this one – it has to be one of the best of all noodle dishes with its blend of flavours and textures.

Dried rice noodles (sen lek) are used in Thailand and, joy of joys, they are now pretty easy to get here, from most good supermarkets. Standard Chinese egg noodles can be used instead, but they lack the silky smoothness of rice noodles.

Serves 2–3

250g (9oz) dried medium rice noodles
4 tablespoons sunflower or vegetable oil
3 garlic cloves, peeled and finely chopped
4 spring onions, sliced
1 egg, lightly beaten
½ teaspoon chilli flakes, or 1 small fresh chilli, deseeded and chopped
3–4 tablespoons fish sauce
1½ tablespoons caster sugar
juice of ½ lemon
110g (4oz) small peeled cooked prawns
85g (3oz) beansprouts
4 tablespoons roasted unsalted peanuts, finely chopped (see opposite)
a small handful of roughly chopped coriander

1 Prepare the noodles according to packet instructions, and drain thoroughly.

2 Heat the wok over a high heat until it begins to smoke. Add the oil, swirl briefly, then add the garlic and half the spring onions. Stir-fry for a few seconds until the garlic begins to brown. Break in the egg and cook for a few seconds, stirring, until it begins to set.

3 Tip in the noodles and stir well, scraping down the sides and underneath so that they mix evenly with the egg.

4 Now add the remaining ingredients in the order they are given (except coriander), stir-frying the noodles briefly between each addition – it's easier to turn and toss them with a pair of forks, than with the spatula. When you get to the peanuts, add just half of them to the pan. Toss and stir-fry everything together for another 30 seconds or so.

5 Divide the noodles between two or three bowls or plates and top each portion with some of the remaining peanuts and spring onions and the coriander.

When the garlic begins to brown, add the egg. When the egg begins to set, add the noodles. Toss with a pair of forks.

need to know

ROASTING PEANUTS You can buy ready-roasted but unsalted peanuts fairly easily, and these are useful for dishes like pad thai. However, peanuts that you have roasted yourself will taste so much better. Either way, make sure that you don't buy pre-salted peanuts or, even worse, peanuts that have been doused in some weird coating.

Roasting peanuts is much the same as roasting any other nuts. If they still have their papery skins on them, roast them as for hazelnuts (see page 70), but if they are pale and naked then obviously you don't have to do all that shaking about in a tea-towel. Let them cool before chopping. If you have a processor, this can be done in seconds, as long as you don't keep going for so long that they turn into peanut butter. Otherwise, it's just a question of attacking them with a knife.

chapter five

Fish

Fish is so quick and easy to cook that it has every right to be considered a convenience food. And a convenience food with a wide range of fabulous tastes and textures, from the small, firm flakes of Dover sole to the big meaty solidity of fresh tuna. Quite why so many people are scared of dealing with fish is something I just don't get. Clearly, the small matter of freshness is an issue. This is not a convenience food that you can stash in the back of the cupboard for some rainy day – perish the thought. So, you have to learn to recognise freshness and buy and eat your fish within a day or so? Hardly a major inconvenience. Think of it instead as a matter of indulging your appetite swiftly. Here it is, take it now, relish every mouthful within a couple of hours…Aaah, the sweet words of temptation. Give in and you can even feel virtuous into the bargain.

Where to Buy Fish

There are three ways to get fish. The first is all neatly packaged, ready prepared, in clear plastic boxes, completely odour-free from the supermarket shelves. The second is from the fish counter of a major supermarket. The third is from a proper independent fishmonger. Actually, there is a fourth, which is to go fishing yourself or get it direct from the fishing boats, but that's a rare option for the lucky and determined few. Let's stick with the first three.

The packaged option is easy, by and large safe, and requires not a shred of expertise on your part. Sounds peachy? Not altogether. Firstly, your choice is remarkably limited and secondly the packaging may well get in the way of checking the real freshness of the fish. You know it won't be inedible, but it may not be in the first flush of delicious youth. Thirdly, you can't ask a piece of plastic for advice, recommendations, or indeed whether bright yellow smoked haddock will be a reasonable replacement for monkfish in the recipe you fancy cooking.

The supermarket fish counter can be every bit as good as an independent fishmonger, though not necessarily. The choice, again, tends to be limited, though not as limited as for packeted fish. You should be able to get advice if the men and women behind the counter are properly trained. They should also be able to prepare the fish exactly as you require for your recipe (scaling, skinning, filleting, beheading and so on). The biggest rub, however, is that centralised methods of buying give the supermarket fish seller little or no control over what he or she puts on the marble slab. As a result, freshness can suffer. If you want to get the best out of supermarket fish, you need to know how to pick out really fresh fish, and not be afraid to ask for it.

In theory, the independent fishmonger should be the best place to buy fish. They are, sadly, an increasingly rare commodity, so if there is one near you, cherish it by shopping there as often as you can. This is the place to go to for the widest choice, for the freshest fish, for the best advice, for the best ideas, and the best service. Or at least it should be, and in most cases is. Never be intimidated – the staff are there to sell you fish, and they are armed with knowledge and skills to help you pick the best for you. Get them to do the work of preparation, too. Think of them as your own personal advisors, and milk them for all you're worth.

Is It Fresh?   Freshness is paramount when it comes to fish. The fresher it is, the better it tastes. Stale fish at best tastes dull and boring. It may be edible in the sense that it won't do you any harm, but it won't give you any pleasure either. And those important nutrients will be diminished, too. Altogether a lose-lose situation.

Picking out properly fresh fish is not hard. The first thing you do is use your nose. Beautifully fresh fish smells of very little except perhaps a whisper of pure ozone. A fishy smell is a clear indication that the fish is past its prime.

The next indicator is the eyes. On a fresh fish the eyes are bright and glassy and raised. As time progresses a milky haze spreads into them, and they sink down into the head. The third indicator is the colour of the gills, which should be a bright, clean pinkish colour, not a dull muddy brown. You can only check this by probing the fish itself, so it may not be too helpful in the middle of the supermarket.

When there is no head to be seen, you will have to judge by the state of the flesh. If it looks firm and pearly fresh then it probably is. Don't buy fillets or steaks which look soft and cotton-wooly, with gaps appearing in the surface – sure signs of staleness.

Storing Fish Get that fish home and into the fridge as soon as you humanly can. Never, ever leave it stewing in the boot of a hot car, or under your desk at work. Once you have got it into the fridge, cook and eat it as soon as possible. Certainly within the next 36 hours, and preferably a good deal sooner. Take it out of the fridge some 15–20 minutes before cooking so that it has time to come back to room temperature.

Cooking Methods

When Is It Done? Over-cooking is to be avoided at all costs with fish. In fact it is far better to marginally undercook it – it will still be perfectly safe to eat, and will taste fine! Always bear in mind that fish will carry on cooking in its own heat after coming out of the pan or oven – another reason to err on the side of undercooking. But how do you tell? No tricks here. With fish on the bone, discreetly poke with a knife – when done the flesh will pull away from the bone with ease. Flat-fish fillets cook in such a brief amount of time that it is virtually impossible to undercook them, but the best check is to press gently – they should feel firm. With thicker steaks and fillets, operate much the same system. Firmness is your best indicator.

Two exceptions to the rule spring to mind: tuna and salmon. Tuna is best treated like an expensive steak, in other words cooked rare in the centre so that it retains maximum flavour and moisture. A firmly cooked tuna steak is an overdone one, and will be dry and stringy. Salmon is an oddball: good cooked right through, which is how we usually get it, but even more succulent and delicious left a tad rare in the very centre. If you don't believe me, try it and see.

Frying One of the best ways of cooking thinner fillets of fish, smaller whole flat fish (such as plaice of lemon sole), and good too for small round fish, such as trout. Begin by putting just enough fat in the frying pan to cover the base, but no more (unless the recipe tells you to use more). Then get it hot, hot, hot. Pat the fish dry with kitchen paper, then lay it in the pan. Hear that noisy sizzle? That's a sign that you're getting it right. A pathetic little sputter or no sound at all? Sorry, the fat is nowhere near hot enough. Once the fish is in and sizzling, LEAVE IT ALONE. Don't start pushing it around or lifting it to check how it's doing. You must let it be for at least 1 minute in the case of very thin fillets (e.g. plaice), or 2–3 minutes for thicker pieces. During this time the fish will brown underneath and, most importantly, detach itself from the pan. Once this has happened, turn it quickly and fry the other side. If you follow these basics, your fish won't stick and collapse in the pan.

Speed is the order of the day here. A thin fillet of fish will need no more than a minute on each side. Allow up to 2 minutes per side for a fillet that is around 1cm thick. Thicker steaks or fillet may need as much as 3 or 4 entire minutes on each side, but rarely more than that.

A whole plaice or lemon sole or, king of all, Dover sole on the bone (and by golly, it tastes all the better for that) should be done after 2 minutes on each side, when cooked to the point that the flesh parts easily from the bone.

Round fish, such as trout, or red mullet take a little longer. Start them off on a high heat, as above, but once both sides have been lightly browned, turn the heat down, and cook for a few more minutes on each side, until the flesh comes away readily from the bone.

Searing and Griddling The difference between these two methods is no more than ridges. Searing is done on a flat heavy-based pan, while griddling is done in a ridged, heavy-based pan. The latter gives you neat brown stripes on your fish, which imitates the look of the outdoor barbecue. It also echoes the smoky scent. Both methods are brilliant for cooking steaks or fatter fillets of larger fish (e.g. salmon). Neither are suitable for thin fillets, or whole round fish.

In both cases the pan needs to be heated to the max (4–5 minutes over a belting heat) before cooking commences. In both cases the absolute minimum of oil is used (very healthy), and in both cases a good deal of smoke is to be expected. Extractor fan to the ready, if you have one. Brush the piece of fish with oil and lay it down on to the metal. Do not attempt to move it now for 2–3 minutes, until it has cooked enough underneath to release itself from the pan. Brush the upper face again with oil, then turn over and sear/griddle the other side. By now the fish should be adequately cooked.

Searing and griddling, incidentally, are particularly suited to tuna and salmon steaks as well as monkfish.

Poaching Poaching is the diametric opposite of searing or griddling. It is as quiet and unassuming and gentle as searing is loud and dramatic and sexy. It can work miracles, and it is a useful way to cook fish to be used for some other dish, as it keeps it moist. Poaching means laying your fish flat in a shallow heatproof dish, adding aromatics such as bay leaves or peppercorns, covering with a liquid, and bringing it oh-so-delicately up to a temperature that lies fractionally lower than simmering. The surface of the water should do no more than tremble and shudder.

Once the bubbles start to stream up to the surface of the water, you know that the heat is over the top. Turn it right down, or draw the pan off the heat.

Many recipes suggest that you turn the heat off as soon as the water reaches poaching point, then cover the pan and set aside for 5–10 minutes or until it cools. Usually this is enough to finish cooking the fish absolutely perfectly. Otherwise the cooking time should be a matter of a few minutes.

Poaching liquids may be as simple as milk (which is later used to make a sauce) or water, with a few herbs and/or other aromatics floating around in it, or a more complicated court-bouillon – a pre-prepared stock of wine, water and aromatics that has already been simmered to draw the maximum flavour out of the additions.

Steaming

Like poaching this is a gentle, damp method of cooking that is admirably suited to fish. Steaming preserves all the innate flavour. Fish is often steamed on a bed of herbs or other ingredients to supplement its flavour. It is possible to steam food without any special equipment (when necessity demanded, I've used a wire sieve balanced over a saucepan and covered with a dome of silver foil), but a proper steamer makes it a far easier operation. They are not too expensive to buy and are also excellent for cooking vegetables.

So, armed with a steamer, the rest is easy. Put water in the base and bring up to a gentle simmer, then turn the heat right down. Prepare your fish and lay it out either on a plate that will sit in the steamer basket, with a gap all around it so that the steam can circulate, or make a little 'basket' for it out of silver foil – or of course you could just lay it straight on the base of the basket, but you lose any juices that the fish exudes. Once you've got your fish nicely settled in the steamer basket, place the basket over the steaming water, and then lay a folded clean tea-towel over the top and clamp on the lid. Make sure that the ends of the tea-towel do not trail down and catch light! The purpose of the tea-towel is to absorb the steam that would otherwise collect on the inside of the lid, then drip down on to the fish, bathing it in pool of water, which is not the point at all. Remember that fish cooks fairly quickly in a steamer, so check frequently, but be very careful not to scald yourself in the steam.

Grilling and Barbecuing

This is the most superb way of cooking fish, utterly fabulous with its toasty browned outside contrasting with the moist tender flesh. And it's strikingly healthy, too. You can't grill or barbecue just any bit of fish, however. Smaller whole fish, such as sardines, trout, mackerel, plaice and soles of either sort were made for barbecuing and grilling. Steaks or thick fillets of bigger fish such as salmon, tuna, monkfish, halibut and the like are also ideal. Thin fillets are useless – they'll turn out as dry as a bone and, worse still, fall apart as soon as you try to move them. One of the few exceptions are mackerel fillets, which can be grilled, as long as the grill pan is lined with foil (but more on that in the recipe on page 152). Fish kebabs are an appealing prospect, but the only fish that can take this treatment are monkfish and tuna. Other fish tend to collapse unless they are wrapped in, say, a strip of bacon or pancetta (actually a surprisingly delicious solution).

With either grilling or barbecuing, you need to make sure first of all that the interior of the fish is protected from the searing power of the heat. In practice this means at the least brushing the surfaces lightly with oil, which helps to seal in moisture. Better still, marinate the fish beforehand in a marinade that contains some oil. Middle-sized round fish (e.g. mackerel or trout) should also be slashed two or three times across the body with a sharp knife on both sides, so that they cook evenly.

Next, make sure that the grill is thoroughly preheated or that the charcoal has reached that all-important white-hot stage before you start to cook. Since fish cooks very quickly, it needs to be close to the heat in order to brown on the outside before it is cooked through. It is a good idea with fish in particular to oil the bars of the grill rack before you start to cook, to minimise the chances of the fish sticking.

Baking and Roasting   Defining the difference between baking and roasting is tricky if not impossible, but with fish I tend to think of roasting as cooking at a high temperature in the oven, with the fish uncovered and exposed directly to the heat. Baked fish are often (but not always) covered and cooked at a lower temperature for a longer time, relatively speaking. Working with these definitions, I would say that roasting produces the most interesting results. Fish cooks quickly, which makes it ideal for high-temperature oven cooking as it rarely has time to dry out before it is cooked (with the exception of thinner fillets, which are generally happier being baked).

So, to roast a fine piece of fish, a cod steak perhaps, or a piece of halibut, lay it in a greased ovenproof dish, brush it with a touch of oil or melted butter, add seasoning, a little slug of wine, maybe, or balsamic vinegar, or just lemon juice. Next place it in a very hot oven (230°C/450°F/Gas Mark 8), and lo and behold, it will be beautifully cooked in around 10–15 minutes.

For a larger chunk of fish, e.g. a whole monkfish tail or a sizeable sea bass, prepare the fish in the same way, but roast at 200°C/400°F/Gas Mark 6 for a few minutes longer – we're talking 20–30 minutes, depending on the size of the fish. Placing a bed of herbs under the fish is a nice touch, or else slice up fennel and onions, blanch in boiling water for 3–4 minutes, then drain well and lay that in the dish, with the fish on top.

Baking instructions usually come as part and parcel of a recipe. You might, for instance, be cooking papillotes of fish in the oven (in other words, fish in a greaseproof paper or silver foil pouch), or making a dish of boned and rolled herring soused in white wine vinegar, oil and water. In these instances baking works well, but it is not generally a method that brings out the best in fish. So, no general advice on baking fish except to forget about it, unless a particular recipe you've been longing to try instructs you to have a go!

Stewing Fish stews are made quite differently from meat stews. This is because fish cooks so very quickly. So the trick here is to make the sauce first (and you can do this a day in advance), then to add the fish to the hot sauce just a few minutes before serving so that it is perfectly cooked. Over-cooked fish in a stew is a mess – it collapses to a mush that is edible but not too appealing. For this reason, and for reasons of food safety, it is not a good idea to reheat leftover fish stew.

Fish stews can be cheap and cheerful (with a sauce made from tinned tomatoes and simple aromatics, and fleshed out with cheaper fish such as coley) or exquisitely grand (tomato again, but perhaps with a shot of Pernod cooked into it, and a mixture of monkfish, squid, prawns, clams and mussels). It's no good deciding that you absolutely must have certain specific fish or shellfish for your stew as you just don't know what will be available and looking perkily fresh at the fishmonger's or supermarket. Remember roughly how much you need, then choose the best of what is on offer.

Grilled Mackerel Fillets with Lemon Chilli Relish

Fish are usually served with a wedge of lemon to squeeze over them, but this unusual sweet sharp relish makes the lemon wedge redundant. It goes particularly well with oily fish like mackerel, but if you fancy serving it with grilled salmon or seared tuna, or even with a nice piece of chicken, go right ahead.

For this recipe, I've chosen to cook mackerel fillets (ask the fishmonger to fillet them for you) because they are so quick, but if you prefer to use whole fish, slash on both sides, brush with oil and grill for around 5 minutes per side.

Serves 4

4 mackerel, filleted
a little olive or sunflower oil
salt and pepper

RELISH
2 lemons
4 tablespoons caster sugar
1 teaspoon coriander seeds, coarsely
    crushed
½ tablespoon black mustard seeds
1 red chilli, deseeded and thinly sliced
2 plum tomatoes, deseeded (see page 8) and
    finely diced

1 First make the relish. Slice the lemons very thinly with a sharp knife, discarding the ends. Save all the juice that is squeezed out as you cut (or at least as much as you can).

2 Lay the lemon slices in a shallow dish in a single layer and pour over enough boiling water to just cover. Let it stand for 3 minutes, then drain. Repeat with a new lot of boiling water, leave to stand for another 3 minutes, then drain again. Cut the lemon slices into quarters.

3 Put the sugar into a saucepan with 6 tablespoons water. Stir over a medium heat until the sugar has dissolved. Add the lemon quarters, the saved lemon juice, the spices and the chilli. Simmer for about 20 minutes, stirring occasionally, until the liquid is very syrupy and the lemon rind is translucent and tender.

4 Take off the heat and stir in the tomato. Leave to cool.

5 Preheat the grill thoroughly. Cover the grill rack with a sheet of silver foil (so that the mackerel won't stick to the bars). Brush the foil with a little oil. Season the cut sides of the fillets with salt and pepper. Lay them, cut-sides down, skin upwards on the foil, and brush the skins lightly with oil. Grill close until the skin has browned nicely. Turn over. The heat of the grill will probably have been enough to cook the fillets right through already, but if they look a touch raw, grill for another minute or two, cut-sides up.

6 As soon as the fillets are cooked, serve with the relish.

Grilled mackerel fillets with lemon chilli relish.

Grilled or Barbecued Sardines Portuguese Style

There are few nicer ways than this to eat sardines. It's how the fishermen along the Atlantic coast of Portugal enjoy them, cooked over an outdoor barbecue, and eaten with their fingers with enormous relish.

When buying sardines, ask if you can touch them before you hand over your money. If they feel soft and cotton-wooly, they are not fresh enough to taste at their best. You want firm-fleshed, silver fish with bright eyes. Don't forget to ask the fishmonger to scale and clean them for you. Neither is difficult to do at home, but they are phenomenally messy. Better that he or she has fish scales all over the shop, than you having them all over the kitchen.

Per person

3–4 fresh, firm sardines, cleaned and
    scaled, heads on
a little olive oil
2 lemon slices, halved
4 small sprigs rosemary, fennel or dill
coarse salt and pepper

TO SERVE
3–4 slices sturdy bread (e.g. pain de
    campagne or ciabatta)
lemon wedges

1 Preheat the grill or barbecue thoroughly. Oil the wire grill rack, or barbecue rack. If you are barbecuing, a double-sided, hinged wire grill makes turning the fish much easier, but remember to grease the insides first.

2 Tuck a half slice of lemon and a herb sprig inside each fish. Brush the outsides lightly with oil. Arrange the sardines on the grill rack and season with salt and pepper.

3 Slide under the grill (or place over the charcoal). Make sure that the sardines are fairly close to the heat. Grill until browned and cooked through on the first side. Turn, season the other side and return to the heat. Cook until done.

4 Pile the steaming hot sardines up on a plate with the bread and lemon wedges piled up beside them. Place a large empty dish on the table too, to take the bones.

5 Now the particularly Portuguese part: each diner takes a slice of bread in one hand, and lays a sardine on the bread. Add a squeeze of lemon juice and then it's time to eat. No cutlery allowed. Just pick the tender, succulent flesh off with your fingers and pop it into your mouth. Pull away the backbone and bits as you get to them and throw on to the discard plate. Eat the rest of the sardine and then you have what is almost the nicest part of all, the delicious bread that has soaked up the juice of the sardine as you were eating. Once that's gone, it's time to start on the next sardine!

Grilled Tuna Steaks with Warm Anchovy, Caper and Sun-dried Tomato Dressing

Spooning a speedily constructed dressing over the steaks as they emerge from the grill gives them an instant lift without detracting from their enticing flavour. Keep the rest of the meal simple – all this needs is a straightforward crisp green salad, or the sweetness of halved cherry tomatoes, and a few new potatoes. Cod or halibut could be cooked in the same way.

Serves 2

2 tuna steaks, cut between 2cm (¾in) and
   2.5cm (1in) thick
a little olive oil
salt and pepper

FOR THE DRESSING

1 heaped tablespoon roughly chopped parsley
2 anchovy fillets, chopped
1 garlic clove, peeled and finely chopped
1 tablespoon capers, rinsed if salted
2 pieces sun-dried tomato, cut into thin strips
1 tablespoon lemon juice
3 tablespoons extra virgin olive oil

1 Preheat the grill thoroughly. Brush the tuna steaks with olive oil and season lightly with salt and pepper

2 Grill the tuna steaks fairly close to the heat for about 3 minutes on each side, until browned, but still slightly pink at the centre.

3 Meanwhile mix all the dressing ingredients in a small saucepan, and warm through gently.

4 Transfer the cooked steaks to individual plates and spoon over the dressing. Serve immediately.

Tartare Sauce

Tartare sauce is mayonnaise spiked with herbs, perky capers and cornichons or gherkins. It goes with most fish, cooked most ways (except perhaps mackerel or herring, which are just too oily for it). It will keep in the fridge, covered, for up to four days.

For four, mix together the following: 200ml (7fl oz) mayonnaise, 20g (⅔oz) very finely chopped shallot or red onion, 1 tablespoon each of finely chopped chives and parsley, ½ tablespoon finely chopped chervil (if you can get it), 1 teaspoon finely chopped tarragon, 1½ tablespoons capers, rinsed and roughly chopped, 1 tablespoon chopped pickled cornichons or gherkins. Taste and adjust seasoning. Cover and store in the fridge until needed.

Plaice with Lemon and Parsley Crust

Very fresh plaice are beautiful creatures, dotted with spots of vivid orange. I love them grilled, but since the flesh is fairly soft, this dish with its crisp crust gives you a brace of contrasting textures that is utterly irresistible.

Serves 2

2 whole plaice, cleaned
60g (2oz) fine, dry breadcrumbs
finely grated zest of 1 lemon
2 tablespoons finely chopped parsley
1 garlic clove, peeled and very finely chopped
1 egg, beaten
a little plain flour
salt and pepper
3 tablespoons olive or sunflower oil
lemon wedges, to serve

1 Trim the fins and tail off the plaice with a pair of sharp scissors.

2 Mix the breadcrumbs with the lemon zest, parsley and garlic in a shallow plate. Place near the stove. Put the egg in a second shallow plate near the stove and the flour in a third. Season the flour with salt and pepper.

3 Heat half the oil in a frying pan large enough to hold one of the plaice. Whilst it is heating up, coat the first plaice in flour, shaking off the excess, then dip into the egg mixture, making sure that it is coated on each side. Transfer to the crumb mixture and pat it on to the fish on both sides.

4 When the oil is hot, lay the fish in the pan and cook over a medium heat for 2–3 minutes on each side until the crust is golden brown, and the fish just cooked through.

5 Keep the first fish warm for a few minutes, while you repeat the whole exercise with fish number two. Serve with the lemon wedges.

need to know

TO COOK ALMONDS Toasting, roasting or frying flaked almonds produces dramatic results, transforming their normal mild, sweet taste into a bigger, feistier number altogether. There are several methods you can use to achieve this modicum of kitchen alchemy. With all three methods, remember that the almonds change from a perfect rich brown, to burnt in a horribly short space of time. So be vigilant as they take on some colour.

1 Preheat the oven to 190°C/375°F/Gas Mark 5. Spread the almonds out on a baking tray and roast for 4–8 minutes, checking frequently and shaking the tray gently so that the almonds brown fairly evenly.

2 Preheat the grill. Spread the almonds out on a baking tray and grill, turning them frequently, until browned. This method often produces some burnt edges, alongside a few paler almonds, but that's quite appealing in its own way.

3 Heat a heavy-based wide frying pan over a medium heat. Add the almonds and shake and turn continuously until browned.

Lemon Sole Meunière

This recipe is deceptively simple. Although there is no great mystery to the cooking method, the results are tremendously good. Some people like to add a few flaked almonds to the butter at the end, frying until golden as the butter darkens, but it is not strictly necessary. The two key things to remember is that the fish should be as fresh as possible, and the first batch of butter must be clarified (i.e. have all impurities removed – easier than it sounds) before frying the fish, otherwise it is likely to burn.

Serves 2

100g (3½oz) unsalted butter
2 lemon soles, filleted
a little plain flour
salat and pepper
15g (½oz) flaked almonds (optional)

TO SERVE
fresh parsley sprigs
lemon wedges

1 First clarify half the butter. Put it into a small pan and melt over a low heat. Now raise the heat a little, and warm up gently until a white scum forms on the surface. Skim off the scum, and then carefully pour the golden, pure melted butter into a small bowl, leaving behind all the white sediment that has settled at the bottom.

2 Spread out the flour on a shallow plate and season with salt and pepper.

3 Heat half of the clarified butter in a frying pan large enough to take half the lemon sole fillets. When it is foaming, quickly coat half the fillets in flour, shake off excess, then lay in the butter. Fry for about 1 minute on each side until golden brown. Lift out and place in a heated serving dish. Keep warm.

4 Tip the used butter out of the pan and wipe the pan clean with a piece of kitchen paper. Heat the remaining clarified butter in the pan, and flour and cook the remaining fillets in the same way.

5 Once again, tip out the used butter and wipe the pan clean. Return to a moderate heat, and add the unclarified butter. Once it has melted, stir in the flaked almonds if using. Cook until the butter darkens to a light hazelnut brown. Immediately spoon over your sole fillets, tuck the parsley and lemon wedges around, and serve straightaway.

Tuna Fishcakes

Everyone loves fishcakes. Even people who don't like fish, oddly enough. Maybe it is the reassuring presence of the potato that makes them so acceptable. Whatever, they remain a stalwart of restaurant fare, but are no hassle to make at home.

These particular fishcakes are made with tinned tuna, but practically any cooked fish can be used instead. For salmon fishcakes, buy 225g (8oz) of salmon fillet, then wrap in lightly oiled foil, and pop into the oven with the potatoes for the last 10 minutes of their cooking time. Or, cook cod in the same way for cod fishcakes. Smoked haddock or smoked cod are also superb – either bake in the oven, or poach in a little milk with a few bay leaves, a slice of onion and 4 or 5 peppercorns.

Serves 4

around 325g (11oz) large potatoes
1 x 200g can tuna steaks
30g (1oz) butter, melted
2 tablespoons finely chopped fresh parsley
3 spring onions, finely chopped
1 tablespoon lemon juice
finely grated zest of 1 lemon
salt and pepper
1 egg, beaten
plain flour

TO COOK AND SERVE

15g (½oz) butter
1 tablespoon sunflower oil
4 lemon wedges (optional)
Tartare Sauce (see page 155), Salsa Cruda
(see page 69) or Salsa Verde (see page 104)

1 Preheat the oven to 200°C/400°F/Gas Mark 6. Bake the potatoes in their skins in the oven until soft – about 1 hour. If you don't have time for this, prick the skins all over with a fork and cook in the microwave on full power until tender.

2 Halve the potatoes while still warm, scoop the flesh out of the skins, and place in a bowl. Drain the tuna and add that to the bowl too, along with the melted butter, parsley, spring onions, lemon juice, lemon zest and some salt and pepper. Add about half the beaten egg. Mix the whole lot together with your hands, squidging up the chunks of potato and tuna, but leaving the mixture slightly rough and uneven.

3 Divide the mixture into quarters. Dust your hands with

Shape into a round flat 'cake'.

Tuna fishcake with
salsa verde.

Coat with flour.

flour, then shape each quarter of the mixture into a round, flat 'cake', about 1.5–2 cm (½–¾ in) thick. Coat each one in flour, then cover loosely and leave in the fridge until almost ready to eat.

4 About 15 minutes before you wish to sit down and eat, put the butter and oil for frying into a frying pan over a moderate heat. As soon as it begins to foam, lay the fish cakes in the pan. Leave until browned underneath, then turn and brown the other side. Serve extremely hot with lemon wedges (if using) and the sauce or salsa that has taken your fancy.

Roast Salmon with Lime

This is an extremely simple way of cooking salmon, but it produces fish that tastes marvellous. The key is partly the lime, of course, but also that the salmon remains a tad translucent and dark pink at the heart. This is what the uninitiated might think of as under-cooked, but you will know better. Take a bite and see just how good it is.

Serves 2

½ tablespoon extra virgin olive oil
2 x 150g salmon fillet slices
juice of ½ large lime, or 1 small lime
1 red chilli, deseeded and finely chopped
   (optional)
salt and pepper
2 lime wedges, to serve

1 Preheat the oven to 230°C/450°F/Gas Mark 8. Use a little of the oil to grease a baking dish just big enough to take the two fillets.

2 Place the fillets, skin-side down, in the dish. Spoon over the remaining oil, the lime juice, chilli if using, and some salt and pepper. Rub the mixture in lightly.

3 Roast for 10–12 minutes. Serve very hot, with lemon wedges.

Roast Salmon with Thyme and Lime Crust

Mix 30g (1oz) slightly stale breadcrumbs with 20g (²⁄₃oz) butter, melted, 1 teaspoon chopped thyme leaves, 1 tablespoon chopped parsley, the finely grated zest of 1 lime (or lemon), a good squeeze of lime juice, and some salt and pepper. Place the salmon steaks in a greased baking dish as above, then pat the breadcrumb mixture evenly over each one. Roast as for **Roast Salmon with Lime** for 15 minutes. Serve with lime or lemon wedges.

Roast Salmon with Spice Rub

Crush 1 garlic clove and mix with ¼ teaspoon cayenne pepper, ¼ teaspoon ground cumin seeds, ¼ teaspoon ground coriander seeds, 1 teaspoon extra virgin olive oil and a squeeze of lemon juice. Rub this mixture all over two salmon steaks and set aside for 30 minutes. Roast as for the **Roast Salmon with Lime**, omitting the lime.

Roast salmon with thyme and lime crust.

Newspaper-baked Trout with Lime, Chive and Chilli Butter

Baking trout in newspaper is an old-fashioned notion, but one that works amazingly well. The damp newspaper steams away merrily in the oven, keeping the fish wonderfully moist, and ensuring that not a mite of flavour is lost.

N.B. By a sheet, I mean one double-page spread.

Serves 4

4 trout
a newspaper
salt and pepper

FOR THE BUTTER
1 fresh red chilli
125g (4½oz) lightly salted butter
finely grated zest and juice of ½ lime
1 tablespoon chopped chives

1 To make the butter, begin by 'roasting' the chilli. If you have a gas hob, spear the chilli on a fork, and hold it in the flame, turning frequently, until blackened and blistered all over. Otherwise, grill, close to the heat, turning frequently, again until blackened. Drop into a plastic bag, seal loosely, and leave until cool enough to handle. Pull off the skin, then discard the stalk and seeds. Chop the flesh roughly.

2 Now process all the butter ingredients together, including the chilli and some salt and pepper. If you don't have a processor, chop the chilli and chives very finely then beat into the softened butter with the lime zest and juice, salt and pepper. Mound into a small dish and chill – or roll into a cylinder in foil so that you can cut thin slices.

3 Preheat the oven to 200°C/400°F/Gas Mark 6. For each trout, take one sheet of a broadsheet newspaper, or two of a tabloid, and wet them thoroughly. Wrap each fish up neatly in the damp paper, and place on a baking tray.

4 Bake for 20 minutes. Let each diner unwrap his or her parcel at the table (make sure there's a handy waste-paper bin), and quickly pass around the flavoured butter while the fish are still hot enough for it to melt into their flesh.

Fundamental Fish Pie

Our very own British fish pie is essentially comfort food of the very best kind. At its most basic it is a soothing supper dish with its milky sauce and mashed potato, but it can be dressed up with prawns and scallops and all manner of herbs and other extras to make a creation that stands well at any dinner party.

Quick it is not. However, when you have the time to spend an hour or two in the kitchen, it is a joy of a dish to make. In traditional recipes the fish is poached in the milk, but in fact the completed dish is in the oven quite long enough to cook the fish through with no preamble, so there is no real need for this. Using raw fish makes the pie a mite quicker to prepare.

Serves 6

675g (1½lb) baking potatoes, scrubbed
4 eggs
75g (2½oz) butter
600ml (1 pint) milk, plus a little extra for the
    potato
2 sprigs parsley
1 small onion, peeled and sliced
5 black peppercorns
1 bay leaf
30g (1oz) plain flour
salt and pepper
450g (1lb) smoked haddock fillet, skinned
    and diced
400g (14oz) coley, hoki or other white fish
    fillet, skinned and diced
110g (4oz) shelled, cooked fresh peas, or
    thawed frozen peas

1 Preheat the oven to 200°C/400°F/Gas Mark 6.

2 Bake the potatoes in the oven until soft, or boil in their skins until cooked. Peel and mash 500g (18oz) of the potato flesh with 1 egg, 30g (1oz) of the butter and enough milk to give a soft consistency.

3 Hard-boil the remaining three eggs (see page 47) and run under the cold tap. When they are cool enough to handle, remove their shells and cut into quarters.

4 Put the milk into a pan with the parsley, onion, peppercorns and bay leaf. Bring gently to the boil, then draw off the heat, cover and leave to infuse for 10 minutes. Strain the milk and discard the onion and seasonings.

5 Make a white sauce (see page 165) with 30g (1oz) of the butter, the flour and the milk. Simmer for 5–10 minutes until thick and season well.

6 Mix the diced fish in a 1.5 litre (2 pint) pie dish (or gratin dish). Scatter over the peas and the quartered eggs. Pour over the white sauce, shaking the dish gently to distribute evenly.

7 Dollop the mashed potato over the top, then carefully smooth it down to cover entirely. Use a fork to make a wavy pattern on the top, then dot with the remaining butter. Bake for 20–30 minutes until lightly browned.

Fancy fish pie.

Fancy Fish Pie

Replace the coley or hoki of **Fundamental Fish Pie** on page 163 with a mixture of scallops, shelled prawns, and/or diced skinned salmon, in whatever proportions suit you and your bank balance. Replace 150ml (5fl oz) of the milk with crème fraîche or double cream. Stir 3 tablespoons chopped dill into the hot white sauce.

If you use a few scallops (and they do transform the pie), separate the orange coral and the white scallop, then pull off the black thread that runs part way around the white meat, and the white knobble on the side. Slice the white cylinder in half horizontally. Mix the coral and whites with the remaining fish.

White Sauce

Never, ever be bamboozled into buying instant white sauce mix – you probably already have the ingredients in your kitchen, and it is genuinely easy to make.

Makes 300ml (10fl oz)

15g (½oz) butter
15g (½oz) plain flour
300ml (10fl oz) milk
salt and pepper
freshly grated nutmeg (optional)

1 Melt the butter in a medium heavy-based saucepan. Stir in the flour until evenly mixed.

2 Take the pan off the heat. Add a slurp of milk and stir it in thoroughly, then repeat until you've added enough milk to make a thick runny cream. Now you can stir in the rest of the milk in big sploshes.

3 Return the pan to a medium heat and bring up to the boil, stirring and scraping the thickening sauce from the base of the pan. Turn the heat down very low, and let the sauce cook gently for at least 5 minutes. This cooks out the taste of raw flour and allows time for it to thicken. In an ideal world, you would let it barely simmer for 10 minutes or even longer, to get a truly first-class flavour.

4 Season the sauce with salt, pepper and nutmeg.

Stir the flour into the butter.

Add milk to make a runny cream.

Stir in the rest of the milk.

Mouclade

A French mouclade is a glorious treat of a dish – a huge steaming mountain of mussels bathed in a velvety sauce lightly spiked with curry. Serve it as a first course, or as a main course, with nothing more than some big chunks of crusty bread for mopping up the sauce, and glasses of chilled white wine to wash it all down.

Serves 4 as a main course, 6 as a starter

200ml (7fl oz) dry white wine
2kg (4½lb) mussels, cleaned and well rinsed
    (see opposite)
1 onion, peeled and chopped
45g (1½oz) butter
2 teaspoons medium curry paste
300g (10oz) crème fraîche
salt and pepper
a little chopped parsley, to serve

1 Pour the white wine into a large, roomy saucepan. Bring up to the boil, then tip in the mussels, clamp on the lid and shake over a high heat until all the mussels have opened. This should take 5–8 minutes. Discard any mussels that stay steadfastly shut.

2 Tip the mussels and their juices into a colander set over a bowl. Transfer the drained mussels to a deep, warm serving dish, cover and keep warm while you make the sauce. Reserve the juices in the bowl.

3 Fry the onion in the butter over a medium heat until tender without burning. Stir in the curry paste, and cook for a further 30–60 seconds. Now tip in the juices from cooking the mussels, tilting the bowl carefully so that the grit at the bottom is not disturbed. Stop pouring just before the grit starts to tip over the edge into the frying pan.

4 Boil hard until reduced by half, then stir in the crème fraîche and boil for a further 2–3 minutes, until thickened. Season with pepper, then taste and add salt only if it needs it (the mussel juice can be quite salty). Pour over the mussels, sprinkle with a little chopped parsley, and serve immediately.

Wash the mussels well, throwing away any that are broken or that gape and do not close when tapped. Remove and discard the beards.

Serve the cooked mussels sprinkled with chopped parsley.

Preparing Mussels Tip the mussels gently into the sink and turn on the cold tap. Now take a mussel and examine it. If the shell is broken, throw it into the bin. If it is whole, but open, tap the shell firmly on the side of the sink. If it closes, then the mussel is alive and kicking and good to eat. If it stays open, boot it out. Now cleaning. Scrape off the barnacles on the outside and pull off the hairy bit, the 'beard', with your fingers. Rinse the mussel under the tap. Place in a bowl, and move on to the next mussel, repeating the whole rigmarole. Once you've worked your way through the whole lot, rinse out the sink, and return the cleaned mussels to it. Cover with cold water and swish them around gently. Let the water settle, then remove the mussels. Repeat if you have time. The mussels are now ready for the pot.

Vegetables and Salads

chapter six

You know the recommendation, I'm sure. We should all be eating at least five portions of fruit and vegetables every day. It's an easy and pleasurable requirement if you let it be, believe me. Most salads are, of course, part of this whole 'let's be healthy' business, but they have a potential far beyond the mere rabbit food image. A plain green salad or tomato salad can be a creation of distinction with a great dressing, but that's merely a launching point for the marvellous, virtually infinite possibilities that salads offer. Invest in a bottle of extra virgin olive oil and some decent wine vinegar, and you're halfway to salad satisfaction.

Potatoes

Everybody loves potatoes. They love them boiled or mashed, baked, roasted or fried. And unlike so many beloved foods, they are cheap and nutritious and available everywhere, from the lowly corner-shop to the grandest of London's food halls. Most of us need no urging to pile the potatoes on the plate; they are, after all, the foundation stone of the European diet, the lovely, satisfying carbohydrate that fills all the gaps in our stomachs. Knowing how to handle them and cook them appreciatively is one of the first things any first-time cook should learn, if they haven't already imbibed the knowledge with their mother's milk.

First-base Potato Knowledge

Which Variety? Potatoes fall very broadly into two categories: floury and waxy. Floury potatoes are main-crop potatoes, in other words potatoes that are fully mature and adult. Their flesh when cooked is soft and mealy, ideal for baking or mashing, or making chips. They can also be boiled, but great care must be taken not to over-cook them, or they start to dissolve into the water. Waxy potatoes include new potatoes, small and immature, and salad potatoes, which are varieties that are still waxy when mature. Waxy potatoes are excellent for boiling, roasting, and, above all else, salads.

Buying Good potatoes are firm and heavy. They should not be wrinkled, but the odd small blemish is not a problem. Soft spots and bruising, on the other hand, is not a good sign. Reject potatoes that have plenty of green patches on them – they have been kept for too long in the light, and have developed toxins that can give you nasty stomach-ache.

Before you hand over the cash, take a sniff at your potatoes, particularly new potatoes. They should smell earthy and fresh. Any hint of a mouldy whiff suggests a potentially mouldy taste. This is especially true of new potatoes that have been out of the ground for too long.

Do not buy potatoes in bulk unless you a) get through them at a rate of knots, and/or b) have somewhere they can be stored in the right conditions.

Storing If you are going to use them up quickly, then you can leave your potatoes in the vegetable drawer of the fridge. Or in a brown paper bag on the vegetable rack. Or in the same brown paper bag on the shelf. That's for a couple of days or so. Prolonged exposure to very low temperatures transforms some of the starch in potatoes to sugars, which is not dangerous or unpleasant, but perhaps not exactly what you want. Prolonged exposure to light is far more serious, as it produces green solanine which is toxic. The green parts can just be cut off, leaving the rest of the potato perfectly edible, but it does seem a bit of a waste for the want of, say, a brown paper bag.

So, the upshot of all this is that ideally you will store potatoes in the dark, somewhere dry and cool, but not too cold.

Preparation Absolute fundamentals are pretty obvious: scrub potatoes in cold water if dirty, or just rinse them well if they are not laden with dirt. Cut away any bruised areas, green patches and any small shoots (the latter two laced with toxic solanine!). The rest depends on the way you intend to cook them.

Boiled Potatoes

I'd like to assume that you know how to boil a potato. Just in case, here is a précis: main-crop floury potatoes should be put in a pan with cold water and salt and then brought up to the boil. New potatoes should go straight into salted boiling water. Simmer old or new until the potatoes are tender – test with a fork, or the tip of the knife. Drain thoroughly. Timing is around 10–20 minutes, depending on size and variety.

Now to details. There is no point peeling new potatoes or salad potatoes. You may, however, choose to scrub very early, small new potatoes, which will remove most of the outer layer of skin. Ideally they should all be of similar size so that they cook evenly. If some are much larger than others, cut them in half or thirds before adding to the pan.

Big floury potatoes are more problematical. If you cook them whole in their skins it takes longer, but they will retain more taste. The skin will pull away easily once the potatoes are cooked (spear each one on a fork so that you can pull off the skin without scalding your fingers), which donates a small measure of economy to the method.

If you peel them first, and cut into smaller chunks, the potato will lose a good deal of nutrients and flavour to the cooking water and will taste duller and more watery. But of course, they will cook far more quickly.

To be honest, I don't often serve plain boiled floury potatoes. They always seem boring in comparison to potatoes cooked in other ways. The one time I do boil them, peeled but only until two-thirds cooked, is when I want to make proper roast potatoes.

Baked Potatoes

Even though the jacket potato is common as muck these days, it still makes a handsome, cheap and comforting meal, topped with butter and cheese, or any one of any number of other fillings (soured cream and chives or baked beans have long been my favoured options). There is absolutely no mystery to baking a potato. Take a largish floury potato (around 200g/7oz is about right), scrub it well, pierce with a fork once or twice (to let steam escape), then bake at around 200–220°C/400–425°F/ Gas Mark 6–7 for 1–1½ hours until tender all the way through. You can speed the process up by pushing a skewer through the centre and out the other side – the metal conducts heat directly to the centre, cooking it inside outwards as well as outside inwards. This will knock some 15–20 minutes off the cooking time.

Some people like to rub oil or salt or both into the skin of the potato before it goes into the oven, but it is not necessary.

Baked potato flesh, incidentally, makes the very best mashed potato or fish cakes, as it retains all its flavour, unlike boiled potato, which will have lost some to the water.

Roast Potatoes

A great roast potato of the very traditional sort should have a crisp, crunchy exterior encasing a blamelessly tender centre.

Here's how to make perfect roast potatoes. It's not quick, but it is worth every second you spend on them. You'll start off with large, floury potatoes – Desirée or King Edwards work well amongst many others. Boil in their skins for 10 minutes, then drain and run under the cold tap. Peel and cut into large chunks. Put enough fat (lard, olive oil, sunflower oil, goose fat, according to your means and preference) into a roasting tin to cover the base generously. Slide it into the oven, preheated to 200–220°C/400–425°F/Gas Mark 6–7. Leave it there for at least 5 minutes, or longer, until extremely hot – this is absolutely critical to success.

Meanwhile, use the prongs of a fork to scrape little ridges all over each surface of every chunk of par-boiled potato. This, too, is critical. Put the potatoes into the sizzlingly hot fat, turn to coat them all over, sprinkle with salt and return to the oven a.s.a.p. Roast for 50–70 minutes, turning the potatoes after the first half hour, and then again 15 minutes later, so that they brown evenly.

Sautéed Potatoes

I'd take sautéed potatoes over chips any time, but especially if I'm the one who has to make them. Like a cross between perfect roast potatoes and chips, they come up trumps every time. Most potatoes can be sautéed, but I particularly favour larger end-of-season new potatoes, or a densely fleshed variety like Cara.

Peel your potatoes and cut into small dice – around 1.5cm (¾in). Pour enough fat (olive oil, sunflower oil, half and half oil and butter, goose fat, lard) into a frying pan to cover the base generously. Heat until very hot, then add the potato dice. There should be a loud sizzle as the fat and potatoes meet. Use a fish slice to keep the cubes turning in the fat, on the move all the time, for the next 10–15 minutes until they are delectably brown on the outside and very tender inside.

Tip them out on to a dish lined with kitchen paper (to absorb excess fat), then pile into a dish and season generously with salt. Alternatively, if you happen to have a clean paper bag handy, scoop the hot sautéed potatoes into that, add salt and scrunch the top of the bag up. Toss the potatoes around in the bag so that the fat is absorbed by the paper at the same time as the salt is evenly distributed. Either way, eat the potatoes swiftly while they are still crisply tender. Or is that tenderly crisp? Let me know.

Mashed Potatoes

For mash you want a floury large potato – the flourier it is, the lighter and nicer your mash will be. King Edwards are good, but if you see Kerr's Pink snap them up straightaway – they cook to the crumbliest, flouriest state ever.

The best mash is made with baked or microwaved potatoes. Cooked in their jackets in the oven, the potatoes do not absorb any extra water. This means that you start off with a perfect, dry-cooked potato mash, with no flavour lost, which guzzles up lots of milk and butter, and so ends up tasting extra good.

Second best mash is made with potatoes that are boiled whole in their skins.

Mustard mash.

This minimises the absorption of water. Mash made with potatoes that have been peeled, cut into chunks and boiled tends to have a more insipid flavour, as some of the potato juices are lost to the water, and the chunks become waterlogged. You can dry the mash off later in the pan to some extent, but this is not entirely satisfactory.

Whichever way you choose, it is easier to mash potato when it is still good and hot, so if they are baked or microwaved, halve the potatoes lengthways and scoop the flesh out of the skins into a large saucepan. Spear the potatoes one by one on a fork, and peel if they have been boiled in their jackets. Drain chunks thoroughly, return them to the pan and 'dry' over a very gentle heat for a few minutes.

Once you have the cooked potato steaming in the pan, add a generous knob of butter – somewhere around 30g (1oz) for each 500g (18oz) of potato. Mash the potato thoroughly with a potato masher or a large fork. For a perfectly smooth and unctuous mash, invest in either a potato ricer, or a vegetable mill. The processor is not a good option, as it turns the starch gluey and rather unpleasant. Whilst mashing, heat a small pan of milk – allow 100ml (3½fl oz) per 500g (18oz) of potatoes.

Put the saucepan of mashed potatoes on a low heat, add salt and a good slurp of milk, then beat hard. Continue beating in the milk until the potatoes have reached the kind of consistency you like. Stir in a generous scraping of fresh nutmeg, then taste and adjust the seasoning.

Mustard Mash   Stir 1 heaped tablespoon of coarse-grain mustard per 500g (18oz) potatoes into the steaming hot mash just before serving. No need for nutmeg.

Irish Champ	Chop up loads of spring onions – 3 for each 500g (18oz) potato. Cook them gently in a knob of butter for a minute or so to soften, then stir into the hot mash.
Crème Fraîche and Rocket Mash	For a thoroughly modern take on mash, try replacing some of the milk with a small tub of crème fraîche. When the mash is fully done, stir in plenty of roughly chopped rocket – 20g (⅔oz) for every 500g (18oz) potatoes.
Cheesy Mash	This can be very self-indulgent. Exact quantities are impossible to give as it depends on which cheese you use, and how cheesy you want your mash to be. There's one French dish, aligot, where you melt in half as much cheese as there is potato! I'm not suggesting that you need go that far, but this is a suit-yourself sort of an affair. Try adding lots of Parmesan and extra butter, or grate in plenty of mature Cheddar, or stir in a generous helping of soft garlic and chive cheese. A spoonful of mustard (English, Dijon or whole-grain) adds a lively kick to the mixture.

Roast Potato Wedges

Save chips for an occasional treat when you are out and about. Roast potato wedges are much less trouble to make at home, and taste every bit as good. Use main-crop potatoes that are not too floury: Desirée or Estima are good.

Per person

1 large baking potato, scrubbed
½ tablespoon extra virgin olive oil or sunflower oil
1–2 whole garlic cloves (in their skins)
coarse sea salt

1 Preheat the oven to 220°C/425°F/Gas Mark 7. Cut each potato into quarters lengthways, but don't peel. Now cut each quarter into two or three long wedges, depending on the size. Ultimately the skin-side of each wedge should be around 2.5cm (1in) across.

2 Put the potato wedges into a shallow ovenproof dish, wide enough to take them in a more or less single layer. A bit of a jumble of overlapping is fine, but if the wedges are piled up too deep, they will sweat and stew instead of browning nicely.

3 Add the oil, garlic and plenty of salt. Turn the whole lot with your hands so that each wedge is coated in oil. Bake in the preheated oven for 45–60 minutes, turning the wedges every 20 minutes or so, until browned on the outside and tender in the centre (check with a skewer or the tip of a knife). Serve hot.

Roast potato wedges with lemon and thyme.

Roast Potato Wedges with Lemon and Thyme

Add a third of a lemon per person, cutting the whole thing, peel and pith and all, into chunks, to the **Roast Potato Wedges** on page 174 before they go into the oven. Tuck 3–4 sprigs of thyme in amongst the potatoes, as well.

Roast New Potatoes

New potatoes, roasted whole in exactly the same way as potato wedges (see page 174), adding a sprig or two of rosemary if you have any to hand, are so delicious – browned on the outside and smoothly tender inside. Make plenty – they'll soon be wolfed down.

Gratin Dauphinoise

Gratin dauphinoise is possible the ultimate, grandest, most sensational way to use a clutch of lowly tubers dug out of the dirt. It might well go on my 'last-meal-before-I-die' menu. It is no more and no less than thinly sliced potatoes, baked slowly in cream until the potatoes are divinely tender, and the top is golden brown. The food police won't like it at all, but everyone else will.

Serves 6

15g (½oz) butter
1 tablespoon plain flour
600–750ml (1–1¼ pints) double cream
1kg (2¼lb) main-crop potatoes, peeled and thinly sliced
1 large onion, peeled, halved and thinly sliced
2 garlic cloves, peeled and finely chopped
salt and pepper
freshly grated nutmeg

1 Preheat the oven to 170°C/325°F/Gas Mark 3. Grease a large ovenproof gratin dish thickly with the butter.

2 Mix the flour with a little of the cream to a smooth paste, then stir back into the cream.

3 Spread a quarter of the potatoes, onion and garlic out in the base of the dish, and season with salt, pepper and a grating of nutmeg. Repeat. Now pour over half the cream then layer the remaining ingredients, finishing up with potato. Do not fill the dish to the brim. Pour over enough of the remaining cream to just cover the potatoes.

4 Bake, uncovered, for about 1½ hours, until the potatoes are tender all the way through, and the top is brown. Serve hot or warm.

Arrange in the base of the dish...

Add a grating of nutmeg.

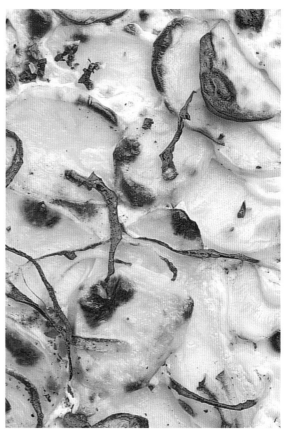
Gratin dauphinoise.

Gratin Dauphinoise with Gruyère

Purists would argue that you shouldn't include cheese in a true gratin dauphinoise, but what does it matter? If you want cheese, use cheese. In this case, enough freshly grated Gruyère to sprinkle lightly over the top of the gratin before it goes into the oven.

Green and Other Vegetables

You might start to feel anxious when told that we should all be eating a minimum of five portions of fruit and vegetables every day. However, let me point out that all it means is, say, a glass of orange juice (not squash) with breakfast, or a piece of fruit sliced on to your cereal, then at lunchtime you could perhaps have a something and salad sandwich and an apple or a pear or strawberries when they are in season, and when it comes to suppertime all it takes is a couple of carrots and a bit of broccoli alongside your main course or a plate of pasta and tomato sauce, followed by a few spoonfuls of Greek yoghurt, topped with raspberries, nuts and a drizzle of golden honey, and you're there.

Buy your vegetables fresh, cook them lightly and appropriately, tart them up speedily with herbs and spices, toasted nuts, a scraping of Parmesan or just a shake of soy sauce, and the whole five-a-day process becomes a positive joy. You may even find you become an insufferably smug six- or seven-a-dayer, and super-healthy into the bargain.

Buying Vegetables

Supermarkets have oodles of lovely vegetables these days, which makes life very simple. Markets, on the other hand, tend to have a more limited range but the prices are much lower. On the whole this means fabulous bargains (especially at farmers' markets where the vegetables are guaranteed local, and picked within the past day or so, but beware. A few deeply unscrupulous stall holders pass off fruit and veg that is way past its prime – perhaps not quite 'inedible' but getting close.

On the whole it is pretty easy to tell when vegetables are fresh and good to eat. For a start they should look sprightly and vigorous and full of promise. A bit of earth clinging on for dear life is often a good sign. Most vegetables should be firm and smooth skinned. Wrinkles, bruises, discoloration, soft patches and mouldy spots are all indications that you should look elsewhere.

It makes a good deal of sense to buy with the seasons, especially when you shop in markets. First of all, produce is fresher and cheaper in season, and secondly, prices are far more encouraging. Above all, you are likely to get much more flavour from vegetables which have been recently plucked from the earth, and have had the benefit of nature's rightful allowance of sunshine and rain.

Storing Vegetables

It is best to buy relatively small quantities of vegetables at a time – just what you can use up in the next couple of days – so that you eat them at their best. Keep them in the vegetable drawer of your fridge, unless you have a handy cool corner to leave them in, in which case a vegetable rack will come in handy, allowing air to circulate around them. Plastic wrapping is only good short term. Better to allow your vegetables to breathe freely – so discard the plastic once you get home.

Preparing Vegetables

Most basic preparation of vegetables is just common sense. They should all be rinsed before use, and those with tough, unsightly or less-than-tasty skins are usually peeled before cooking. The recipes and notes throughout the book will give you more details.

Cooking Vegetables

Boiling A misnomer. Most vegetables should be simmered. So, half fill a saucepan with water, add a good pinch or two of salt and bring up to the boil. Add the prepared vegetables (which should all be of a similar size – halve or quarter larger pieces if necessary), bring back to the boil, then turn the heat down, so that the water does no more than simmer lazily. As soon as vegetables are al dente (tender but with a slight firmness at the centre) or fully tender, depending on the vegetable and your taste, drain thoroughly. If not serving immediately, run them under the cold tap to prevent further cooking in their own heat. Drain again.

Return to the pan, and add a knob of butter if you wish. Keep warm and serve swiftly.

If you take care not to over-cook them, many vegetables can be boiled in advance, then reheated with a knob of butter, or a little extra virgin olive oil, over a low heat.

Frying You would be surprised at how many vegetables respond well to frying. There's onion, obviously, courgettes (with garlic – mmm), cucumber (yes – honestly – fry in chunks over a brisk heat, then finish with a dash of cream, a squeeze of lemon juice, salt and pepper), carrots (divinely sweet and tender after lengthy, slow frying), mushrooms, peppers, shredded cabbage and so on.

Frying vegetables falls into several different categories. The slow and gentle approach is the one that is used for onions in particular, at the beginning of a recipe, to bring out their full sweetness, without actually letting them brown. Don't rush this process. It takes a good 10 minutes or longer to fry chopped onion to the proper degree of tenderness and translucence, without letting it brown. Carrots also need a slow approach, so that they are cooked through, but the temperature can go a little higher so that they do brown.

More tender vegetables (e.g. courgettes or sliced peppers) respond best to a medium-hot and fairly fiery session in the frying pan. Turn them frequently, but let them catch a little here and there in the heat, so that they are peppered with brown, though not actually burnt! Scoop out pieces of vegetable that colour early and keep warm, while you wait for the rest to finish cooking. The higher temperature means that oils (e.g. olive or sunflower oil) are preferable to butter, which burns easily.

High-temperature frying is essential for mushrooms in particular, and for sautéing diced vegetables (see sautéed potatoes on page 172 for more on this), or vegetables with a high water content, such as cucumber.

Stir-frying   Many vegetables are just brilliant stir-fried. Turn to the stir-frying chapter on page 135 for more on this.

Grilling   Grilling is a great way to cook many quick-cooking vegetables (peppers, courgettes, sliced aubergine, sliced onion, and so on), bringing a warm smokiness to the flesh that is entirely appealing. However, the big disadvantage is that you can't get an awful lot under your average kitchen grill. This doesn't matter if there are just one or two of you to feed, but any more than that and you have a problem on your hands. You could transfer the whole lot to the barbecue, but that may not be possible.

Anyway, if you do want to grill veg, here are the basic rules: slice or cut vegetables into pieces that are big enough not to get lost between the bars of the grill rack. Brush them lightly with oil, or steep in a marinade for a short while. Preheat the grill thoroughly, then arrange the vegetables on the grill rack, and grill about 10cm (4in) from the grill until browned. Turn with kitchen tongs, and brush the other side again with oil before sliding them back under the grill again. Though you don't want to actually burn them (with the exception of peppers, which are a unique case), the odd slightly charred edge or corner is a good and tasty thing. Serve the vegetables hot as they are, or toss with a garlicky dressing and serve warm or cold.

Griddling   Griddling produces a similar effect to grilling or barbecuing (and suits the same vegetables), but is only good for small quantities of vegetables. It also produces copious amounts of smoke, so turn the extractor fan on to full power or open all the windows. Get the griddle pan frighteningly hot, oil or marinate the vegetables, then lay on the hot ridges of the pan. Leave until the underneath is striped with brown, then turn and cook the other side. Serve the vegetables hot, or toss with a simple vinaigrette (see page 189) and serve warm or cold as a salad.

Roasting   This is one of the best of all ways of cooking many types of vegetables. I really, really, really love roast veg. Why? With no water to draw out flavour, every last iota of taste is kept and concentrated in the roasting tin, and the high heat produces splashes of caramelisation, which make everything taste even better.

Then there is the fact that roasting is so very easy – put everything in one large tin or dish, put it in the oven and take it out 45 minutes later. It's convenient – once the vegetables are in the oven, they just need to be stirred occasionally and meanwhile you can get on with the rest of the meal, or read the newspaper or do whatever else needs doing – and there's only one dish to wash up, too.

First choose your vegetables. One type all on its own is good. A mixture is good. All of the following can be successfully roasted: tomatoes (halved), peppers (cut in strips or large chunks), courgettes (cut into 5–7.5cm/2–3in) lengths, cabbage (quartered or cut into eighths through the stalk if large), carrots (whole if small, halved or quartered if large), parsnips (whole if small, halved or quartered and cored if large), fennel (quartered through the stalk), Jerusalem artichokes (whole, unpeeled), onions (cut into wedges), pumpkin and winter squash (cut into wedges about 3cm/1¼in thick, skin on, or 5cm/2in cubes), and probably several others that escape me for the time being.

Preheat the oven to 220°C/425°F/Gas Mark 7. Put all the prepared vegetables in a roasting tin, or shallow ovenproof dish in a closely packed single layer. Drizzle over a good measure of olive oil, season with salt and pepper, add sprigs of herbs such as thyme or rosemary, whole cloves of garlic, a few chopped chillies if you wish, then turn everything with your hands so that all the vegetables are coated in oil and seasonings. Roast for around 40–50 minutes, turning the vegetables after 30 minutes and then again after another 10–15 minutes. They are done when all the vegetables are very tender, with appetising touches of brown-black here and there. Serve hot or warm.

French Beans with Almonds and Cream

Most fresh green beans need to be topped and tailed. This means cutting off the tips at both ends (see page 9). Back in the old days, it was also the moment when you pulled away tough fibres running down the 'seams', but modern varieties have usually had these strings bred out of them. They will appear only when vegetables are over mature.

Runner beans also work well in either of these recipes – great in August when they are incredibly cheap and plentiful. Top, tail and cut into chunks or strips.

Serves 4

450g (1lb) French beans, topped and tailed
salt and pepper
30g (1oz) butter
15g (½oz) flaked almonds
1 small onion, peeled and chopped
120ml (4½fl oz) whipping or double cream
a dash of lemon juice

1 Cook the beans in boiling salted water for around 4 minutes until barely tender. Drain thoroughly. Put a couple of pieces of kitchen paper on a plate.
2 Melt half the butter in a frying pan and stir-fry the almonds until golden brown. Scoop out on to the kitchen paper, which will absorb excess fat.
3 Add the remaining butter to the pan and, when foaming, add the onion. Fry gently until tender without browning.
4 Now add the beans, stir about for a minute or so, then add the cream, salt and pepper. Bring up to the boil, then let it bubble for a minute or two until the cream has reduced (boiled down) to a sauce that coats the beans nicely.
5 Stir in a squeeze or two of lemon juice (just to heighten the flavours), then taste and adjust seasoning. Finally stir in the almonds and serve.

French Beans with Cumin and Almonds

Cook the beans as above, but omit the almonds. Add 1 teaspoon ground cumin to the frying pan with the beans. Forget about the cream and lemon juice. All you need do is turn the beans in the butter with the onion and cumin for 2–3 minutes until very hot.

Sautéed Cabbage with Garlic and Lemon

Like sprouts, cabbage has a dubious reputation. Treated properly, however, it can be extremely delicious. The name of the game is brevity, whether sautéing as here, or boiling. For a plain but tasty result, cook shredded cabbage in a relatively small amount of boiling water for 3–4 minutes, possibly 5, but absolutely no more. Lengthy boiling not only makes it slimy and unpleasant, but also produces that ghastly over-cooked cabbage scent that lingers so grimly, ever more stale, in pubs and schools and other institutions where cooking is not their foremost concern. Drain the cabbage swiftly and run immediately under the cold tap for a few seconds. Drain well and serve with a large knob of butter, just to reassure one and all that this is now something special to be savoured, rather than dreaded.

Serves 4

½ small head white cabbage
3 tablespoons extra virgin olive oil
2 large garlic cloves, peeled and chopped
1 dried hot red chilli, crumbled, or 1 fresh
    chilli, deseeded and chopped (optional)
juice of ½–1 lemon
salt

1 Halve the half head of cabbage, then slice out the tough central core. Slice the remaining cabbage very thinly.
2 Take a wide deep frying pan and heat the oil in it over a high heat. Add the cabbage, and sauté, turning it regularly, until it begins to soften, and get frizzled with brown here and there.
3 Add the garlic and chilli if using, and sauté for another 2–3 minutes.
4 Squeeze over plenty of lemon juice and season with salt. Taste and add more lemon juice if you'd relish a sharper zing to parry with the cabbage and chilli.

Roast Tomatoes with Fennel Seeds

For plain roast tomatoes, roast as outlined below, leaving out the fennel seeds and possibly the thyme. Not only are plain roast tomatoes terrific as a side dish, but they can also be tossed into hot pasta, along with any juices in the dish. Serve with plenty of freshly grated Parmesan – they need nothing more.

Serves 4

3 tablespoons extra virgin olive oil
6 plum tomatoes or other medium-sized
  tomatoes
½ tablespoon fennel seeds
3 garlic cloves, unpeeled
2 sprigs thyme
salt and pepper
caster sugar

1 Preheat the oven to 220°C/425°F/Gas Mark 7. Smear 1 tablespoon oil over the base of a large ovenproof dish.
2 If using plum tomatoes, cut them in half from stem end to base. If using round tomatoes, cut them in half around the equator, i.e. halfway between stem end and base. Arrange the tomatoes, cut-sides up, in a cosy layer in the dish.
3 Scatter fennel seeds evenly over the tomatoes. Tuck the garlic and the thyme down amongst them. Season with salt, pepper and a few pinches of sugar. Drizzle over the remaining olive oil.
4 Bake for 40–45 minutes until the tomatoes are very tender, and browning here and there at the edges. Eat hot, warm or at room temperature.

Roast tomatoes with fennel seeds.

Stir-fried Vegetables with Black Bean Sauce

Use this as a primer for any mixed vegetable stir-fry, adding the vegetables that take longest to cook first. Remember not to over-crowd the wok at any point, or you will end up stewing the vegetables instead of stir-frying.

You could replace the black bean sauce with oyster sauce (from Chinese stores, and there is even a vegetarian version), or you could leave the sauce out altogether and finish with a tablespoon of sesame oil tossed in at the end (and perhaps a little more soy).

I like to eat this as a main dish, on top of a big bowl of rice, but it can also be served as a side dish with perhaps some grilled lamb chops.

Serves 3–4

2 garlic cloves, peeled and finely chopped
1.5cm (¾in) piece fresh root ginger, peeled and finely chopped
110g (4oz) tender-stem broccoli, halved lengthways, and cut into 2.5cm (1in) lengths
2 carrots, peeled and cut into thin matchsticks
1 red pepper, deseeded and cut into strips
¼ white cabbage, core removed, thinly shredded
2 tablespoons sunflower or vegetable oil
1 tablespoon soy sauce
2–3 tablespoons black bean sauce

1 Prepare all the vegetables, and gather all the ingredients around the hob.

2 Place the wok over a high heat and leave until it smokes. Keep the heat high throughout the cooking process. Now add the oil, swirl around once or twice, then throw in the garlic and ginger. Stir-fry for 10–20 seconds until beginning to colour.

3 Next add the broccoli and the carrot and stir-fry for around 2 minutes. Then add the red pepper and the cabbage, and continue to stir-fry for another 3–4 minutes, until crisp-tender and patched with brown here and there.

4 Spoon in the soy sauce and the black bean sauce. Toss to mix, and serve immediately.

Broccoli al Diavolo

This is a pleasingly quick and easy way to inject a shot of raunchy life into broccoli; it's an idea that comes straight from southern Italy, where they know a thing or two about garlic and chilli and enjoying their meals to the max.

The trick with broccoli is to realise that the florets (the 'flowery' darker green bits at the top) and the stem cook at different rates. Also, that the stem is actually the best bit of all. So, first slice off the stem(s) and peel the lower thicker parts which can have a tough skin. Slice. Next break up the top into small pieces. Bring a large pan of water to the boil, add the slices of stalk, simmer for 1–2 minutes, then add the florets. Simmer for a few more minutes (around 4–5) until the florets are just tender, but not yet mushy. Run under the cold tap to halt the cooking. Drain again.

Cover the base of a frying pan with extra virgin olive oil, heat over a medium heat, then add 2–3 chopped cloves of garlic. Let them sizzle for a few seconds, just to perfume the oil, then add 1 dried red chilli, broken into three or four bits. Stir, then pile in the broccoli – just enough to give a single layer of bits in the pan, with a little room to move them around. Fry gently for a few minutes, turning the broccoli occasionally, until it is hot. Season with a little salt and pepper and serve.

Ginger-glazed Carrots

Peel medium to large carrots thinly, top and tail, then cut into slices, or thin batons. Simmer in salted water for a few minutes until al dente. Drain, run under the cold tap to halt cooking, then drain again thoroughly.

Put the carrots into a saucepan with a large knob of butter, and enough ginger beer to come about halfway up the carrots. Sprinkle over a little caster sugar and season with salt. Bring up to the boil, stirring occasionally, then boil until the ginger beer has more or less all boiled away, leaving the carrots glazed with a sweet, buttery gingery glaze. Taste and add more salt if needed.

Salads

Salads are dishes of glorious, mind-boggling diversity. Anything goes (within reason), but there are certain combinations that will always loom large as golden examples of how wonderful a salad can be, and a few of those are included below. The principles of making a salad are not complicated, but success relies on good ingredients matched and mixed with attention to detail.

First Principles of Salad Making

A salad consists of two elements. The first is the substance of the salad, the solid matter, such as lettuce leaves, or tomatoes, or grated carrot, or pasta and so on. The second is the all-important dressing, which is, I think, the defining element.

Leaves and the Rest

Green salad.

Whatever goes into a salad, it should be in prime condition. No dressing, however delicious, can mask limp leaves, over-ripe tomatoes, or wrinkly peppers. All kinds of things can be combined, but take a few minutes to consider whether they will work together. Often, the best salads are the simplest – just two or three main ingredients and no more, so that each flavour can be savoured. So, don't think of the salad bowl as an economical dustbin replacement, but more as a place where you can put together a salad that will look every bit as sensational as it will taste.

Raw ingredients must taste fresh and lively and full of vigour. This usually means that the salad is best composed as near to eating as possible, but of course there are always exceptions to this rule. We'll come to those later.

Salad leaves need to be treated with due respect. Prepare them as late as you can, and keep them stashed in plastic bags or tubs in the fridge until shortly before serving. Much the same goes for all the crisp raw salad vegetables that might accompany the leaves, such as radishes or cucumber or raw peppers. By the time you've arranged everything in your salad bowl – with the dressing in the bottom and the salad servers crossed over it, to keep most of the leaves out of the dressing – they will have lost their ice-box chill (just as well, as all but a handful of salads taste best at room temperature).

A straightforward green salad can be made with just one variety of lettuce, in which case you should choose one with clear character, such as Cos or Webb's Wonder, or Little Gem, or a mixed bunch. With a mixed bunch, the ideal is to choose contrasting tastes and textures, so you might, for instance, combine shredded Cos, with watercress or rocket for pepperiness, lamb's lettuce for tenderness, and frisée for bitterness.

Cooked salad ingredients (e.g. beans, grilled peppers, pasta) are different to raw ones. They obviously need advance attention because they have to be cooked and cooled. The trick here, though, is to make the dressing while they are cooking, so that you can toss them in it whilst they are still warm. As they cool down they draw the dressing right into them, which makes them taste especially good.

Remember that all those cooked, bland, starchy ingredients, like rice, potatoes, pasta and lentils, which all make excellent bases for salads, need a relatively sharp dressing to balance the starch. Make it more pokey than usual, and use plenty, adding it while the ingredients are still hot.

The Dressing   When it comes to dressing a salad, the possibilities are legion. However, the most useful dressing of all, the one that goes with practically anything you care to mention, the one that is open to almost infinite variation, is the vinaigrette, also known as a French dressing. At its purest it consists of no more than vinegar (or lemon juice), oil, salt and pepper. Nothing to it, eh? Well, you would be surprised how often people get it wrong, for all that. The key is balance – too much vinegar ruins any salad, too little leaves it tasting naked and dull.

As important is using good oils and good vinegars. So invest in a bottle of decent extra virgin olive oil and another of decent white or red wine vinegar, and you've made a fine start. If you eat lots of salads, then you might like to add a small bottle of walnut or hazelnut oil to your collection as well as a bottle of balsamic vinegar (buy the most expensive you can afford – you really can taste the difference). These are the first steps on a voyage of discovery that will take you way beyond the scope of this book.

Do not be lazily seduced into buying bottles of ready-made dressings. You save yourself very little time, and inevitably lose out on flavour and variety.

Basic vinaigrette   I've been making this since I was a little girl (and it still tastes as good). It will dress a green salad to feed six people. Even if you are just making a salad for two people, it is still worth making up the full quantity, as what is not needed can be stored in the fridge in a screw-top jar for another day. Vinaigrette keeps almost indefinitely. Whisk 1 tablespoon red or white wine vinegar, ½ teaspoon Dijon mustard, 2 pinches caster sugar and plenty of salt and pepper together in your salad bowl. Gradually whisk in 4–5 tablespoons extra virgin olive oil, a spoonful at a time. With energetic whisking the oil and vinegar should emulsify to make a thick dressing but don't worry if this doesn't happen – it is not critical. Taste the dressing and adjust seasonings, adding more oil, vinegar or salt if necessary. The degree of sharpness required will depend on the ingredients for the salad. For green leaves and tomatoes and the like, the dressing should have a touch of sharpness but not so much that it makes your mouth uncomfortable. For starchy ingredients the vinegar needs to be more dominant but still not overwhelmingly aggressive.

Or, instead of whisking the vinaigrette in the salad bowl, put all the ingredients into a screw-top jar. Screw on the lid tightly and shake with enthusiasm. Again taste and adjust the balance of flavours according to the salad you are putting together.

Basic vinaigrette variations Replace some or all of the oil with other oils such as hazelnut or walnut (great on green salads dressed up with toasted hazelnuts or walnuts), or pumpkin seed oil. Try using balsamic vinegar, sherry vinegar or tarragon vinegar instead of wine vinegar. Instead of using Dijon mustard, replace with a heaped teaspoon of coarse grain mustard. Whisk ½ crushed garlic clove into the vinegar with the mustard. Replace the salt with 2 teaspoons soy sauce, and whisk a teaspoon of honey in with the vinegar instead of sugar. Or, for an Italian/Greek vinaigrette, simply whisk the juice of ½ lemon with some salt and pepper and 6 tablespoons extra virgin olive oil (no mustard). And so it goes on – you've got the idea, so make up some more of your own.

Danish Cucumber Salad

This was one of my mother's favourites and remains one of mine. It must be made at least an hour in advance, which can be helpful at times, and keeps for two or three days in the fridge if necessary.

Serves 4

1 large cucumber
1 level tablespoon salt
1 rounded tablespoon caster sugar
3 tablespoons white wine vinegar
finely chopped parsley or dill

Peel the cucumber, then cut into thin slices. Mix with the salt, sugar and vinegar. Leave for an hour or more in the fridge, stirring occasionally. When ready to serve, drain off the liquid and place the cucumber in a serving dish. Scatter over the parsley or dill.

Tomato and Basil Salad

The tomato salad is one of the aristocrats of the salad kingdom. It can be made quickly and goes perfectly with any number of other dishes, from cheese on toast to roast lamb. The trickiest part here is finding really good tomatoes, but even that is so much easier these days. Look out for tomatoes that are vine-ripened or 'grown for flavour' or just look interesting and inviting. What you are searching for is the magic of sweetness and tartness combined, along with a deep tomatoey nature.

Per person

1–2 medium ripe tomatoes
1–2 teaspoons vinaigrette (see opposite)
2 large basil leaves, torn up

Slice the tomato(es) and arrange on a plate. Drizzle over the vinaigrette. The salad can be finished and served straightaway, but can also be left for an hour or so before serving. Just before placing on the table, scatter with the basil.

Tomato and mint salad   Replace the basil leaves with mint leaves – every bit as good.

Tomato and mozzarella salad   Slice half a 150g (5oz) ball of mozzarella per person. Arrange on a plate alternating with the tomato slices, then dress (you may need a little more vinaigrette) and finish with torn-up basil leaves.

Tomato and black olive salad   Make a tomato salad, and finish either with torn-up basil, or chopped parsley or chopped chives, then dot with black olives – 3 per person should do nicely.

Tomato and red onion salad   Make a tomato salad, and scatter with thinly sliced rings of red onion (or shallot) and torn-up basil.

Tomato, orange and olive salad   Make a tomato salad, and alternate slices of tomato with slices of peeled, sweet orange. Dress with vinaigrette, scatter with chopped chives and then dot with black olives.

Chickpea, Courgette and Carrot Salad

This cooked vegetable salad is just what's called for if you are barbecuing, especially as it can be made up to 24 hours in advance. The flavour improves with a spot of hanging around. You could also serve it as a starter, on its own, perhaps adding a little crumbled feta cheese for good measure, or put it on the table with a simple lunch of cheese, sliced ham or salami, a green salad and bread.

Serves 6

400g (14oz) carrots, peeled and cut into
    batons (see below)
salt and pepper
400g (14oz) courgettes, sliced about 5mm
    (¼in) thick
1 x 400g can chickpeas, drained and rinsed
a handful of mint leaves, half shredded

DRESSING

2 teaspoons tomato purée
1 tablespoon white wine vinegar
1 teaspoon caster sugar
1 teaspoon Dijon mustard
4 tablespoons olive oil

need to know

SALAD TIPS AND TECHNIQUES

BATONS   For medium-sized carrots, all you need do is cut them across into sensible lengths – let's say around 3–4cm (1¼–½in), then quarter each piece lengthways. Bigger, fatter winter carrots will need to be cut into similar chunks, then carefully sliced into three or four lengthways, and again at right angles into three or four.

SHREDDING   To shred herbs, or spinach or other green leaves, pile 4–5 leaves on top of each other, then roll up tightly. Slice thinly to produce fine shreds.

1 Bring a large pan of salted water to the boil. Add the carrots, bring back to the boil and simmer for 3 minutes, then add the courgettes. Bring back to the boil, simmer for 1 minute, then drain. Run under the cold tap and drain again, thoroughly.

2 Meanwhile, to make the dressing, whisk the tomato purée with the vinegar, sugar and mustard, then gradually whisk in the olive oil. Taste and adjust the seasoning.

3 Mix the cooked vegetables, while still warm, with the chickpeas, the shredded mint leaves and enough dressing to coat. Leave to cool.

4 Serve at room temperature, scattered with the remaining whole mint leaves. (If not serving immediately, cover with clingfilm and chill, without adding the whole mint leaves, until half an hour before you intend to sit down and eat. Take the salad out of the fridge and let it come back to room temperature, scatter over the whole mint leaves, and tuck in.)

Greek Salad

What a wonderful salad this is! It is just one of the cleanest, most energising salads I know, perfect for a spot of light lunch with nothing more than a slice or two of excellent bread, but discreet enough to serve as a side salad with perhaps a pile of grilled sardines, or cold roast chicken.

Serves 4–6

½ cucumber
6 Cos lettuce leaves, shredded (see opposite) or torn
3 really good, ripe tomatoes, cut roughly into chunks
½ red onion, peeled and very thinly sliced
16 plump black olives (Kalamata olives are perfect for this)
85g (3oz) feta cheese, crumbled

DRESSING
2 teaspoons dried oregano
juice of ½ lemon
3 tablespoons extra virgin olive oil
salt and pepper

1 Either simply cut the cucumber into quarters lengthways, then slice each quarter thickly, or for a more soigné look, peel the cucumber, then cut in half lengthways. Scoop out the seeds with a teaspoon and discard. Now slice the cucumber into half moons about as thick as a one-pound coin.

2 Take a salad bowl and pile in the lettuce. Add the cucumber, tomato, red onion and olives and mix all the ingredients together.

3 To make the dressing, whisk together the oregano, lemon juice, olive oil and some salt and pepper. Taste and adjust the seasoning.

4 Just before serving, scatter the feta cheese over the top of the salad. Whisk the dressing again to mix back together, then spoon over the salad. Toss at the table.

Panzanella

Food writers endlessly urge readers to toss salads at the last minute, but for once here is a recipe where the salad is best made and tossed at least an hour before serving. Panzanella is an Italian peasant salad. It was a thrifty way to use up stale bread, which would absorb the delicious juices of tomatoes mixed with vinegar and olive oil. Nowadays, chefs and cooks across the world make it just because it tastes so good.

Serves 6

2 large thick slices sturdy bread (e.g. pain de campagne)
500g (18oz) of the ripest, reddest tomatoes you can find
1 red onion, peeled and finely diced
2 celery stalks, thinly sliced
½ cucumber, diced
6 tablespoons extra virgin olive oil
2 tablespoons red wine vinegar
salt and pepper
caster sugar (optional)
a big handful of basil leaves

1 Cut the crusts off the bread. If your bread is fresh you will need to dry it out. Turn the oven on to a gentle 110°C/225°F/ Gas Mark ¼. Lay the bread directly on the shelf in the centre of the oven and leave for between 30 and 60 minutes until pretty dry. Cut into 1.5cm (¾in) cubes, or break into small pieces. Place in the bottom of a capacious salad bowl.

2 Add the tomatoes, onion, celery and cucumber. Spoon over the oil and vinegar and sprinkle with salt and pepper. If the tomatoes were a bit on the dull side, add a pinch or two of sugar to bring out the flavours.

3 Use your hands to mix all the ingredients together, scooping right down to the bottom of the bowl to make sure that the bread is mixed in too.

4 Set aside the handsomest sprig of basil for decoration. Tear up the rest of the leaves roughly, then mix them into the salad too. Cover loosely with clingfilm, then leave at room temperature for up to an hour, or in the fridge for up to 3 hours.

5 Turn the mixture again just before serving. Taste and adjust seasoning. The idea is that the bread breaks up as you turn the salad, so don't worry that it doesn't stay in perfect cubes. Place the reserved sprig of basil on the top, and serve.

Panzanella.

Salade Niçoise

A dish for a summer's day. The classic version is made with canned tuna, but for a modern twist, use fresh tuna, grilled or barbecued. Brush 500g (18oz) fresh tuna steaks (cut 2–2.5cm/ ¾–1in thick) with a little extra oil. Grill or barbecue over very hot charcoal for about 2 minutes on each side. Cut into large cubes, and toss with the salad ingredients.

Serves 4

400g (14oz) small new potatoes, boiled
110g (4oz) green beans, topped and tailed
    and cut in half
8 Cos lettuce leaves, torn up
225g (8 oz) cherry tomatoes, halved
1 x 200g can tuna steak, drained and flaked
12–16 black olives, stones in
3 hard-boiled eggs, quartered
8 canned or marinated anchovy fillets

VINAIGRETTE
1 garlic clove, peeled
coarse sea salt
1 tablespoon red wine vinegar
generous ½ teaspoon Dijon mustard
a pinch of caster sugar
salt and pepper
4–5 tablespoons extra virgin olive oil
2 tablespoons chopped chives

1 To make the vinaigrette, crush the garlic to a paste with some coarse salt. Work in the vinegar, mustard, sugar, and some salt and pepper. Whisk in the oil a tablespoon at a time. Taste and adjust seasoning, then stir in the chives. Set aside until needed.

2 If the potatoes are very small (walnut sized) leave whole, otherwise halve or slice thickly, pulling off as much of the skin as comes away easily. Toss with a tablespoon or so of the dressing.

3 Boil the green beans in salted water for 4–5 minutes until just tender. Drain and run under the cold tap to stop them cooking any further. Toss with about ½ tablespoon of the dressing.

4 Place the remaining dressing in the bottom of a large salad bowl. Place the lettuce over the dressing, then add the potatoes, green beans, tomatoes, tuna and olives, mixing them lightly without actually delving right down to the dressing itself. Arrange the egg and anchovy fillets decoratively on top.

5 Take the salad to the table and toss just before serving.

Salade niçoise made with fresh tuna.

chapter seven

Puddings, Cakes and Biscuits

We don't need them, but life wouldn't be quite as sweet without. Most of us love the occasional pudding or slice of cake, or just a couple of biscuits with a cup of coffee or tea. They don't have to be grand or complex, but even the most homely of sugary treats is a bonus. Creating a fabulous pudding, or divinely moist cake, is a true labour of love (or is it just greed...?), the kind of thing that you know will bring smiles to the faces of everyone who gets a taste. Build up a basic repertoire of favourites that you can fall back on at a moment's notice, and you'll swiftly earn a reputation as a fine and generous cook.

Puddings

Chocolate

Apparently, placing a picture of a chocolate pudding or cake on the front of a food magazine increases the sales instantly. That puts it up there with the late Diana, Princess of Wales, and a few other rare individuals. Chocolate is the new sex? Well, maybe, but given the choice I'd rather have both.

The moral, as far as I see it, is that every cook should have at least two fantastic chocolate recipes up their sleeve. They don't have to be complicated or exotic to hit the mark time and time again. In fact, I've always found that the simpler, more fundamental chocolate puddings (chocolate mousse, vanilla ice-cream with chocolate sauce, chocolate cake, even chocolate cornflake crispies) are the ones that give more pleasure than any others.

Which Chocolate? The general rule is to cook only with good-quality plain chocolate, with a high percentage of cocoa solids. This is easy to pick out from the crowd, as bars of plain chocolate almost invariably have this percentage printed on them. It should be at the very least over 60 per cent and, better still, over 70 per cent. Good-quality chocolate does not contain vegetable fat or vast amounts of sugar. Once you start noticing these things, you'll be amazed at how low the percentage of cocoa solids is in a cheap bar of chocolate.

Classy chocolate, with its full 70 per cent or more of cocoa solids, has an intense and penetrating flavour that is perfect for most cooking as it will be softened by other ingredients. However, I've found that when making something as minimalist as a chocolate mousse, the flavour can be too strong for many people, especially children. Two possible solutions – either add cream to the mousse, or use a really tip-top milk chocolate made without vegetable fats, instead of the plain chocolate.

With white chocolate, the first thing to check is that you are actually buying white chocolate. There's a good deal of white chocolate flavour stuff hanging around, and that is not what you want. Price is your best guide in this instance.

Melting Chocolate

Melting chocolate is easy, but it can go wrong. I speak from bitter experience. I will try to guide you away from disaster, but it is likely to happen to you at least once, when your attention is caught by something else just at the wrong moment. Don't let all of this put you off cooking with chocolate, but just make sure that you know the way it works.

The first thing to do is find a heatproof bowl that will sit comfortably on top of a small or medium-sized saucepan, with the base suspended a fair way from the bottom of the pan. Now put about 2.5cm (1in) water into the pan, and sit the bowl on it again. Check the base of the bowl. If it is damp, tip out some of the water, or replace the pan with a slightly smaller one.

Next, put the pan with its water on the hob to heat up. The bowl meanwhile sits on the table, while you break your chocolate up into squares and drop them into it. This is the point to add butter, or brandy, or concentrated coffee, or other liquid flavourings. Once the water in the pan is simmering, turn the heat off, then sit the bowl on the pan. Leave it there for 2–3 minutes, then lift the bowl off the pan, and stir. Let it stand for 3 or 4 minutes. The heat of the bowl will carry on melting the chocolate. Stir again – if the chocolate has all melted, but the base of the bowl is still hot, stand it in cold water to help cool it down. If there are still some smallish lumps of chocolate, keep on stirring – they will soon melt. If absolutely necessary (for instance, when melting a considerable amount of chocolate), repeat the whole process.

The reason for all this on/off business is that it takes no more than a few seconds for chocolate to go from the state of 'melting nicely' to the state of 'ruinously over-heated'. Better to err on the side of caution. When chocolate is over-heated, it seizes up like concrete and nothing much can be done to restore it to the divine, smooth runny state that you are after.

You can also melt chocolate in the microwave. Break it up into a microwave-proof bowl, cover tightly with clingfilm, and then heat on low-medium power in short bursts of about 1 minute, stirring between each burst. Don't overdo it, and remember that often you need do no more than stir to dissolve residual lumps of chocolate.

Once your chocolate has melted nicely, leave it to cool down until tepid. Never ever mix it with anything colder (e.g. yolks of eggs straight from the fridge). This, too, makes it seize up. Never ever let any water or watery liquid get into it at this stage. This also makes it seize up. After that, it is all plain sailing.

Put pieces of chocolate in a heatproof bowl over a pan of simmering water (the bowl must not touch the water).

Leave to melt slowly, stirring occasionally, until it becomes smooth and runny, perfectly melted chocolate.

Simple Chocolate Mousse

There are few chocolate recipes more elementary than chocolate mousse, but it always thrills people, unless they are from that very weird clan of oddballs who don't like chocolate.

Incidentally, should you want to make this for more people, or perhaps even just for you on your own, you need 60g (2oz) chocolate for each egg. Multiply up as you will. Note, too, that the eggs in chocolate mousse are uncooked, so it is not suitable for very young children, pregnant women, elderly souls or serious invalids (see page 43).

Serve the mousses with single cream or, if you prefer, top each one once set with a swirl of whipped cream. You could also scatter on something like flaked almonds and chopped stem ginger as in the photograph.

Serves 4

110g (4oz) plain chocolate
2 room-temperature eggs, separated

1 Break up the chocolate and melt over a pan of simmering water (see pages 200-1). Cool until tepid.
2 Beat the egg yolks into the chocolate one by one.
3 Whisk the egg whites until they form soft peaks. Stir one spoonful straight into the chocolate to loosen the mixture, then fold the rest of the whites in until no specks of white remain.
4 Spoon into either four individual ramekins, or one larger bowl. Chill until set (allow a good 4 hours for this).

Whisk egg whites.

Stir in a spoonful of whites...

then fold in the rest.

Chocolate mousse with toasted almonds and stem ginger.

Boozy Chocolate Mousse

To give **Simple Chocolate Mousse** an extra, grown-up sort of a kick, add 2 tablespoons of something strong and alcoholic to the broken-up chocolate before you start to melt it. The traditional addition is brandy, but you could use any number of other spirits or liqueurs – try whisky, rum, Malibu, Tia Maria, Grand Marnier or Cointreau.

Chocolate Mousse with Toasted Almonds

Make the mousse as on page 202, and top each pot with a generous helping of lightly toasted flaked almonds (see page 156). A mutually enhancing pairing of tastes and textures.

Chocolate Mousse with Toasted Coconut

Make either a plain chocolate mousse (see page 202), or a boozy mousse laced with Malibu (see above). Toast either ordinary desiccated coconut or coconut flakes as if they were flaked almonds (see page 156), and sprinkle over the top of each mousse just before serving.

Mocha Mousse

Mocha indicates a mixture of coffee and chocolate, and that's exactly what this is. Make the **Simple Chocolate Mousse** on page 202, adding a teaspoon of best-quality instant coffee granules to the chocolate as it melts.

Ginger and Chocolate Mousse

For those with a taste for preserved stem ginger, melt the chocolate (see page 202) with a tablespoon of the syrup from the ginger jar. Once you have folded the whites into the chocolate, fold in 1 sphere of stem ginger that has been very finely chopped.

Petits Pots au Chocolat

As smooth and rich as chocolate mousse is foamy, these little pots of chocolate are another brilliantly simple chocolate pudding.

You can leave them plain – just a devastating blend of chocolate, cream and a touch of egg – or you can add complementary flavours, as you can with a mousse.

Serves 5–6

450ml (15fl oz) single cream
150g (5oz) plain chocolate, roughly chopped
4 egg yolks
45g (1½oz) caster sugar

1 Preheat the oven to 130°C/270°F/Gas Mark 1.

2 Bring the cream gently up to the boil, then take off the heat.

3 Mix the egg yolks and sugar.

4 Stir the chocolate into the hot cream until completely melted in. Pour into the egg yolk mixture and whisk together.

5 Strain the mixture into a jug, and pour into five to six small custard cups or ramekins or even small espresso cups if you have enough of these.

6 Stand the cups in a roasting tin and pour enough boiling water around them to come almost halfway up their sides. Slide into the preheated oven and cook for 40–60 minutes until just set, but still slightly soft in the centre. Lift out of the roasting tin and leave to cool, then slide them into the fridge to chill.

7 Bring back to room temperature before serving.

Petits Pots au Chocolat à l'Orange

Pare the zest off half an orange and add to the pan with the cream. Bring up to the boil, then take off the heat, cover and leave in a warm place for 10 minutes or so to infuse. Heat up again, take off the heat, and stir in the chocolate. Carry on with the recipe as above, but stir in 2 tablespoons Grand Marnier or Cointreau before straining into the ramekins.

Petits Pots au Chocolat et Romarin

'Romarin' is rosemary, which goes amazingly well with chocolate. To add a subtle rosemary scent to your petits pots, infuse the rosemary in the cream as for the orange (see page 205), then carry on with the basic recipe from page 205 (no added booze).

Ice-Cream Sauces

As quick puddings go, there is little to beat a few scoops of rich vanilla ice-cream smothered in an unctuous and decadent sauce. Not that it has to be vanilla ice-cream, though vanilla does show off the glory of practically any sweet sauce to great effect. Still, if you've got a penchant for ginger ice-cream or strawberry ice-cream to the exclusion of all else, that's fine. It will still taste glorious with a sexy drizzle of hot chocolate sauce melting down into it.

Hot Chocolate Sauce

Made with water, this sauce is pretty devastating, but it becomes richer if you make it with milk. For something truly epic, replace half the milk with single cream. Wow!

It can be made in advance, and reheated when you're ready to indulge.

Serves 4–6

175g (6oz) plain chocolate, broken into
squares
30g (1oz) cocoa powder
175g (6oz) caster sugar
300ml (10fl oz) water or milk

1 Put all the ingredients into a saucepan and stir over a low heat until the sugar and chocolate have completely dissolved.
2 Raise the heat and bring to the boil, then reduce the heat again and simmer for 8 minutes, stirring occasionally. That's it. Now it's ready to pour.

Butterscotch Sauce

Butterscotch sauce has no scotch in it, but it does contain butter! The major ingredients, however, are cream and light muscovado sugar, which is what gives most of the flavour. It is devastatingly sweet, so a little goes a long way.

Serves 4–6

175g (6oz) light muscovado sugar
60g (2oz) unsalted butter
2 tablespoons golden syrup
a pinch of salt
150ml (5fl oz) double cream

1 Put all the ingredients into a saucepan and stir over a low heat until the sugar has completely dissolved.
2 Bring up to the boil, stirring, then take off the heat. All done, and ready to go.

need to know

TO MEASURE GOLDEN SYRUP Hold your tablespoon in the flame of a gas hob, or dip the bowl end into boiling water, then quickly slide it down into the can of golden syrup. If it is really hot the syrup will sizzle in a satisfying manner. Scoop out the tablespoonful you need, then watch as it slides off the spoon straight into the pan. Repeat for however many spoonfuls the recipe demands.

Raspberry Sauce

This is what is known in restaurant circles as a 'raspberry coulis' – a smart name for something made speedily from just three ingredients. It is best made in the summer with fresh raspberries, but when the season is over, you'll find that frozen raspberries can be used very successfully instead.

ripe raspberries (thawed if frozen)
lemon juice
icing sugar

1 Rub the raspberries through a sieve, to make a purée and to remove the seeds.
2 Stir in a few squeezes of lemon juice (as well as improving the flavour, it also helps to keep the colour bright and true), and icing sugar to taste.

Sieving raspberries for raspberry sauce.

Vanilla ice-cream with raspberry sauce

Strawberry Sauce

Hull and quarter ripe strawberries. Mash with a fork, then rub through a sieve. Sharpen with lemon juice and sweeten with icing sugar as for **Raspberry Sauce** (see page 207).

Blueberry Sauce

When blueberries are cooked, their flavour becomes quite superior – almost perfumed – and twice as nice as when raw. They still need a little lime or lemon juice to make up for their natural lack of acidity, but even so, it takes very little time to make a superb, dark purple sauce that is good served hot or cold.

Serves 4

250g (9oz) blueberries
1 cinnamon stick
85g (3oz) caster sugar
1 tablespoon lime or lemon juice
2 tablespoons water

1 Put all the ingredients into a small saucepan and bring up to the boil. Simmer for 5 minutes.
2 Taste and add more sugar or lime juice as needed. Stir well. Serve hot or cold.

Crumbles

The fruit crumble is one of the most formidable institutions of Great Britain. What self-respecting household would do without it? Economical, seasonal, open to endless variation, and always welcome, a crumble is hardly a work of art, but it is a thing of considerable beauty. The pleasure one gets from pulling a perfectly browned crumble out of the oven, fruit juices bubbling up around the edges, is surely almost equal to that derived from actually eating it.

Once you know how to make one crumble, you can turn your hand to any number of variations. Blackberry and apple is an absolute classic, but autumn is also a high time for pear and ginger crumble. Rhubarb crumble is the stuff of legends, but I'm incredibly partial to damson crumble, or gooseberry crumble, or apricot or…and so the list goes on.

I'm never quite sure whether I prefer to eat my crumble with cream or custard, but there's no doubt that one or other is necessary. Cream should be honest single or double and runny, not extra thick, and custard should definitely be home-made, so turn to page 220.

A Few Quick Crumble Notes

- The layer of fruit under the crumble needs to have a touch of acidity to balance the sweetness. This is why fruits like rhubarb, gooseberry, plums and cooking apples are so good in crumbles. If you use fruits lacking acidity (e.g. bananas or blueberries), add some lemon juice or lime juice to compensate.
- The layer of fruit under the crumble shouldn't be too acidic. This is largely a matter of trial and error. Use more sugar with sourer fruits, less with sweeter ones.
- Don't pack down the layer of crumble. Just scatter it on lightly, so that the texture remains crumbly when cooked. If you pat it down enthusiastically, it will become too heavy and soggy.
- The crumble mixture can be made a day or two in advance and stored in the fridge, if it makes life any easier. Or if you want your own personal crumble, make up the whole batch, use just enough for yourself and freeze the rest for a later occasion.

Blackberry and Apple Crumble

It almost goes without saying that the best blackberry and apple crumble is made with wild blackberries, gathered on a chilly September afternoon. Their taste is so very superior to that of cultivated blackberries, spiced also by being free for the taking.

The proportion of blackberries to apples is variable, depending on how many blackberries you've gathered and how many got eaten on the way home.

Serves 6

600g (1lb 6oz) more or less cooking apples
400g (14oz) more or less blackberries
110–150g (4–5oz) caster sugar

CRUMBLE
225g (8oz) plain flour
a pinch of salt
110g (4oz) caster sugar
175g (6oz) chilled unsalted butter, diced

1 Begin by making the crumble mixture. Mix the flour, salt and caster sugar in a bowl and add the butter. Rub in using the tips of your fingers, until the mixture resembles coarse breadcrumbs. Chill until needed.

2 Preheat the oven to 180°C/350°F/Gas Mark 4. Peel, core and slice the apples. Mix with the blackberries and caster sugar in a pie dish. Smooth down lightly.

3 Scatter the crumble thickly over the surface of the fruit, without pressing it down. Bake for some 35–40 minutes until golden brown, with the juices bubbling up around the edges. Serve hot or warm with custard (see page 220), cream or vanilla ice-cream.

Add butter to the flour mix.

Rub in with the fingers...

until it resembles breadcrumbs.

Blackberry and apple crumble.

More Crumbles Please

Here comes the mix-and-match section. Lots of ideas to play around with, so that no two crumbles are ever identical, unless you want them to be.

Ways to vary the crumble topping

• Replace one-third of the flour (see page 210) with the same weight of ground almonds – almonds and fruit go notoriously well together. Or try the same thing with ground hazelnuts.
• Stir a handful of desiccated coconut into the made-up crumble.
• Replace half the caster sugar (see page 210) with light muscovado sugar to give a butterscotch taste.
• Sift a teaspoon of cinnamon or mixed spice or ground ginger together with the flour.
• Stir the finely ground zest of 1 orange or 1 lemon into the crumble mixture. Squeeze some of the juice (especially orange) over the fruit.
• Mix a handful of pine nuts, or roughly chopped pecans, walnuts or hazelnuts, in with the crumble topping.
• Once you have put the crumble on top of the fruit, scatter flaked almonds over the top of the crumble.

Ways to play with the layer of fruit

• Combine different fruits to create an infinite number of possibilities: apple and blueberry; or mixed summer-pudding fruits – raspberries, redcurrants, gooseberries, tayberries; apricot and redcurrant; pineapple and rhubarb; plums and blackberries; cherries and blueberries, greengages, purple plums and golden plums; plum and peach.
• Mix sliced or chopped preserved stem ginger with slices of ripe pear, or short lengths of rhubarb.
• Sprinkle 1 or 2 tablespoons sloe gin or crème de mûre or crème de cassis over red fruits.
• Use vanilla sugar, or light muscovado or demerara sugar, to sweeten the fruit.
• At Christmas, mix cranberries, mincemeat, orange zest, a slug of brandy, and sugar for the base of your crumble.

Orange Fried Bananas

Choose firm large bananas for this pudding and be prepared for a surge of ecstasy at first mouthful. And second, and third....The flavour of cooked bananas is just amazing, particularly when doused in sticky sauce.

Weigh out the ingredients and squeeze the orange juice in advance, but peeling the bananas and the cooking are definitely last-minute processes.

Serves 2–3

3 bananas
30g (1oz) unsalted butter
150g (5oz) caster sugar
juice of 1 large orange
½ teaspoon vanilla extract
scoops of vanilla ice-cream, or double cream, to serve

1 Peel the bananas and cut into 1cm (½in) thick slices, on the diagonal, so that they turn out as stretched ovals.

2 Melt the butter in a wide frying pan over a medium heat. When it is foaming add the banana slices. Fry until beginning to patch with brown underneath. Turn over and fry for 2 or 3 more minutes.

3 Now sprinkle over the caster sugar. Turn the pieces so that they are nicely coated, then pour in the orange juice and the vanilla extract. Stir the bananas, turning gently, until the orange and sugar have melded together to form a thick, sticky, irresistibly scented sauce.

4 Serve immediately, with ice-cream or a little double cream.

Fry bananas in foaming butter and, when slightly brown, add the sugar. The orange juice and sugar form a thick, scented sauce.

Flaming Butterscotch Apple Slices

Most fun you can have with a frying pan? It's got to be a spot of flambéing. There is nothing more dramatic than a sudden burst of flames rocketing up out of the pan, shimmering blue and gold and red for a minute or so until they die down. The taste is as good as the show. So, for these brandy-flamed apples, crowd the whole gang into the kitchen to watch the spectacle, before tucking into the richly sauced, tender slices of fruit.

Again, measure everything out in advance, but leave the preparation of the apples and the cooking until the last minute. I use a mixture of butter and oil here, as apples take a little longer to cook than bananas or pineapple, and it reduces the risk of burning the butter. Don't peel the apples. The peel not only looks good, but also prevents the softening slices collapsing to a mush.

Incidentally, this is also very good made with pears instead of apples. You might want to emphasise the pear flavour by using Poire William, a clear pear-scented spirit from France, instead of the Calvados or brandy.

Serves 4

30g (1oz) butter
1 tablespoon sunflower oil
5 eating apples, cored and cut into eighths
150g (5oz) light muscovado sugar
4 tablespoons Calvados or brandy
200ml (7fl oz) double cream or 200g (7oz)
   crème fraîche

1 Melt the butter with the oil in a wide, heavy frying pan. When it is foaming, add the apple slices. Fry over a moderate heat, turning occasionally, until golden brown on both sides.
2 Spoon over the sugar, then turn the apples so that they all get doused in sweetness. Next tip in the Calvados. Stir, then give it a few seconds to warm through.
3 Now for the fun. If you cook on gas, just tip the pan gently towards the flame. Before the liquid spills out, it will whoosh up very dramatically in flames. Do not be taken aback. This is flambéing. Just let it flame away, shaking the pan gently, until the flames die down of their own accord. If you cook on an electric hob, light the Calvados with a match, at arm's length.
4 Now stir in the cream or crème fraîche. Let the whole lot bubble down for a few seconds until the cream has thickened to a sexy, saucy consistency. Serve at once.

Tip in the Calvados.

Lemon ice-cream with strawberry sauce and prosecco – an ice-cream soda for grown-ups.

Lemon Ice-cream

I discovered this many years ago, and it has remained a favourite quick pudding. Like the lemon posset overleaf, it seems so easy that it hardly counts as a recipe. Make it a day in advance so that it has time to freeze.

Although it is good all on its own, I love it served either with a raspberry or strawberry sauce (see page 208) to make it look more dressy. Or, when I'm feeling extra generous, I serve it Venetian style. In other words, I put a scoop of lemon ice-cream in each person's glass, drizzle over some strawberry sauce, and then top the whole lot up with Italian prosecco, or Spanish cava (sparkling white wines). A kind of grown-up ice-cream soda.

Serves 6–8

5 lemons
1 x 400g can sweetened condensed milk

1 Squeeze the juice out of all five lemons, then strain to remove stray pips and pulp.
2 Scrape the condensed milk into a bowl and gradually whisk in the lemon juice. Spoon into a shallow freezer container and cover.
3 Slide into the freezer and leave until frozen.
4 Transfer the ice-cream from the freezer to the fridge about 20 minutes before serving so that it has time to soften a little.

Lemon Surprise Pudding

This is a pudding that has been around for decades, but still delights and indeed surprises people who have never come across it before. The surprise element... I hesitate as this feels a bit like giving away the end of a film...the surprise element is that as it cooks, the pudding separates into two distinct layers. On the top is a light lemony sponge that gradually morphs into a tart lemon custard hidden underneath.

Serves 6 people

100g (3½oz) unsalted butter, plus a little extra for greasing
200g (7 oz) vanilla sugar or plain caster sugar
3 lemons, juice of all 3, finely grated rind of 2
4 medium eggs, separated
75g (2½oz) plain flour
500ml (18fl oz) milk

1 Preheat the oven to 180°C/350°F/Gas Mark 4. Butter a 2 litre (3½ pint) shallow, oven-to-table dish.

2 Cream the butter with the sugar and lemon zest. Beat in the egg yolks one by one. Don't panic if the mixture curdles.

3 Next beat in the flour, a spoonful at a time, alternating with slurps of milk and then lemon juice.

4 Once that is all in, whisk the egg whites until they form stiff peaks, and fold lightly into the lemon batter.

5 Pour the mixture into the baking dish, and then stand the dish in a roasting tin. Pour enough boiling water around the dish to come about halfway up the sides. Bake for 40–45 minutes until golden brown. Serve hot, warm or cold.

Lemon Posset

Lemon posset is quite the most extraordinary pudding I know. Three simple ingredients, three minutes' cooking and hey presto, an exquisite lemon cream.

Serves 8–10

1 litre (1¾ pints) double cream
275g (10oz) caster sugar
juice of 4 lemons

1 Bring the cream and sugar slowly up to the boil in a large heavy-based pan, stirring until the sugar has dissolved. Let the cream boil for exactly 3 minutes.

2 Draw off the heat and stir in the lemon juice. Strain into a bowl and then pour into eight to ten small ramekins. Leave to cool, then chill for at least 4 hours, before serving.

Baked Rice Pudding

This is the very best rice pudding ever. It is cooked very, very, very slowly, so that the rice guzzles up nearly all the milk, forming a golden brown crust on the top, tasting of caramel and childhood.

It only works if you use proper short-grained pudding rice and full-cream milk. I've tried it with skimmed and it is nowhere near as good. When I was little, rice pudding was always served with a dollop of red jam perched jauntily on top, and being something of a traditionalist, that's how I still like to do it. For a change, however, try it with a blueberry sauce instead (see page 208).

The vanilla pod, though expensive, is well worth including. After all, it can be re-used as long as you rinse it thoroughly after the meal.

Serves 4–5

30g (1oz) unsalted butter
85g (3oz) pudding rice
45g (1½oz) caster sugar
1 vanilla pod (optional)
a pinch of salt
700ml (1¼ pints) creamy milk

TO SERVE
strawberry jam, raspberry jam or
   coarse-cut marmalade

1 Preheat the oven to 140°C/275°F/Gas Mark 1. Smear the butter around the base and sides of a sturdy ovenproof dish.
2 Pile in the rice, sugar, vanilla pod (if using), salt and 500ml (18fl oz) of the milk. Stir, then place in the oven and leave for 1 hour.
3 Stir in half the remaining milk and cook for another 1 hour.
4 Stir in the last of the milk and return to the oven for a final hour, until the mixture has thickened and a golden brown skin has formed on the surface.
5 Serve the pudding hot or warm, each helping topped with a spoonful of jam or marmalade.

need to know

VANILLA PODS These should be regarded as investments, as they can be used five or six times over, as well as producing a good supply of vanilla sugar. To give a strong flavour to a custard or other mixture, slit the vanilla pod along its length, and with the tip of a sharp knife, scrape out the tiny black, paste-like seeds into your liquid. Add the split pods as well.

Once the vanilla pod has been used, rinse it really well in warm water, dry thoroughly, then bury it in an airtight jar of sugar. Tuck it in the cupboard for at least four days, and lo and behold, you have made your own vanilla sugar to be used in cakes and puddings, imparting a light scent of vanilla. Leave the pod in the jar until next time you need to use it.

Tartes Fines aux Pommes

These apple tartlets are made of little more than shop-bought puff pastry, apples and sugar, but they look a million dollars and taste divine. Serve with cream or ice-cream. There's no need to peel the apples – the tartes will look prettier if you don't.

Serves 4

500g (18oz) puff pastry
plain flour for dusting
2-3 good, juicy eating apples
15g (½oz) unsalted butter, melted
3–4 tablespoons caster sugar
2 tablespoons apricot jam

Cut pastry using a side plate as a template.

'Knocking up'.

Arranging apple slices in a circle.

1 Roll the pastry out on a lightly floured board, to a thickness of 3mm (⅛in). Cut out four 15cm (6in) circles, using a side plate as a template. Lay on a lightly greased baking sheet, without overlapping. Using the side of a knife, tap all the way around the edges of each circle, pushing the pastry very slightly inwards. This is called 'knocking up' and will encourage the puff pastry to rise. Chill in the fridge for 20–30 minutes.

2 Preheat the oven to 220°C/425°F/Gas Mark 7. Place a second baking sheet in the oven to heat up.

3 Quarter each apple, then core and slice each quarter thinly. Fan the apple slices out in a circle on the pastry as shown in the photograph. Repeat with the remaining apples and pastry.

4 Brush the bare edges of the pastry lightly with melted butter. Sprinkle a quarter of the caster sugar over each circle of pastry.

5 Place the baking sheet with the tartes on it directly on the hot baking sheet in the oven to give an instant blast of heat to the bases. Bake for 5 minutes, then reduce the heat to 190°C/375°F/Gas Mark 5 and continue cooking for another 15 minutes. Check after 10 and cover lightly with foil if the pastries are threatening to burn.

6 Some 3 or 4 minutes before the tartes are done, heat the apricot jam gently with 1 tablespoon water, stirring until evenly mixed and runny. As soon as the tartes come out of the oven, brush the apple slices lightly with the runny jam – you're bound to dislodge a few as you do this, but just nudge them back into position. Serve hot or warm.

Custard

The finest pouring custard is made with egg yolks, milk or cream and sugar and perhaps a drop or two of vanilla. The rub is that the minute it is over-heated it will curdle. So, I usually opt for second-best pouring custard, adding a spoonful of cornflour to stabilise the mixture. The consistency is not quite so perfect, but all anxiety is dispelled, and that to my mind is worth a great deal.

Remember that a pouring custard does not have to be very thick. The idea is to aim for a slightly thickened mixture, not a stand-your-spoon-up-in-it sauce. Using an extra egg yolk will produce a slightly thicker custard.

Makes about 300ml (10fl oz)

300ml (10fl oz) full-cream milk, or half and half milk and single cream, or all single cream
1 vanilla pod, or ¼ teaspoon vanilla extract
15g (½oz) caster sugar
3 egg yolks
½ tablespoon cornflour

1 Heat the milk and/or cream with the vanilla pod if using, until it boils.

2 Meanwhile beat the caster sugar with the egg yolks and cornflour in a bowl until smooth.

3 Pour the hot cream into the egg mixture, stirring constantly.

4 Rinse out the saucepan, and pour the custard back into it. Set over a very low heat, stirring all the time, until the custard has thickened enough to coat the back of the spoon (see opposite). Try not to let it boil. Serve hot or warm.

5 In the miserable event that it should get too hot and start to curdle, take it swiftly off the heat and beat vigorously until smooth.

need to know

COATING THE BACK OF THE SPOON
Means just what it says. Look at the back of the spoon you are stirring the custard with. It should be coated thinly in custard. Double-check by running your finger down it. It will leave a clear trail through the custard when it has thickened enough.

Beat the sugar, yolks and cornflour.

Stir in the hot cream.

Cakes and Biscuits

Whilst they are not the stuff of everyday cooking, cakes and biscuits are undoubtedly a good thing. You can buy them ready-made but there's much to be gained from a spot of baking, and I'm not just talking calories. Taste is inevitably the first bonus. Commercial cakes cannot hold a candle to the plainest, freshly baked cake, all light, moist golden crumb and buttery sweetness. And as for a finger of shortbread, so meltingly short and crumbly that it almost breaks your heart to swallow the last morsel – sorry, but the packeted version is a miserable pastiche.

Another mega-plus is the unparalleled satisfaction to be had from baking your own cakes and biscuits. There's a kind of warm glow, stemming perhaps from nostalgia for childhood, or a natural human instinct to cosset and nurture, or perhaps just because they look so very appealing and promise such pleasure. And you can't possibly ignore the fact that friends and family lucky enough to be invited to share your lovingly crafted efforts will be impressed and suffused with gratitude. Not bad going, really.

The point is that it is worth acquiring a small repertoire of basic baked goods that you can turn out at the drop of a hat. Tea parties (anything from a slice of cake and a cup of tea with your best mate, to a full-blown spread complete with lacy doilies and cucumber sandwiches) are a fantastically easy way to entertain. Far less time-consuming than a proper dinner party, the tea party also comes garnished with a delightful air of frivolity.

Who could resist?

Basic Cake-making Etiquette

Begin with the best. Cakes are all about pleasure and indulgence, not about nutrition or survival. You will be baking them occasionally, as a treat, so when the moment comes, splash out on the best ingredients. That means the very best unsalted butter, not the bargain basement pack (and don't even think margarine); the freshest, organic or free-range eggs; unrefined sugar with its delicate modicum of extra taste; golden Jersey cream; jam packed with real fruit; expensive darkest plain chocolate (more on that on page 199) and so on. Yes, you'll have to shell out a few pence more, but there's absolutely no doubt that it will show from the moment the first bite is taken.

Cake Tins   Size matters. It is asking for trouble to use the wrong-sized tin. Even a measly 1 or 2.5cm (½ or 1in) difference in diameter can wreak havoc. Use a tin that is too big and you may well find that you end up with a large biscuit instead of the plump cake you were aiming at; with a tin that is too small, the mixture will take far longer to cook than it should, and is more likely to burn on top long before the inside is set. Sorry, but there is no way round this one.

So, before you set your heart on baking the stunning cake of your dreams, check that you own the right-sized tin. If not you must either borrow or buy it, or switch to a recipe that matches your bake-ware. Guesswork is risky with cakes, so if in doubt get out the ruler and double-check.

When buying a cake tin, choose one with a removable base to make extracting the cake an easy affair. Non-stick tins are a good idea but by no means necessary as it takes no more than a couple of minutes to line a tin with non-stick baking parchment, or to grease and flour it.

Preparing the Tin   The first thing to do when baking a cake is to turn on the oven. The second is to prepare the tin. Most recipes will begin with instructions on how to do this: greasing, flouring, lining base and sides and so on. I happen to be a complete coward in this respect, but a lazy coward, so my advice is nearly always to 'base-line' the tin and grease the sides. This involves minimum fiddle, whilst at the same time ensuring that you will be able to turn the cake out.

1 Make sure you buy a roll of baking parchment – this non-stick paper is the saving of amateur bakers. Greaseproof paper is not the same thing, so don't use it instead.
2 Unroll a length of baking parchment, and place the removeable base of the tin on it. Hold it down firmly with one hand, and draw a circle around the edge. Return the base to the tin. Cut out the circle of baking parchment.
3 Using either a butter paper (i.e. the wrapper from a pack of butter) or a knob of butter and a wad of kitchen paper, grease the base of the tin lightly (this helps to hold the baking parchment in place), and the sides of the tin thoroughly.
4 Lay the circle of baking parchment in the base of the tin, centring it exactly, and press down lightly. The tin is now ready for use.

Measurements   Baking cakes and biscuits is the one area where measurements must be 100 per cent accurate. The exact ratio of sugar to butter to eggs to flour is critical to success. Guesswork, improvisation or mere approximation are totally unadvisable.

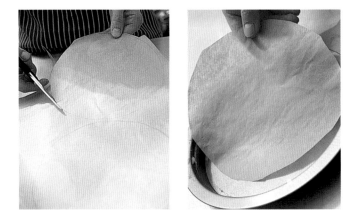

Method
The aim when making a cake batter is to create a structure that will capture lots of air. As it bakes, the bubbles of air expand, the cake rises and everyone is happy. There is no doubt that traditional methods of making cakes, by which I mean creaming butter and sugar or whisking yolks and sugar, whisking and folding in whites, produce the finest, lightest cakes of all. You can cut corners, saving time and reducing washing up, by using the all-in-one method, in other words by piling all the ingredients into the mixing bowl, adding extra baking powder to make up for the loss of air, and beating everything together until smooth. The result is more than acceptable but falls a few paces short of perfection. In the cake recipes below, I offer both options – it's up to you to decide which way to go.

If you decide to tread the traditional route, this is what you will need to know:

Creaming butter and sugar Put softened butter (i.e. butter at room temperature) and sugar in a large bowl. Using a large wooden spoon, start mashing them together, then beat hard until the two have combined to make a light, fluffy mixture, granules of sugar no longer visible. The idea is to dissolve the sugar into the butter and begin to bring air into the mixture. If you have a food processor or, better still, a food mixer or a hand-held mixer, this can be achieved in seconds. Allow some 5 minutes for this when powered by human elbow-power alone.

Whisking eggs/egg yolks and sugar Put whole eggs, or yolks as the recipe tells you, into a bowl and whisk together with a balloon whisk or spoon whisk. Keep going until the mixture becomes very, very pale and thick. Lift the whisk out and drizzle a figure of eight on the surface. If it disappears instantly, keep right on whisking. If it remains visible on the surface, the eggs and sugar have been perfectly amalgamated. As with the creaming, the purpose is to dissolve the sugar and incorporate air.

Whisking and folding in egg whites In some cake recipes the eggs need to be separated carefully (see page 44). Once the rest of the batter has been made, and not before, whisk the egg whites until they reach soft peak stage (see page 46). Stir a tablespoonful of the whites into the batter to slacken the mixture, then fold in the remainder with a large metal spoon. Once again your aim is to get as much air as possible into the cake; a metal spoon crushes out less air than a wooden one. Slide the edge of the spoon down into the whites and batter, right down to the bottom of the bowl, then through and up, turning the spoon to fold the mixture back on top of itself. Keep on doing this, working swiftly but smoothly, until the whites have been completely mixed into the batter, with no flecks of white spotting the mixture.

Dropping consistency For most cakes, the batter needs to have a good dropping consistency. This means that the batter drops off the spoon easily when it is tapped on the side off the bowl.

Cooking the cake The oven must be thoroughly preheated. If using a fan oven, the temperature should be set 10 degrees lower than the standard temperature. Arrange the shelves so that the cake can sit right in the centre of the oven, where it will cook more evenly. Slide the cake in, close the door, set the timer to 5 minutes less than the given time (to allow for the vagaries of individual ovens) and walk away. Do not disturb the cake while it cooks, unless you smell burning.

When the timer rings, open the oven door and pull the cake out. The surface should have coloured to a golden brown. Press the centre gently. If the cake feels firm, the dip bounces back swiftly, and the edges are pulling away from the sides of the tin, then it is most likely done. Double-check by plunging a skewer right down into the centre of the cake. If it comes out clean and dry, then the cake is baked.

When the cake feels squidgy, the dip stays dipped, and the skewer emerges sticky with cake batter, return the cake instantly to the oven and give it another 5–10 minutes' baking before checking again. If necessary, cover the surface of the cake with a loose sheet of silver foil or baking parchment to prevent the surface darkening.

Turning out   Once the cake is cooked, leave it in its tin on a wire rack for 5–10 minutes to firm up. Some extra-delicate cakes may even need to cool completely in the tin, but be guided by your recipe. Run a knife around the sides, hugging it close to the tin. Stand a jam jar on the work surface, then centre the cake tin on top of the jam jar. Ease the sides down, leaving the cake and base of the tin perched on the jar. Return to the wire rack to finish cooling, then slide the cake off the base of the tin on to a serving plate.

Admire your handiwork.

Biscuit Basics

Equipment   The two items of kitchen paraphernalia that are essential for biscuit making are solid, flat baking trays or sheets (which don't have sides at all), and non-stick baking parchment. As for the rest – biscuit cutters, wire cooling racks, palette knives and so on – you can always improvise. I often use a small or medium glass as a biscuit cutter, or simply cut dough into squares or rectangles with a knife, instead. The grill rack can stand in as a cooling rack (as long as it is thoroughly clean), and any wideish table knife or fish slice can replace a broad-bladed palette knife.

Doughs   Biscuit doughs are many and various and it is extraordinary how small changes in quantities of one or other of the ingredients can change the whole nature of the biscuit. The base of most biscuits, however, is a substantial blend of butter, flour and sugar. Don't over-work the dough, or it will produce a tougher biscuit.

Most biscuit doughs freeze well. This is handy if you only want a few biscuits at a time. Cut out and bake what you need, then wrap the remainder in clingfilm and freeze for a later date. The dough is best used within the next month.

Biscuit doughs often spread in the heat of the oven, so always leave plenty of room between biscuits on the baking tray (which will, of course, be lined with non-stick baking parchment). It's better to bake several batches than to try to squeeze too many on to the tray at the beginning.

Baking biscuits   This is the make-or-break sector of home-biscuit production; timing is all. With their high sugar and fat content, biscuits speed swiftly from brown to burnt. Just 2 or 3 excess minutes can be all it takes to do serious damage. Indeed most biscuits are best removed from the oven when they have reached no more than a pale hint of a tan. All those luscious American-style cookies lose their melting texture if they are at all over-cooked.

So, you must check your biscuits regularly as they cook, and never, ever, ever rely on cooking times given in recipes. All ovens vary a little, and for most cooking purposes it doesn't matter too much. With biscuits, it does. Start checking your biscuits several minutes before they are due to emerge from the oven, and keep a careful eye on them if they need to go back.

Are they done? This is not necessarily an easy question to answer. It's fine if the biscuit in question is meant to brown, but for something like shortbread, which barely turns a few shades darker, it is largely a matter of guesswork. There is no reliable test, and often biscuits that seem soft and crumbly as they come out of the oven, firm up beautifully as they cool. Not helpful, I know. Just be guided by descriptions of colour in the recipe and do your best. Experience will make matters easier, and while you are waiting to gain it, be comforted by the fact that marginally under-cooked biscuits still taste pretty good, even if the texture is all wrong.

Cooling Unless a recipe deliberately instructs you to whip the biscuits straight off the baking tray on to a wire cooling rack, it is a good idea to leave them on the tray, undisturbed, for some 5 minutes or so to firm up and settle, before transferring to the rack to cool completely.

Storing Cakes and Biscuits

Always store cake and biscuits in airtight containers, but not the same one. Cake and biscuits should be kept apart so that the biscuits do not absorb the inherent moisture in the cake and go soggy.

You don't need a fancy storage tin – a plastic ice-cream tub will do, as long as there are no gaps around the sides.

Victoria Sponge

The apex of plain cake-making, the Victoria sponge is always a winner. It can be dressed up and dressed down, but remains welcome at every tea party, from the church fête ('Would you care for another slice, Vicar?') onwards. What more can you ask of a cake?

The lightest Victoria sponge is creamed and whisked properly, but a very creditable one can be turned out using the all-in-one method.

Serves 6–8

175g (6oz) softened butter
175g (6oz) caster sugar
3 large eggs, beaten
175g (6oz) plain flour
2 teaspoons baking powder (all-in-one method only)

FILLING AND TOPPING
raspberry or strawberry jam or lemon curd
lightly whipped fresh cream (optional)
icing sugar

1 Preheat the oven to 170°C/325°F/Gas Mark 3. Base-line two 20cm (8in) cake tins (see page 223).

All-in-one method
2 Put all the ingredients for the cake, including the baking powder, into a large mixing bowl. Beat together incredibly energetically until smoothly mixed. The final batter should be of dropping consistency, but if it is a little too thick, beat in a tablespoon or two of water or milk.
3 Divide the mixture between the two cake tins and smooth down lightly. Bake for approximately 30 minutes, until the surface springs back when lightly pressed with a finger. Cool for 5 minutes in their tins, then turn out and finish cooling on a rack.
4 Place one of the cakes, curved side down, on a serving plate. Spread jam or lemon curd over the flat upper side, followed by whipped cream if using, and sit the second cake neatly on top, curved side upwards.
5 Dust lightly with icing sugar and your Victoria sponge is ready to serve.

need to know

DUSTING If you want to dust the top of a cake or pudding with icing sugar, and you don't own an icing sugar shaker (and why should you?), use a small sieve. Hold the sieve over the cake and spoon some icing sugar into it. Tap the side of the sieve gently, moving it around above the cake until evenly coated in icing sugar.

Classic cake

1 Cream the butter and the sugar together until light and fluffy.

2 Beat in the egg, a teaspoon at a time, until about half of it is incorporated, gradually adding a little more at a time afterwards. The idea here is to prevent the mixture curdling. Not the end of the world, but your cake won't rise quite so well if it does.

3 Sift in roughly a quarter of the flour, then fold in carefully with a metal spoon. Repeat until all the flour has been incorporated. Test for dropping consistency (see page 225). If the batter is too firm, beat in a tablespoon of hot water.

4 Divide between the two prepared cake tins and smooth down lightly. Bake for 25–30 minutes until the cakes spring back when the top is pressed gently. Cool for 5 minutes in the tins, then turn out and finish cooling on a wire rack.

5 Sandwich together and finish as for the all-in-one Victoria sponge.

Orange or Lemon Sponge

Fold the finely grated zest of 1 large orange or lemon into the **Victoria Sponge** batter. Sandwich the cakes together with lemon curd, or fine-cut marmalade.

need to know

LEMONS are irreplaceable in the kitchen. It's always worth keeping a few in your fruit bowl, or in the vegetable drawer of your fridge, because you just never know when you'll need them. Especially when it comes to cakes and puddings. The penetrating sharpness of lemon juice slashes through the intensity of sugar, and the richness of cream. Lemon juice also seems to work a sort of alchemy, often producing unexpected results. No doubt the laws of chemistry and physics could explain them, but I prefer to believe in magic.

Always zest a lemon before squeezing the juice – never the other way round!

Double Chocolate Cake

This chocolate cake boasts a double helping of chocolate (in the form of real chocolate and cocoa powder) for a wildly big hit of chocolate heaven. Swathed in a fudgy chocolate cream all over the outside and the inside, it becomes a king amongst chocolate cakes.

Serves 8–10

110g (4oz) plain chocolate, broken into squares
200g (7oz) self-raising flour
30g (1oz) cocoa powder
a pinch of salt
175g (6oz) unsalted butter, softened
60g (2oz) light muscovado sugar
110g (4oz) caster sugar
4 eggs, separated
3 tablespoons milk
1 teaspoon baking powder (all-in-one method only)

CHOCOLATE FUDGE CREAM

200g (7oz) plain chocolate, broken into pieces
175ml (6fl oz) double cream
225g (8oz) icing sugar

1 Preheat the oven to 180°C/350°F/Gas Mark 4. Grease and base-line (see page 223) two 20cm (8in) sandwich tins (shallow cake tins).

2 Melt the chocolate in a bowl (see page 200-201), and cool until tepid. Sift the flour with the cocoa and salt.

Classic method

3 Cream the butter with the two sugars. Beat in the melted chocolate and then the egg yolks, one at a time.

4 Fold in one-third of the flour, then 1 tablespoon milk. Repeat until all of the flour and milk have been used up.

5 Whisk the egg whites until they form soft peaks. Beat a tablespoonful into the chocolate batter, then fold the remainder in lightly with a metal spoon. Now go to step 6.

All-in-one method

3 Beat the melted chocolate, flour mixture and all remaining cake ingredients together until smooth. Now go to step 6.

6 Divide the mixture between the two cake tins and smooth down lightly. Bake for 30 minutes until just firm. Test with a skewer. Let them cool in the tins for 5 minutes, then turn out and finish cooling on a wire rack.

7 While the cake is baking, make the chocolate fudge cream. Melt the chocolate in a bowl. Put it back over the heat, and gradually beat in the cream. Once it is all in, take off the heat. Sift the icing sugar and beat into the chocolate and cream mixture, to get a smooth, fudgy blend.

8 Sandwich the two cakes together with one-third of the chocolate fudge cream. Spread the rest over the top and sides, roughing it up here and there with a fork.

Creaming butter and sugar.

Whisking egg whites.

First egg white in the chocolate mix.

Folding egg white into the mix.

Chocolate and Pecan Brownies

The brownie is one of America's great gifts to the world. I imagine that they were discovered by accident one wet Sunday afternoon, when someone whisked the chocolate cake out of the oven a mite too early. 'Disaster – the cake has sunk! Too late now. I'll have to cut it up and pretend that it was meant to be like that.' Everyone loved it and begged for more.

This illustrates the most important principle of brownie-making (apart from using tip-top quality chocolate (see page 200); unlike cake, it must never be cooked until a skewer comes out totally clean! Over-cooking produces an over-chewy brownie instead of an immorally fudgy one.

Makes around 16

110g (4oz) plain chocolate, broken into squares
110g (4oz) unsalted butter
125g (4½oz) caster sugar
175g (6oz) light muscovado sugar
1 teaspoon vanilla extract
2 eggs, beaten
150g (5oz) plain flour
a generous pinch of salt
110g (4oz) shelled pecan nuts, chopped

1 Preheat the oven to 170°C/325°F/Gas Mark 3. Base-line a 20cm (8in) square shallow baking tin (see page 223).
2 Put the chocolate and the butter into a bowl and melt gently over a pan of barely simmering water (see pages 200–201). Stir in the two sugars and the vanilla extract.
3 Beat in the eggs, one at a time, and then mix in the flour, salt and the pecans. Don't over-do the mixing. Oddly, but successfully, a brownie batter is better if it is a little unevenly mixed. And you really don't want to get too much air into the mixture. Think fudgy all the way.
4 Scrape into the prepared tin. Bake in the centre of the oven for about 30-40 minutes until set but not solid. Cool in the tin, then cut into squares. Store those squares that are not gobbled up within the next hour in an airtight tin.

Warm Brownies with Ice-cream and Raspberry Sauce

To turn your latest batch of brownies into a highly fashionable and wicked pudding, pile a couple of still warm squares of brownie on to each person's plate, or into bowls. Top with a scoop of ice-cream, and spoon over some freshly made **Raspberry Sauce** (see page 207). Top with a few whole raspberries and hand round.

Chocolate and pecan brownies.

Shortbread

One of the best of all biscuits, shortbread should be buttery and very short or, in other words, firm to the touch yet meltingly crumbly in the mouth. It is easy to make and requires only four ingredients – flour, cornflour, butter and sugar.

Makes 10–15 fingers

175g (6oz) plain flour
100g (3½oz) cornflour
85g (3oz) caster sugar
175g (6oz) unsalted butter, softened

1 Preheat the oven to 180°C/350°F/Gas Mark 4.

2 Mix the flour, cornflour and sugar, then work in the butter to give a soft dough. Alternatively, just put everything in the bowl of the processor and process until the mixture forms a ball.

3 Press the dough into an 18cm (7in) square baking tin with your fingers as evenly as possible. Prick all over with the tines of a fork. Bake for 30-35 minutes, until the surface is lightly coloured but not brown.

4 Take out of the oven, and cut straightaway into fingers, then leave to cool in the tin. When cold, break the fingers apart. Store in an airtight container.

Petticoat Tails

This is the pretty name for wedges of shortbread cut from a circle. If you don't have the right-sized tin to make the fingers as above, this is the best alternative. Roll or press the dough out directly on a baking tray to form a circle around 1cm (½in) thick. Neaten it up around the edges and prick all over with a fork. Bake as above. As soon as it comes out of the oven, divide it into 12 wedges, then leave to cool. Break up into individual 'petticoat tails' and store in an airtight tin.

Chocolate Shortbread

To make chocolate shortbread, replace 30g (1oz) of the cornflour (see above) with cocoa.

Orange Shortbread

To make orange shortbread, mix the finely grated zest of 2 oranges into the dough opposite.

Orange shortbread fingers.

White Chocolate and Pecan Cookies

American cookies are sweet and soft and slightly chewy, at their best still a mite warm from the oven. The trick here, as with American brownies (see page 232), is not to over-cook them – too long in the oven and they crisp up into biscuits. They should never darken to more than a pale, pale tan.

The gentle sharpness of dried apricot balances the insistent sweetness of white chocolate. Do make sure that you buy real white chocolate buttons (or use real white chocolate, roughly chopped) not a second-rate, cheap white candy.

Makes 20 x 7.5cm (3in) cookies

150g (5oz) butter, softened
150g (5oz) caster sugar
225g (8oz) self-raising flour
1 tablespoon milk
60g (2oz) shelled pecan nuts, roughly
    chopped
100g (3½oz) white chocolate drops
100g (3½oz) ready-to-eat dried apricots,
    roughly chopped

1 Preheat the oven to 190°C/375°F/Gas Mark 5. Line two baking trays or sheets with non-stick baking parchment.
2 Beat the butter and sugar with a wooden spoon until light and fluffy, then work in the flour and milk to make a stiff dough.
3 Mix in the pecans, chocolate and apricots.
4 Roll dessertspoonfuls of the mixture into balls, then place on the baking trays, leaving a 7.5cm (3in) gap between each ball, to allow for spreading. Use the prongs of a fork to gently press each ball down to form a rough disc, about 1cm (½in) thick.
5 Place both trays in the oven and bake for 10–14 minutes, swapping the trays around halfway through the cooking time. Take the trays of biscuits out of the oven when they have turned slightly more coloured, but are still barely brown. Cool for 5 minutes on the tray, then transfer to a rack to finish cooling.

Milk chocolate and raisin cookies Replace the white chocolate (see page 235) with 110g (4oz) roughly chopped milk chocolate, and replace the apricots with 110g (4oz) raisins (for a real kick, soak them in rum or brandy for an hour or two before using, but drain them well before adding to the dough). Leave out the pecans, or replace with chopped roasted hazelnuts.

Dark chocolate and raspberry cookies A sophisticated cookie, for those of you with dark tastes. Replace the white chocolate with 110g (4oz) best dark chocolate, roughly chopped, and replace the apricots with 150g (5oz) raspberries. Omit the pecans.

Angelica, apricot and almond cookies – the three 'As' Replace the white chocolate with 85g (3oz) candied angelica, roughly chopped, and replace the pecans with nibbed, or halved almonds. Leave the apricot just as it is.

Smarty-arty cookies Replace the chocolate with 175g (6oz) Smarties or chocolate M & Ms. Leave out the apricots and pecans altogether.

Toffee and dried cranberry cookies Replace the chocolate with hard toffees, each one quartered, and replace the apricots with dried cranberries. No need for nuts.

And more
You get the picture, don't you? Raid the larder, the sweetie counter, the squirrel's hoard, and even the fruit bushes to add variety to your cookies. As well as all the above, what about trying a handful of chopped preserved stem ginger, or some sultanas, or a few chopped dates? Dried or fresh blueberries are good in the mix as well, but never add too many as the juices will run while cooking and could turn your gorgeous cookies into purple-blue flops.

Index

almonds, toasting, 156

angelica, apricot and almond
cookies, 236

antipasti, Italian, 32

apples: blackberry and apple crumble,
210

flaming butterscotch apple slices,
214

tartes fines aux pommes, 218–19

apricots, tagine of lamb with, 132

avocados: guacamole, 40

bacon, 19

fried onion and bacon omelette, 56

baking: fish, 150–1

potatoes, 171

balsamic vinegar and tarragon
marinade, 102

bananas, orange fried, 213

barbecuing, 95, 149–50

basil: home-made pesto, 71

sugo al pomodoro e basilico, 69

basting meat, 110, 117

beef, 95, 105, 111–12, 122, 125

beef stew with mushrooms and
Guinness, 126–7

beef with carrots, 128

daube de boeuf, 128

grilled steak, 96

Jamaican beef stew, 128

spaghetti with meatballs, 72

steak teriyaki, 105

tagliatelle Bolognaise, 73–4

biscuits, 226–7, 234–6

blackberry and apple crumble, 210

blueberry sauce, 208

boiling: eggs, 47

potatoes, 170–1

vegetables, 179

Bolognaise sauce, 73–4

bouquet garni, 20

braising meat, 122–33

bread: bruschetta, 35–7

croûtons and croûtes, 18

broccoli al diavolo, 187

brownies, 232

browning meat, 124

bruschetta, 35–7

burgers, lamb, 98

butter beans, Jamaican beef stew with,
128

butters, flavoured, 103

butterscotch: flaming butterscotch
apple slices, 214

sauce, 207

cabbage with garlic and lemon, 183

cakes, 222–6, 228–33

cannellini beans: Italian bean and
vegetable soup, 26

tuna and bean salad, 35

carrots: beef with carrots, 128

carrot and coriander soup, 22

chickpea, courgette and carrot
salad, 192

ginger-glazed carrots, 187

carving chicken, 118

casseroles, 122–33

champ, Irish, 174

cheese: blue cheese butter, 103

cheesy mash, 174

double cheese omelette, 55

gratin dauphinoise with Gruyère,
177

grilled goat's cheese salad, 40

for pasta, 65–6

penne with Gorgonzola, spinach
and hazelnuts, 70

pizzas, 80–2

soup garnishes, 18

tomato and mozzarella salad, 191

chicken, 95, 105, 123, 125

chicken fajitas, 108–9

classic chicken stock, 16

escalopes with mustard and crème
fraîche, 106–7

grilled chicken, 100–1

microwave chicken stock, 15–16

rich chicken casserole, 129–31

roast chicken, 116–21

stuffing, 121

chickpea, courgette and carrot salad,
192

chilli: deseeding, 9

sauces, 138

chocolate, 199–206

chocolate and pecan brownies, 232

chocolate shortbread, 234

cookies, 235–6

double chocolate cake, 230–1

hot chocolate sauce, 206

melting, 200–1

mousses, 202–4

petit pots au chocolat, 205–6

coffee: mocha mousse, 204

cooking terms, 11

coriander leaves: salsa verde, 104

coriander seeds: carrot and coriander
soup, 22

courgettes: chickpea, courgette and
carrot salad, 192

courgette and pancetta risotto, 88

sautéed courgette, prawn and
chorizo omelette, 56

cranberries: toffee and dried cranberry
cookies, 236

cream, soup garnishes, 18

crème fraîche and rocket mash, 174

croûtes, 18
croûtons, 18
crumbles, 209–12
cucumber salad, Danish, 190
curried parsnip soup, 22
custard, 220

Danish cucumber salad, 190
daube de boeuf, 128
deglazing pans, 124

eggs, 42–61
   cooking methods, 47–50
   egg-fried rice, 91
   folding in, 46–7, 225
   fried eggs with coriander, cumin
     and balsamic vinegar, 50
   frittate, 57–61
   lemon scrambled eggs, 51
   omelettes, 52–6
   separating, 44–5
   whisking whites, 45–6, 225

fajitas, chicken, 108–9
figs with Parma ham, 38
fish, 145–67
   cooking methods, 147–51
   fancy fish pie, 164
   fundamental fish pie, 163
   SEE ALSO INDIVIDUAL TYPES OF FISH
fish sauce, 137
fishcakes, tuna, 158–9
flour, 76, 123
French beans: with almonds and
    cream, 182
   with cumin and almonds, 182
frittate, 57–61
fruit: crumbles, 209–12
   SEE ALSO INDIVIDUAL TYPES OF FRUIT
frying: eggs, 47–8

fish, 147–8
   meat, 104–9
   vegetables, 179–80

garlic, preparing, 7
garnishes, for soups, 18–19
goat's cheese SEE cheese
gratin dauphinoise, 176–7
gravy, 120
Greek/Middle Eastern mezze, 34
Greek salad, 193
griddling, 11, 148, 181
grilling: fish, 149–50
   meat, 95–101
   vegetables, 180
guacamole, 40

hazelnuts, roasting, 70
herbs: bouquet garni, 20
   chopping, 8
   soup garnishes, 18
hors d'oeuvre Provençal, 31

ice-cream: lemon, 215
   sauces for, 206–8
   warm brownies with, 232
Irish champ, 174
Italian antipasti, 32
Italian bean and vegetable soup, 26
Italian vegetable soup with pasta, 27

Jamaican beef stew, 128

kitchen utensils, 10-11
kneading pizza dough, 77–8

lamb, 95, 105, 111–12, 123, 125
   grilled lamb chops, 100
   lamb burgers, 98
   roast leg of lamb, 115

roast rack of lamb with parsley and
    orange crust, 113
   tagine of lamb with apricots and
    almonds, 132
leeks: rich chicken casserole, 129–31
lemon, 229
   grating, 9
   lemon ice-cream, 215
   lemon posset, 216
   lemon scrambled eggs, 51
   lemon sponge, 229
   lemon surprise pudding, 216
lemon sole meunière, 157
liquidisers, 17

mackerel fillets with lemon chilli
    relish, 152
maître d'hôtel butter, 103
mangetout, stir-fried ginger pork with
    cashew nuts and, 141
marinades for meat, 102
mashed potatoes, 173–4
mayonnaise: tartare sauce, 155
meat, 93–133
   frying, 104–9
   grilling, 95–101
   resting after cooking, 94–5
   roasting, 110–21
   stewing and braising, 122–33
meatballs, spaghetti with, 72
Mediterranean marinade, 102
Mediterranean medleys, 29–34
melon with Parma ham, 38
mezze, 34
mocha mousse, 204
mouclade, 166–7
mousses, chocolate, 202–4
mushrooms: mushroom and pancetta
    (or bacon) frittata, 61
   mushroom omelette, 55

mussels: mouclade, 166–7

mustard mash, 173

noodles, Thai stir-fried, 142–3

olive oil, soup garnishes, 18–19
olives, 31–4
   tomato and black olive salad, 191
omelettes, 52–6
onions: fried onion and bacon or
      pancetta omelette, 56
   preparing, 6-7
   roast tomato and onion soup, 24–5
   tomato and red onion salad, 191
oranges: orange fried bananas, 213
   orange shortbread, 235
   orange sponge, 229
   petit pots au chocolat à l'orange,
      205
   tomato, orange and olive salad, 191

pad thai, 142–3
pancetta: courgette and pancetta
      risotto, 88
   mushroom and pancetta frittata, 61
   sugo all'Amatriciana, 69
panzanella, 194
Parma ham: melon or figs with, 38
   pizza con prosciutto e olive, 81
parsley: parsley and lemon stuffing,
      121
   potato, parsley and garlic soup, 21
   salsa verde, 104
parsnip soup, curried, 22
pasta, 63–75
   cheese for, 65–6
   cooking, 64–5
   Italian vegetable soup with, 27
   pasta frittata, 61
   sauces for, 67–9

peanuts, roasting, 143
penne with Gorgonzola, spinach and
      hazelnuts, 70
peppers: preparing, 8-9
   pepper and basil frittata, 61
pesto, home-made, 71
petticoat tails, 234
pizzas, 76–83
plaice with lemon and parsley crust,
      156
poaching: eggs, 49–50
   fish, 148–9
pork, 95, 105, 111–12, 123, 125
   grilled pork chops, 101
   sticky spare ribs, 112
   stir-fried ginger pork with
      mangetouts and cashew nuts, 141
potatoes, 169–77
   cooking methods, 170–4
   fundamental fish pie, 163
   gratin dauphinoise, 176–7
   potato, parsley and garlic soup, 21
   roast new potatoes, 176
   roast potato wedges, 174–6
   tuna fishcakes, 158–9
prawns: egg-fried rice, 91
   Thai stir-fried noodles, 142–3
puddings, 199–221

ragù bolognese, 73–4
raspberry sauce, 207, 232
rice, 84–91
   baked rice pudding, 217
   cooking, 85–6
   egg-fried rice, 91
   risotto, 84, 86–8
roasting: fish, 150–1
   meat, 110–21
   potatoes, 172
   vegetables, 181

rosemary and garlic butter, 103

salads, 35, 40, 188–97
salmon, roast, 160
salmonella, 43, 116, 117
salsa cruda, 69
salsa verde, 104
sardines, grilled or barbecued
      Portuguese style, 154
sauces: gravy, 120
   ice-cream sauces, 206–8
   for pasta, 67–9
   salsa cruda, 69
   salsa verde, 104
   tartare sauce, 155
   tomato sauce for pizza, 80
   white sauce, 165
sautéed potatoes, 172
sautéeing, 11
scallops: fancy fish pie, 164
scrambled eggs, 48–9
searing fish, 148
shortbread, 234–5
Smarty-arty cookies, 236
smoked haddock: fundamental fish
      pie, 163
   smoked haddock and shrimp
      chowder, 28
sole meunière, 157
soups, 13–28
soy sauce, 136–7
spaghetti with meatballs, 72
Spanish chaciñas plate, 33
spare ribs, sticky, 112
spinach, penne with Gorgonzola,
      hazelnuts and, 70
sponge cakes, 224–5, 228–9
spring onions: Irish champ, 174
starters, 29–41
steak SEE beef

steaming fish, 149

stews, 122–33, 151

stir-frying, 135–43

stocks, 15–16

strawberry sauce, 208

stuffing, parsley and lemon, 121

sugo al pomodoro, 69

sugo all'Amatriciana, 69

sugo all'Arrabiata, 69

sweating vegetables, 14

tagliatelle Bolognaise, 73–4

tartare sauce, 155

tartes fines aux pommes, 218–19

Thai stir-fried noodles, 142–3

toffee and dried cranberry cookies, 236

tomatoes: panzanella, 194

   pizza alla marinara, 82

   preparing, 8-9

   roast tomato and onion soup, 24–5

   roast tomatoes with fennel seeds,

   184

sauces, 67–9, 80

tomato and basil omelette, 56

tomato and basil salad, 191

tomato and black olive salad, 191

tomato and mint salad, 191

tomato and mozzarella salad, 191

tomato and red onion salad, 191

tomato and spring onion frittata,

   58–9

tomato, orange and olive salad, 191

topping and tailing, 9

tortillas: chicken fajitas, 108–9

trout, newspaper-baked with lime,

   chive and chilli butter, 162

tuna: grilled tuna steaks, 155

   salade Niçoise, 196

   tuna and bean salad, 35

   tuna fishcakes, 158–9

vanilla pods, 217

vegetables, 169–87

   cooking methods, 179–81

   good vegetable soup, 20

   Italian bean and vegetable soup, 26

   Italian vegetable soup, 27

   soup garnishes, 19

   stir-fried vegetables with black

     bean sauce, 186

   stock, 16

   sweating, 14

   SEE ALSO INDIVIDUAL TYPES OF

   VEGETABLE

Victoria sponge, 228–9

vinaigrette, 189–90

white sauce, 165

wild rice, 85

woks, 135–6

yeast: pizza dough, 76–7

yoghurt marinade, spiced, 102

Acknowledgements

I'd like to thank everyone listed below for one or more of the following: forbearance, patience, back-up, laughter, hard work, vision, photography, cooking, friendship, companionship, organisational skills, reassurance, entertainment, honesty, cups of coffee, cups of tea and many more fine qualities that have made this book what it is.

The roll-call is as follows: Denise Bates and all at HarperCollins, Martine Carter, Susan Fleming, Borra Garson, Georgia Glynn Smith, Christine Wood, Eliza Baird, Annabel Hartog, Jennine Hughes, Charles Jackson, Pixelle and all who sail in her, Juliet Rickard and the late, much missed Jim Rickard, Michelle Wadesley, Sarah Widdicombe. Jennifer Wilson, and no doubt many more who will, I hope, forgive me for not mentioning them by name.

And last and most special of all, Florrie and Sidney, tasters in chief.